I0729663

CHRIS DORLAND: FUTURE RUINS
Robert Hobbs

CONTENTS

Future Ruins and Haunted Screens in the Post-Digital Present 2

Introduction: Art as History 2

Chapter One: Memoryscapes (2001–7), Paradoxical and Anamorphic Views 4

    The Specter of Simulation
    Anamorphosis, Illusion, and Dystopian Vision
    Architectures of Past Futures
    Painting as Translation, Painting as Ruin
    Painting as Inquiry and Ideological Contradiction
    Spectral Forms and Historical Fragments
    Photocopied and Photorealist Representations

Chapter Two: Simulations, Logos, and Prototypes (2007–14),
Trompe l'Oeil Painting and the Financial Crisis 12

    Simulating the Simulated: Painting in a Post-Authentic Age
    Hyperreality as Method
    Expo 67 and the Soviet Pavilion: Red Specters and Broken Icons
    The Great Recession, a Major Crack in Dorland's Ideological Screen
    Neoliberal Branding and Accelerationist Irony
    Logos and Prototypes: Branding as Visual Philosophy
    Painting as Speculative Technology

Chapter Three: Scanners and Alumacores (2009–19), Painting by Other Means 20

    Scanner Aesthetics and the Technical Turn
    Cognitive Assemblages and Distributed Subjectivity
    Capitalist Painting
    Advertising and the Anatomy of Desire
    Alumacores: Machinic Surfaces and Neo-Noir Interfaces
    Civilian's Architectural Field
    Artistic Influences as Semiological Ghosts
    Hauntological Ghosts in the Machine
    The Posthuman Eye and the Ghost in the Machine

Chapter Four: Screenscrapes and Their Whiteouts (2020–Present),
Digital Fragments, and Semiotic Ghosts 28

    The Studio as Laboratory
    Glitches
    Whiteouts and the Breakdown of Representation

Ghosts in the Archive: Hauntology and the Loss of Memory
Painting as Interface: Toward a Hybrid Vision
Sensation and the Diagram: Deleuze, Lyotard, and the Logic of Collapse
The Cybernetic Sublime: Goldstein, Heidegger, and Broken Tools
Technogenesis and Recursive Creation
The Ethics of Representation After Technological Failure

Coda: Dorland's Eloquent Ruins as Semiotic Phantoms,
Theorizing His Aesthetic Interventions 35

Endnotes 36
Index 40
Glossary of Terms 46

Inventory **49**
Memoryscapes 49
Simulations, Logos, and Prototypes 53
Scanners and Alumacores 67
Screenscrapes 85
Interface 111

Acknowledgements **119**
Colophon / Credits **120**

**FUTURE RUINS AND HAUNTED SCREENS
IN THE POST-DIGITAL PRESENT**

**INTRODUCTION
Art as History**

Canadian-born American artist Chris Dorland (b. 1978) has emerged as a key figure in contemporary art's engagement with digital media, simulation, and systems aesthetics. Poised at the complex intersection of postcybernetic theory and painterly abstraction, Dorland's most recent work visualizes how algorithmic culture reshapes perception, subjectivity, and materiality. Drawing from traditions of glitch art, surveillance aesthetics, and postmodern appropriation, Dorland constructs a world where the promise of digital transparency collapses into visually persuasive conflations of excess and fragmentation. His canvases are not merely representations of network culture; they constitute the very surfaces upon which the violence of mediation inscribes itself.

Dorland's paintings explore the phantom ruins that haunt the past, present, and future perspectives of our ever-changing world. His first mature works, titled *Memoryscapes* (2001–7), focus on futuristically oriented antecedents refracted through the lens of antiquated and abandoned world's fair sites. Between 2007 and 2014, he concentrated on the

Simulations, large-format paintings resembling Xerox copies that construct hyperrealities. The *Logos* and *Prototypes* series, produced during this same period, employ abstraction and visual rhetoric to critique the branding mechanisms of neoliberal capitalism. In his *Scanners* (2009–16), Dorland juxtaposes low- and high-brow materials to create visual friction between sleek consumer images and austere minimalist references. With the *Alumacores* (2017–19), he turns toward hard-edged, machine-printed surfaces, embedding visual data within industrial substrates. Most recently, the *Screenscrapes* series (2020–ongoing) assembles digital debris into densely layered compositions where glitches and ghostlike signals proliferate, revealing a haunted terrain in which the seams between human vision and machinic perception have frayed.

From childhood, Dorland was prepared to assume the historical role his work now expresses. His father, a respected film critic and cyberpunk enthusiast, introduced him to this genre's dystopian views of the future. At the same time, his mother, a noted feminist scholar, immersed in postmodern theory, with a library of *Semiotext(e)* volumes, nurtured Dorland's early exposure to French thinkers like Jean Baudrillard and Paul Virilio. Graffiti in Montreal's alleyways, a Xerox of Baudrillard's "The Evil Demon of Images," and a first encounter with J. G. Ballard's *Concrete Island* shaped the interconnected coordinates of a sensibility attuned to simulation, collapse, and estranged temporality.

Instead of interpreting Dorland's work as an image to be deciphered or a symptom to be historicized, this study approaches his art as a theoretical act in its own right—an interface where material process, visual culture, and philosophical speculation converge. My aim is not to confine the work to interpretive certainty but to maintain an active and generative dialogue with it: to respect its surfaces, to follow its glitches, and to trace the recursive loops of meaning and unmeaning it sets in motion. Dorland's paintings do not merely represent the postdigital condition—they inhabit it. They enact theory through form, conjuring what British theorist Mark Fisher might call the ruins of lost futures or what Baudrillard might recognize as the ghost logic of simulation. My method blends art historical analysis with theoretical reflection as it considers the structures of painting, the glib psychology of advertising, and the haunted frequencies of cybernetics and post-humanism. In this way, the following chapters are not only about Dorland's work, but they are also shaped by it; they are impacted by its recursive logic, seductive contradictions, and refusal of closure. This is a study not of fixed meanings but of unstable signs. Not specific answers, but sites of ongoing thought.

Accordingly, *Chris Dorland: Future Ruins and Haunted Screens in the Postdigital Present* explores how the artist's evolving body of work engages with the ideological foundations of modernism, critiques the commodifying power of image culture, and examines the glitches that fracture digitally produced realities. Instead of fixed definitions, I theorize meaning in a dynamic and constructive manner by engaging with the philosophical and cultural frameworks that animate Dorland's work. This interpretive method intends to model ways of thinking alongside the work—a cohabitation of critical method and aesthetic encounter.

CHAPTER ONE
Memoryscapes (2001–7), Paradoxical and Anamorphic Views

It is precisely when it appears most truthful, most faithful and most in confor-
mity to reality that the image is most diabolic.
—Jean Baudrillard, "The Evil Demon of Images," 1984

Rather, it is once again the principle of *seduction* that needs to be invoked in
this situation: according to Manichaeism, the reality of the world is a total
illusion: it is something which has been tainted from the very beginning; it
is something which has been seduced by a sort of *ir*real principle since time
immemorial. In this case what one has to invoke is precisely this absolute
power of illusion—and this is indeed exactly what the heretics did. They based
their theologies on the very *negation* of the real. Their principal and primary
convention was that of the non-reality, hence of the non-rationality, of the
world. They believed that the world, its reality, is made up only of *signs*—and
that it was governed solely through the power of the *mind*.
—Jean Baudrillard, "The Evil Demon of Images," 1984

[C]yberpunk's infatuation with boundary crossing, most evident in its transgres-
sion of the traditional boundaries between organic and inorganic, natural and
artificial, human and machine, results in a decentering of the human subject.
—Claire Sponsler, "Cyberpunk and the Dilemmas of Postmodern Narrative:
The Example of William Gibson," *Contemporary Literature*, 1992

The Specter of Simulation

In 1995, when aspiring artist Chris Dorland was seventeen and still living in Montreal,
his mother, a burgeoning feminist with a recently earned PhD,[1] presented him with a
Xerox copy of French sociologist Jean Baudrillard's insightful essay "The Evil Demon of
Images."[2] In this piece, Baudrillard explores the Manichean sources that enabled him to theorize how illusions have seduced humanity. He specifically refers to the Latin word *illudere*,
meaning "a play on actuality," to emphasize the Manichean view of the world as composed
of signs that constitute the models he calls "simulationist" or "hyperrealist," which precede
and haunt the alleged reality they represent.[3]

Anamorphosis, Illusion, and Dystopian Vision

In my opinion, this radical undermining of everyday life by the models representing it can
be compared to the distinct perspective offered by anamorphic views. In art, anamorphosis,
which can be both literal and figurative, often take the form of sideways perspectives, as
compellingly exemplified in Hans Holbein the Younger's painting *The Ambassadors* (1533).
In this work, a prominent white blob in the lower-central section of the canvas appears as a

skull when viewed from the right. Initially resembling an artistic mistake, this mysterious shape creates a new perspective on the two depicted envoys and the many objects on the shelves between them by underscoring the transience of their worldly pursuits and passions. We might conclude that Holbein's anamorphic skull distills the unknown within the context of these scientific and cultural accessories, and this uncertainty in life is the type of conundrum Dorland embraces in many of his works.

Dorland recalls Baudrillard's essay as formative.[4] Its radical take on the playful illusions shaping our everyday lives undoubtedly influenced his early reading of J. G. Ballard's 1974 novel, *Concrete Island*, and Dorland's regard for it has been pivotal to his worldview. This book undermines dominant models of modernity regarding speed and progress by presenting a series of intersecting superhighways on the outskirts of London from the anamorphic position of a desolate crevasse—the book's island—which is wedged among overpasses and ramps and cluttered with culverts, tunnels, and the wrecked carcasses of automobiles and trucks. The book's main character, architect Robert Maitland, becomes permanently stranded in this remnant of land at the margins of the modern world after a blown-out tire puts him there. Ballard's *Concrete Island*, therefore, relies on his readers' familiarity with technology's smooth efficiency to contrast it with the postindustrial fissure that constitutes Maitland's anamorphic Hell. Not only does the book present a stark contrast to Ballard's readers' everyday world, but it also implicitly emphasizes how constructed and artificial their lives are.

Dorland's intensely positive response to this novel, which he describes as "probably the first real aesthetic experience I had, after which I felt I could fully pursue my own interests with confidence,"[5] was undoubtedly catalyzed and perpetuated by the many cyberpunk films he enjoyed watching in the 1980s and '90s—experiences he shared with his father, Michael Dorland, a noted Canadian film critic,[6] who also relished this genre. Several of these science-fiction films explore a doomsday paradox, presenting impending events that serve as figurative anamorphs capable of influencing their origins and outcomes. The future merges with the present in both *The Terminator* (1984) and *Terminator 2: Judgment Day* (1991). In the former, there are unsuccessful attempts to change the course of history by killing, in 1984, the character Sarah Connor to prevent her from bearing the son who, in 2029, will save humankind from the machinations of the hostile artificial intelligence Skynet, creator of the assassin called "the Terminator." Of particular importance to Dorland is the villainous character T-1000 in the second *Terminator* film, a shape-shifting cybernetic entity made from the liquid metal known as mimetic poly-alloy, which allows him to assume identities of the people and objects he encounters, provided they are of comparable volume. "Ever since I was a kid," Dorland recounted in 2023, "I've been obsessed with the metal alloy skin of the T-1000 in *Terminator 2*. I love this idea of an ever-changing, flexible, and smart skin that can adapt like a shape-shifting lizard."[7] In addition to his attraction to the various chimeras and the volatility of this terminator, Dorland was intrigued by his ability to "become a [different] sentient being[s]."[8] These and other cyberpunk films instilled in Dorland an appreciation for anamorphically dystopian futures and their potential impact on the present; they also fostered in him a fascination with how the present and the future can be implicated and deeply intertwined with one another. "As a kid," Dorland recalled in 2024, "I was obsessed with the future," before acknowledging, "now, we live in the future, and it is terrifying."[9]

The resulting "cognitive estrangement"[10] between the present and future—a term coined by sci-fi specialist Darko Suvin for extraordinary breaks occurring in this genre—creates a space where familiar elements are distanced and defamiliarized to establish the distinct perspective I associate with nonliteral and figurative anamorphism. Dorland's fascination with *Concrete Island*, particularly its dislocated protagonist marooned in a postindustrial crevasse, aligns with this estranged vision. Like Ballard's narrative, Dorland's work subverts modernity's linear and predominantly optimistic temporality by positioning viewers within a collapsed perspective in which progress ultimately creates its own ruin.

Dorland's primary source for understanding a contingent present and a sobering future is the 1984 dystopian novel *Neuromancer* by fellow Canadian William Gibson. In 1993, Dorland's father intended to give his son this novel but could only find a copy of the author's second volume in the Sprawl trilogy, *Count Zero* (1986).[11] Soon thereafter, the younger Dorland was able to obtain a copy of *Neuromancer*. In direct opposition to earlier expansionist-oriented science-fiction works featuring adventurer-scientist heroes who colonialize new and future realms, cyberpunk explores a more democratic view of humanity, which has been advanced through the post–World War II interdisciplinary science of cybernetics and its reconsideration of human cognition as comprising sets of informational patterns. This perspective places it on par with the far less hierarchical and undoubtedly more egalitarian realm inhabited by animals and machines. Reinterpreting cybernetics as the basis for a punk aesthetic, cyberpunk presents a gritty, stark, and graphic view of technology that blurs distinctions between humans and machines and includes, according to science fiction critic Istvan Csicsery-Ronay, "a rich thesaurus of metaphors linking the organic and the electronic." Csicsery-Ronay has also highlighted one of this genre's chief qualities when he describes it as "fundamentally ambivalent about the breakdown of the distinctions between human and machine, between personal consciousness and machine consciousness."[12] Not surprisingly, Csicsery-Ronay has also referred to Jean Baudrillard as cyberpunk's most notable philosopher,[13] particularly for his eloquent, yet sometimes hyperbolic, writings about science fiction and simulationist theories, which align him and his work with the view that reality is an elaborate construct, continuously created and recreated by models that displace it.

This genre's jaundiced view of multinational capitalism's efforts to change and sometimes attempt to perfect humanity is crucial to cyberpunk and Dorland's art. This is an imperative reflected in some well-known cyberpunk films. Examples include the Nexus 4 replicants in *Blade Runner* (1982), the crime fighter perfected by Omni Consumer Products in *RoboCop* (1987), the implanted memory of an extraordinary Mars vacation adventure in *Total Recall* (1990), and the simulated reality that relies on humans as energy sources, which intelligent machines have harnessed in *The Matrix* (1999).

Architectures of Past Futures

While *Neuromancer* is impactful for Dorland's *Screenscrapes*, which he initiated in 2020, his earliest mature paintings are deeply influenced by Baudrillard's concept of hyperreality, which this artist has literalized through the actual models for the future presented at various world's fair sites. Large corporations or individual nations often sponsored these buildings to showcase their capabilities in developing viable templates for the future. Dorland considers his first mature work to be the 2001 painting that he connects with the Firestone Pavilion for the 1939 New York World's Fair. "But it wasn't until 2002," he later pointed out, "that I got going . . .[,] that I saw the value in that older painting and recuperated it and now consider it the first mature piece."[14]

Dorland's painting was inspired by the 1990s Firestone Tire controversy, where hundreds of people died in crashes caused by defective tire treads that separated at high temperatures—a dynamic situation that resonates with Dorland's early and long-standing fascination with Ballard's *Concrete Island*. He was also aware of Firestone's initial dominance in the natural rubber industry during the 1920s, after it had secured a ninety-nine-year lease from the Liberian government for a million acres, thereby enabling the company to cultivate African rubber plants. Recognizing that Firestone asserted its influence at the 1939 New York World's Fair by commissioning a namesake pavilion, Dorland was intrigued with how this architectural model of a positive future, along with those sponsored by other corporations and countries at various world's fairs, eventually went awry. Planned amid the Great Depression and intended to celebrate American prominence and the country's promise of future economic prosperity, the 1939 New York World's Fair's theme was "Building the World of Tomorrow," and its opening declaration was "Dawn of a New Day."

For attendees of this world's fair, its self-congratulatory mission may have seemed reasonable and encouraging, but the future has not supported such anticipated optimism and brash commercial opportunism, as evidenced by Firestone's continued, yet misguided, "new day" near the century's end. At that time, it was embroiled in a series of lawsuits revealing its administrators' scandalous calculation that paying off its legal judgments would be far cheaper than recalling its defective tires. "The juxtaposition of the lawsuit, which had unfolded in real time, alongside the nostalgic old picture of the pavilion," Dorland reflected in 2006, "made fireworks go off. I saw the gap between the utopian promise that capitalism had successfully sold to North America after World War II and the destructive drive for profit that capitalism now represents."[15]

This was not the only breach vital to Dorland's formulation of this painting. Although he was influenced by both past and present Firestone accounts, along with the enhancements achieved by the company through its Depression-era world's fair pavilion, Dorland ultimately preferred a different entry's streamlined architecture as a model for his painting: Borden Milk's one-story building, designed by the esteemed New York architectural firm Voorhees, Gmelin, and Walker. Dorland replaced the Borden Pavilion with the Firestone one, even as he continued to consider his painting's content in relation to the other building and the company's later calculated disdain for its customers. There may have been some irony in Dorland's choice, as the immensely popular Borden Pavilion, praised for its futuristic farming, featured a Rotolactor machine that milked fifty cows twice daily, thereby producing a beverage that indirectly symbolized nurturance, progress, and American ingenuity.

Painting as Translation, Painting as Ruin

Although Dorland's easel-sized canvas was hand-painted, he relied on computer imaging to formulate its composition by helping him to decide which aspects of this streamlined modern building to emphasize and which to erase. "I do most of the plotting and figuring out beforehand on the computer," Dorland explained in 2006. "My process is getting more and more layered. There are many steps that involve scanning, printing, and drawing," he added. "I usually make five to ten versions of each painting on the computer. Once I'm done, I select the print I like best. Only then do I get around to the actual painting. From then on, the only thing I care about is the energy of the object I'm working on." Dorland added by stating, "For me, painting is an act of translation and reconstruction."[16] Since his depicted structure represents an outdated model, he decided to give the building the patina of age by rubbing the painted surface of the canvas with brown shoe polish. Thus, his use of computer imaging, layering, and degradation emerges not as an ingenious technical effect but rather as an epistemological intervention. This process enacts the very instability his works theorize, making them not only images of ruins but also enacted theories of ruination. This and his other *Memoryscapes* depicting no-longer-extant or vestiges of world's fair sites become archival machines that sift through the sediment of capitalism's abandoned fantasies. Such works resist closure; they represent absences that trouble the authority of presence and easily determined meanings. In the *Memoryscapes*, traces are evident in the obsolescent architecture of world's fair sites and in the gaps between reference and representation, past and future, promise and failure.

Similarly themed paintings in this series required finding additional real-life equivalents for the futuristic models he liked to represent. While he played on other antiquated modern pavilions like his Firestone-Borden one in his *Memoryscapes*, Dorland occasionally distanced his views of these past models of the future through a range of high-key palettes that sometimes lend his subjects an eerily science-fictional air. Among his more striking *Memoryscapes* is the wonderfully futuristic General Motors Pavilion from the 1939 New York World's Fair, conceived as a Mark Tansey–type monochromatic painting. This depicts a group of people standing on a moving platform while looking down at a model of the future created by renowned American industrial designer Norman Bel Geddes. Other Dorland pavilions focusing on the 1964 New York World's Fair and Montreal's Expo 67 were primarily conceived in saturated hues, endowing them with a spooky and, at times, uncanny quality.

When painting was being challenged by photo-based art and late Minimalist and neoconceptual work, Dorland remained unwaveringly committed to this medium. He was clearly "aware," as he pointed out, "that being a painter is a weirdly old-fashioned vocation that can seem increasingly out of step with society even though painting's resiliency is pretty nuts." He recalled devouring his mother's copy of *Art After Modernism: Rethinking Representation*, edited by Brian Wallis and published by New York's New Museum of Contemporary Art. The book was tremendously important to him in the mid-1990s, and he continues to revere artist/critic Tom Lawson's essay "Last Exit: Painting" for its subversive approach. According to Lawson, some recent painting had been capable of redefining and upgrading this traditional genre, which had become one of the art world's most revered yet outmoded signs of "personal authenticity" in the late twentieth century, and it did so by "reveal[ing] its falseness." Referring to David Salle—one of Dorland's early and long-term heroes—as an example, Lawson writes,

> Salle's paintings remain significant pointers indicating the last exit for the
> radical artist. He makes paintings, but they are dead, inert representations of

the impossibility of passion in a culture that has institutionalized self-expression. They take the most compelling sign for personal authenticity that our culture can provide, and attempt to stop it, to reveal its falseness. The paintings look real, but they are fake. They operate by stealth, insinuating a crippling doubt into the faith that supports and binds our ideological institutions.

Over the years, Lawson's observations have inspired Dorland in his quest to elevate his painting beyond conventional personal and authentic attitudes toward this medium. He has consequently aimed to discover ways to comment on contemporary social, historical, cultural, economic, and political realities. Thus, he has allegorized painting in relation to world's fair architectural models by asserting a simulational or hyperreal status for his artworks and their ongoing representational value. During this early period, Dorland's paintings abandoned the real for the hyperreal: as models, they preceded the future realities they intended to predict.

The fundamental discrepancy between the Firestone Pavilion's idealistic vision of its future and the company's later dystopian, calculated perspective was critical for Dorland, who was haunted by dreams of unrealized futures that had spiraled out of control, and by the abandoned and partially dismantled world's fair pavilions he saw in books and encountered in his hometown, Montreal, where he often passed remnants of one of the most successful twentieth-century world's fairs, Expo 67. Dorland's exploration of the gaps between the past and the present, as well as anticipated and actual futures, became a defining method for his own last-exit paintings.

Dorland's canvases are very much in sync with Lawson's trenchant essay; moreover, they parallel, in many respects, William Gibson's first piece of cyberpunk fiction, titled "The Gernsback Continuum" (1981). Dorland does not recall reading this fictional account at the time, even though he now views it as extraordinarily pertinent to his early work, once it was brought to his attention. I am therefore confident in using it as a diagnostic tool for placing in perspective the significance of both Dorland's focus on the 1939 New York World's Fair pavilions and their diminished historical roles, especially since Gibson's remarkable account correlates well with Dorland's *Memoryscapes* and their role in conveying some "myths of progress."

Painting as Inquiry and Ideological Contradiction

Before discussing "The Gernsback Continuum," I would like to briefly summarize and reaffirm certain points from my discussion. Thus far, we have seen that Dorland's *Memoryscapes* illuminate how painting functions as a mode of historical inquiry rather than merely as a medium for personal expression or aesthetic freedom. His artworks transcend the simple depiction of outdated architectural styles or retro-futuristic visions, instead functioning as proposals within the broader theoretical framework of simulation, anamorphosis, and the collapse of ideological projections. Drawing from the speculative architecture of historical world's fairs, Dorland's paintings underscore the interplay of signs detached from their meanings, revealing how former utopias have decayed into ideological remnants. Individual *Memoryscapes*, therefore, function as theoretical objects. They enact French philosopher Jacques Derrida's often-cited *différance*—the deferral and displacement of meaning—through painterly strategies that foreground simulation, fragmentation, and visual uncertainty. Thus, Dorland's choice to depict the 1939 Firestone Pavilion through Borden Milk is not a symbolic substitution but an allegorical maneuver. It reframes the architecture of corporate futurism as a site of ideological contradiction, namely, the promise of technological abundance that conceals extractive and exploitative practices.

Spectral Forms and Historical Fragments

To return to Gibson's "The Gernsback Continuum," the story pays homage to Hugo Gernsback, the publisher of the popular 1920s magazine *Amazing Stories*, the first publication entirely dedicated to science fiction. In his narrative, Gibson's early 1980s hero, an unnamed American photographer, is hired by a British firm to find and photograph surviving Art Deco and Art Moderne buildings for a proposed coffee-table book on 1930s North American futuristic design, titled *The Airstream Futuropolis: The Tomorrow That Never Was*. While working in the southwestern United States, the photographer uncovers "odds and ends of futuristic Thirties and Forties" buildings, including "movie marquees ribbed to radiate some mysterious energy, the dime stores laced with fluted aluminum, the chrome-tube chairs gathering dust in the lobbies of transient hotels. . . . [In short,] mirage-like images constituting an architecture of broken dreams . . . a shadowy America that wasn't . . . [there, yet still contains remnants of] fifth-run movie houses like temples of some lost sect that worshipped blue mirrors and geometry." While this assignment might seem innocuous, Gibson's photographer becomes ensnared in "too many fragments of the [past futuristic yet unfulfilled] Dream waiting to snare me," causing the recognizable boundaries between present and past worlds to blur and merge. Immersed in his subject, Gibson's on-site narrator begins to hallucinate about the futuristic architecture and envisions its inhabitants as blond, well-scrubbed figures who resemble idealized Nazi types.

When this photographer complains to his U.S. agent, Merv Kihn, about fragments of unrealized futures manifesting as disturbing phantasms, Kihn responds, "I'd say you saw a semiotic ghost. . . . They're semiotic phantoms, bits of deep cultural images that have split off and taken on a life of their own, like the Jules Verne airships that those old Kansas farmers were always seeing. "To cure himself of these phantom-like harbingers of aborted futures, the photographer takes Kihn's advice and immerses himself in the dystopian aspects of his contemporary world, including low-brow TV game shows, soap operas, hardcore pornography, crime stories, and various forms of corruption in the news. The type of science fiction that Gibson embraces in "The Gernsback Continuum" represents a once-anticipated yet misguided future that haunts the present. A few years later, this concept intrigued British cultural critic Mark Fisher, one of Dorland's favored authors, who wrote: "The future is always experienced as a haunting: as a virtuality that already impinges on the present, conditioning expectations and motivating cultural production." This idea became critical for Dorland and his work, as I will demonstrate. Although such past iterations of anticipated futures, represented in depictions of world's fair pavilions and viewed through the lens of Baudrillard's simulational models, may constitute a haunting, as Gibson suggests, it is one, in this artist's words, of "sweet sadness, represent[ing] a kind of longing."

In addition to presenting the Borden Pavilion as a misaligned image foreshadowing Firestone's ill-fated future, Dorland created paintings in the early 2000s that focused on other world's fair sites, including the aforementioned 1964 New York World's Fair pavilions and Montreal's Expo 67. Particularly significant are Dorland's depictions of R. Buckminster Fuller's three-quarter geodesic dome, which constituted the U.S. Pavilion for Expo 67. Dorland recalls first becoming aware of this fair site as an eight-year-old in 1986 when his father described it as a destroyed image of progress. The building originally housed a collection of contemporary art by notable artists such as Helen Frankenthaler, Robert Indiana, Jasper Johns, Roy Lichtenstein, Barnett Newman, and Robert Rauschenberg, among others. Nine years later, all that remained of this edifice was the metal lattice that had served as the armature for the acrylic panels enclosing the structure, which had melted in a 1976 fire, thus leaving the dome a shell. The Canadian government then commissioned in 1990 a reworking of its denuded carcass to serve as the site for its Biosphere.

Dorland's most notable depiction of Fuller's dome is a painted paper collage featuring iterative images reproduced on a black-and-white laser copier he had recently purchased. Wanting the work to resemble a photocopied representation rather than a painting, Dorland emphasized the seams formed by the different pieces of paper, thus creating the illusion that the dome's surface had been fractured. The breakup of this structure shares similarities with the work of British expatriate photorealist painter Malcolm Morley, who had served as an informal mentor to Dorland in the early 2000s. Dorland was particularly drawn to Morley's belief in representing the world through visual nuclei. According to Morley:

> I take painting very literally to be a thing to do with seeing. I want to know
> what perception is in terms of painting. . . . I want the eyes to float and bob
> like buoys on the wetness of the painted surface. . . . [With the grid] I get
> a concentration of a kind of molecular-bunching-up of seen things. I can avoid
> figure-ground problems. Normally, you spend all the energy on the figure,
> and you just fill in the ground. This way everything is ground.

As his collaged geodesic dome indicates, Dorland was particularly pleased with the lessons learned from Morley, especially with his desire to distance himself from his work by making it appear more photocopied. These approaches subsequently became the mainstays of future series, such as his *Simulations*, *Alumacores*, and *Screenscrapes*.

Instead of adjudicating meaning from a position of interpretive mastery, I have sought in this chapter to model an interpretive approach informed by critical theory—one that is sensitive to history's constructedness, representation's mediating function, and the spectral types of logic that animate Dorland's practice. In doing so, I have aimed to position the *Memoryscapes* not merely as aesthetic statements but, more importantly, as discursive formations: paintings that initiate the process of the hyperreal or simulational conditions under which they were created and through which they continue to signify.

CHAPTER TWO
Simulations, *Logos*, and *Prototypes* (2007–14), Trompe l'Oeil Painting and the Financial Crisis

Simulation is no longer that of a territory, a referential being, or a substance.
It is the generation by models of a real without origin or reality: a hyperreal. . . .
It is . . . the map that precedes the territory—the precession of simulacra.
—Jean Baudrillard, "The Precession of Simulacra,"
Simulacra and Simulation, 1983

These works, which I referred to as "*Simulations*," morphed out of the older
landscape works as I became more interested in simulating the effects of printing and the mechanical aspects of painting. I felt the older paintings were
too nostalgic for the source material, and I wanted to mechanize my processes
in order for the paintings to look like they were printed. I devised a whole
technique for that effect. I bought a Xerox laser printer and started to use that
for collages which later became the source inspiration for the paintings.
—Chris Dorland, email to author, April 16, 2023

I define neoliberalism as a specific mode of capitalist production (Marx),
and a form of governmentality (Foucault), that is characterized by the following
specific factors:
    The dominating influence of financial institutions, which facilitate trans-
fers of wealth from everybody else to the already extremely wealthy (the "One
Percent" or even the top one hundredth of one percent).
    The privatization and commodification of what used to be common
or public good (resources like water and green space, as well as public
services like education, communication, sewage and garbage disposal, and
transportation).
    The subjection of all aspects of life to the so-called discipline of the
market.
    The definition of human beings as private owners of their own "human
capital." Each person is thereby, as Michel Foucault puts it, forced to become
an entrepreneur of himself. In such circumstances, we are continually obliged
to market ourselves, to brand ourselves, to maximize the return on our
"investment in ourselves."
—Steven Shaviro, *No Speed Limit: Three Essays on Accelerationism*, 2015

Simulating the Simulated:
Painting in a Post-Authentic Age

Chris Dorland's practice from 2007 to 2014 reflects a shift from model-based allegories of
abandoned futures to works that question the very process of reproduction and simulation.

Instead of viewing these new paintings as a linear evolution or mere reflections of biographical or historical facts, my theoretical interpretation suggests that they serve as epistemological inquiries into the status of images, technologies of reproduction, and the psychic aftershocks of late capitalism. Dorland's *Simulations*, *Logos*, and *Prototypes* are not simply aesthetic responses to historical crises such as the 2008 financial collapse; they are, as I will demonstrate, critical enactments of the structural instabilities introduced into perception and subjectivity by neoliberalism and technological mediation.

In Baudrillardian terms, Dorland's *Simulations* do not depict reality; instead, they perform the collapse of the real into the hyperreal representations of the future that both precede and supplant reality. Their Xerox-like surfaces and digitally layered effects are not incidental; they constitute a painterly strategy that foregrounds mediation itself. Here, painting becomes a recursive medium: it simulates simulation. In doing so, Dorland's work questions the ontological status of images in a culture saturated by digital reproduction while eschewing nostalgia for the hand and related claims to authenticity.

Hyperreality as Method

Chris Dorland's *Simulations* are hyperreal in two ways: they depict models that precede reality and imitate the mechanical copying process used to realize them, so that they function both literally and representationally as hyperreal images. Additionally, they are high-tech yet mysterious and science-fictional yet believable, even though they resemble photographic negatives presented as positive images. These evocative paintings thus obscure their handmade origins while pointing to mechanical affiliations, making them exceedingly simulational.

This series also invites a reevaluation of the paintings' long-assumed emotional effects. The works' photomechanical appearance, cool detachment, and the removal of the artist's hand as a marker of selfhood all emphasize painting's loss of expressive privilege. Instead of lamenting this loss, Dorland's work theorizes it as hyperreal and transforms painting into a critical site for aesthetic and ideological condensation.

These canvases originated as collaged images, which Dorland allegorically equates with "the breakup of illusions symbolizing capitalism's cracking and falling apart." The change began in 2007, prior to the 2008–9 Great Recession, recognized as the most extensive global economic crisis since the Great Depression. In addition to reflecting the impact of this financial catastrophe, Dorland's *Simulations* can be understood in terms of the internal development of his art, where prior artistic investigations have led him to create photomechanical collages. In these later works, he employs both the appearance of laser printing and the fragmentation of images as modi operandi for his trompe l'oeil *Simulations*. Sources for this series include Andy Warhol's silkscreens, as well as the combination of laser printing and painting techniques used by slightly older contemporaries like Wade Guyton, Kelley Walker, and Christopher Wool.

Expo 67 and the Soviet Pavilion:
Red Specters and Broken Icons

In approximately a dozen of his *Simulations*, Dorland focused on Expo 67's Soviet Pavilion. He pointed out that he was uninterested in this pavilion's history and was far more intrigued with visually breaking apart aspects of this building before recombining them into new, more abstract configurations. However, his choice of red for many of these works, a color he has often termed "infrared," provides a subtext for his elaborately broken up and reframed images of the Soviet Pavilion, since this thermal-imaging technique is employed in specially constructed cameras to study heat patterns generated by humans and animals, making it eminently suitable for surveillance technology. Not actually a hue, infrared is an electromagnetic wavelength with a specific heat-radiation frequency invisible to the human eye. Although infrared is imperceptible, Dorland characterizes it in his painting as a hot crimson to heighten the impact of his Soviet [Red] Pavilion renditions through the implicit contrast effected by his heated-up characterizations that ironically contrast with the historical stalemate then typifying the Cold War, at the time a major political concern.

Originally, the entire 1967 world's fair exposition was to be held in Moscow to honor the fiftieth anniversary of the October Revolution. However, the political fallout from the deposition of Nikita Khrushchev, combined with the projected costs for such a global event, were reasons the Soviet Union abandoned this undertaking, thus providing Montreal with the opportunity to celebrate its founding by hosting this international exposition. Expo 67's theme was "Man and His World," and the Soviets dovetailed this concept with the related slogan "In the Name of Man, for the Good of Man." Nevertheless, such lofty sentiments, along with the gender biases that were being questioned in the 1960s, quickly became outdated. These exalted catchphrases reveal the prejudicial views of the exposition organizers, highlighting how ideologically driven world's fairs can be, making them hyperreal aspirational models in line with Baudrillard's theories. Such mottos support my assertion that Dorland's *Simulations* align with William Gibson's "Gernsback Continuum" as incomplete yet hopeful futures that have run amok. In this way, these works represent the aborted models, "semiotic ghosts," and the remnants of dreams and unfulfilled expectations that define Expo 67's legacy.

The Great Recession, a Major Crack in Dorland's Ideological Screen

Dorland continued working on the *Simulations* through the Great Recession, which constituted an immense personal crisis, becoming a major watershed that forced him to rethink his former enthusiastic embrace of the United States' highbrow and popular cultures, extending even to its financial system. Consequently, he felt the need to reconsider his art and its direction. Known also as the Global Financial Crisis, the Great Recession was catalyzed by the predatory lending of subprime mortgages that targeted low-income homebuyers. Offering prospective purchasers enticingly low deposits—and sometimes none at all—in addition to reduced initial monthly payments with adjustable rates and periodic balloon payments, stockbrokers packaged these toxic assets in bundles, comprising hundreds and even thousands of mortgages, which they sold as mortgage-backed securities. Initially, these stocks proved to be commercially viable, since mortgages have traditionally served as low-risk options for banks and accredited investors as well as pension and hedge funds. However, between 2004 and 2006, when the U.S. Federal Reserve was forced to raise interest rates from 1 percent to 5.25 percent, businesses holding subprime adjustable-rate mortgages followed suit, and the resulting jumps in monthly house payments led to massive foreclosures. House prices fell approximately 30 percent in value; unemployment doubled to more than 10 percent; and the S & P 500 dropped 57 percent from its highest point. Six million property owners around the globe lost their homes, necessitating huge governmental bailouts. Unemployment during the Great Recession eventually topped two hundred million people worldwide; $16 trillion in American wealth was lost; and the art market reported a decrease of $15 billion in sales. For Dorland, these changes in the economy were emotionally devastating due to his prior belief in the American system of government and its economy, even though the market for his early paintings remained strong during this period. "It was as if we were all living in *The Truman Show*," Dorland recollected in 2024. "[Like being in] some giant mechanical dome we can't visualize. That's why the financial crisis was so powerful; it was a significant crack in the ideological screen."

When Dorland recalls the onset of the Great Recession, he focuses on several events that exemplify its social and economic magnitude and collapse. The first was the widely publicized auction of British artist Damien Hirst's work at Sotheby's in London. This highly promoted sale, titled "Beautiful Inside My Head Forever," occurred on September 15, 2008. It featured a $240,000 three-volume catalog and an elaborate opening party where 1,500 guests were served foie gras wrapped in gold leaf. The subsequent auction generated over $200 million in sales, making it the most lucrative single-artist event of its kind in history. Coincidentally, the morning after this extraordinary event, the highly respected 158-year-old American financial firm Lehman Brothers closed due to its $600-billion debt, leaving approximately 25,000 of its workers unemployed and marking the largest bankruptcy in American history.

Another financial calamity that deeply troubled Dorland was financier Bernie Madoff's admission, on December 10, 2008, that rising interest rates were forcing him to disclose his company's fictitious assets of $64 billion. In doing so, Madoff unveiled his firm's decades-long secret orchestration of the largest financial Ponzi scheme in U.S. history. Madoff had lost the savings of thousands of investment groups, including pension funds, in addition to the personal wealth of many affluent and average individuals. Dorland was both intrigued and repelled by the callousness and duplicity of this "financial sociopath," who was also labeled a "serial financial killer."

Marking some of the most devastating aspects of the Great Recession, these occurrences proved to be enormously depressing for Dorland; they also emboldened him to rethink and indirectly critique in his work the late twentieth-century revival of unrestricted capitalism from the nineteenth century known as "neoliberalism." First broadly acknowledged in the 1980s through the policies of politicians like Margaret Thatcher and Ronald Reagan as well as the economist and Federal Reserve chair Alan Greenspan, neoliberalism was based on the extensive proposition of privatizing the public sphere, deregulating the corporate domain, and lowering personal income and corporate taxes by cutting public support for essential services such as education, water, electricity, and prisons. After the onset of the Great Recession, when governments were forced to prop up their economies, neoliberalism's laissez-faire platform was significantly compromised. For some, this political and economic theory had lost its appeal, even though its views on capitalism continued to attract adherents from both the right and the left. Dorland was convinced that he needed to change his work by incorporating aspects of capitalism and approaching it with dry humor and irony. Instead of creating the kind of smart work that had garnered his *Memoryscapes* and *Simulations* an impressive following of collectors and dealers, Dorland began contemplating the potential of dumb and humorous artworks. This new initiative resulted in hundreds of scanned works on paper that layered advertisements collected from both low- and highbrow magazines, as well as books.

Neoliberal Branding and Accelerationist Irony

Dorland found the branding of individuals, prized by neoliberals for its ability to commodify many aspects of people's lives, both intriguing and insidious. He believed that such individuals, who were open to marketing themselves, had been brilliantly portrayed by American author Bret Easton Ellis's character Patrick Bateman in *American Psycho*, a controversial thriller published in 1991 that was later adapted into a well-received film in 2000. According to film critic Scott Tobias, Bateman's character was inspired by the U.S. Constitution's Fourteenth Amendment, which enabled corporations to be treated as individuals, making the type of business Bateman embodied a "psychopath[ic]" one. A wealthy Manhattan investment banker who attended Exeter and Harvard, Bateman epitomized yuppie culture, fashion, and consumerism. Idealizing Donald Trump as his hero, Bateman kept a copy of this corporate TV personality's *The Art of the Deal* on his desk and dreamed of receiving an invitation to accompany this media figure and fellow suntanning enthusiast on his yacht. Beneath Bateman's cloak of worldly surfaces, emptiness, and greed lurked a serial killer, a fitting personification of certain business types whose nefarious practices contributed to the Great Recession. For Dorland, *American Psycho* was significant because it implicitly critiqued well-entrenched and intransigent corporate culture, extending even to its key players. At the time, Dorland was intrigued by how corporations affect culture. To this day, he remains an Ellis fan and listens to his weekly podcasts while working in the studio.

To address neoliberalism, Dorland needed to understand how and why others continued to subscribe to it, which led him to the theory known as accelerationism. This composite view combines political and economic concepts with cyberpunk, suggesting that computers are ideal tools for accelerating capitalism, allowing it to reach its eventual denouement—a conclusion that even Karl Marx had left open-ended. Philosopher and cultural critic Steven Shaviro states, "*Accelerationism* is best defined—in political aesthetic and philosophical terms—as the argument that the only way out [of capitalism] is the way through. In order to overcome globalized neoliberal capitalism, we need to drain it to the dregs, push it to its most extreme point, and follow it into its furthest and strangest consequences."

Accelerationism is the brainchild of several philosophers, including Nick Land and Sadie Plant, who worked in the mid-1990s following the fall of the Berlin Wall, which marked for them the end of Socialism in Eastern Europe and the de facto hegemony of capitalism. These academics were affiliated with the University of Warwick in the United

Kingdom and identified themselves as members of the Cybernetic Culture Research Unit (CCRU). Their professed exemplar was the protean cyborg T-1000 from *Terminator 2*, and their aim, according to British journalist and historian Andy Beckett, "was to meld their preoccupations into a groundbreaking, infinitely flexible intellectual alloy—like th[is] shape-shifting cyborg." CCRU members were committed to investigating capitalism's limits and its ultimate end. Accelerationism received its name in 2010 when critical theorist Benjamin Noys disparaged it as such. Elaborating on the role of T-1000 and its relevance to accelerationism, Noys explains, "Accelerationism, here and elsewhere, answers this problem by fusing the man of flesh and blood with the iron man—integrating man and machine, or person and machine, to fuse and infuse living labor into dead labor. This will mutate into the cyborg fantasy of the 'man-machine.'" Despite CCRU accelerationists and others subscribing to this designation combining fantasy and reality in their economic predictions for the future, and although their calculations enticed many into their fold, Dorland and his art required additional incentives to move forward. He found motivations for his art in the theories advanced by French author Paul Virilio, a close friend of Jean Baudrillard, and the ideas propagated by Mark Fisher.

Although he had a background in stained glass that allowed him to collaborate with prominent twentieth-century French artists such as Georges Braque and Henri Matisse, Virilio later emerged as a leading proponent of the theory he terms "dromology" (derived from the ancient Greek noun *dromos*, meaning a race or racetrack) to highlight speed's significant impact on modern life. Instead of equating dromology solely with velocity, Virilio prefers to consider it in relation to the interplay among phenomena and the foundations of modern technological society. Since speed often emphasizes force without limits, it frequently leads to accidents, which Virilio views both negatively as destructive chaos and positively as productive chaos, thereby fostering new concepts and attitudes. To illustrate his ideas, Virilio enriches his writing with a wealth of fragments, facts, individuals, histories, and images. Rather than embracing the notion of a cyborg— a blend of human and machine—like the accelerationists do, Virilio upholds the more conservative concept of integrated natural human bodies. By doing so, he assigns technical accessories to the subordinate role of prostheses, which can destabilize individuals. This dynamic relates to his perspectives on the significance of accidents and chaos while preserving many traditional notions of human stability and continuity.

Virilio's critical entanglement resonates in Dorland's early aesthetic formation. The artist's enthusiasm for cyberpunk cinema, his engagement with Baudrillard's and Virilio's theories, and his exposure to feminist and poststructuralist thought through his parents' intellectual milieu are not incidental to his development; they form the discursive infrastructure from which his art emerges. These paintings are not nostalgic; they are hauntological. They participate in what Mark Fisher refers to as "lost futures," where the spectral remnants of failed ideologies continue to shape the present.

A postgraduate student at the University of Warwick during the 1990s, Mark Fisher had a much greater impact on Dorland's developing thought than Virilio's writings, especially his book *Capitalist Realism: Is There No Alternative?* With its main title, a play on *socialist realism*, Fisher's book reframes capitalism. The subtitle directly refers to Margaret Thatcher's often-cited neoliberal assertion, "There is no alternative." Despite the seeming inevitability of Thatcher's stance, which she utilized to great advantage, Fisher was much more optimistic about the future and viewed capitalism as both an ideology and a dominant economic position. He consequently titled his first chapter "It's easier to imagine the end of the world than the end of capitalism," which he attributes to the theorists Fredric Jameson and Slavoj Žižek.

In his text, Fisher also cites the French psychoanalyst and psychiatrist Jacques Lacan, who offers a truly viable strategy against capitalism's hegemony in terms of the Real, which cannot be imagined or signified. Fisher describes it as "an unrepresentable X, a traumatic voice that can only be glimpsed in the fractures and inconsistencies in the field of the apparent reality." As we will see, Dorland required more than a decade to formulate ways to allude to the Real in his art by presenting breaks in the world's ideological fabric that I will refer to as "whiteouts," which become a major component of Dorland's most recent body of work, his *Screenscrapes*. The mysterious whiteouts that haunt the distinctly artificial intelligent realm defining this series might be viewed as an ironically wry transposition of British philosopher Gilbert Ryle's well-known critique, the ghost in the machine, which challenges the Cartesian idea of the soul or mind being lodged within the body or machine, a notion subsequently deemed an unequivocal categorical error.

Logos and *Prototypes*:
Branding as Visual Philosophy

Between 2010 and 2014, Dorland sought a new direction, resulting in two new series: *Logos* and *Prototypes*, which were informed by his shifted perspectives on American capitalism, as well as his understanding of CCRU's accelerationism, Virilio's dromology, and Fisher's capitalist realism. He reflected on these challenges in the following statement:

> This [the years 2010–14] was an exploratory phase. I needed to expand my
> project significantly and needed to inject a sense of capitalism into the work.
> My paintings weren't being interpreted properly. I began a few new series
> during this time. There were the ongoing *Simulations* that continued to evolve
> and become more abstract as well as a series of *Logos* paintings as well as
> works that explored imagery from advertising.

In consideration of these groups of paintings, the 2008 financial crisis serves not only as a backdrop but also as a break, an occasion for Dorland's previously mentioned "crack in the ideological screen." His engagement with accelerationist theory, cyberpunk aesthetics, and corporate advertising, however, is a nuanced critique rather than a straightforward moral denunciation. By utilizing the visual languages of advertising, finance, and surveillance, he reveals their constructed nature and internal contradictions. The *Logos* paintings, for example, do not mock branding; rather, they perform its logic to the point of dry absurdity, thus disturbing the viewer's ability to distinguish critique from complicity.

This ambivalence aligns with key accelerationist propositions, specifically, that capitalism's contradictions cannot be resolved through resistance alone and must be pushed to their limits. Dorland's engagement with the CCRU, Virilio's dromology, and Fisher's capitalist realism should be viewed as a constellation of critical tools, each providing a means to conceptualize how speed, repetition, and collapse shape our psychic and visual environments. I should emphasize at this point that his paintings are not mere illustrations of these ideas; instead, they represent theoretical acts that model their force.

Dorland views his *Logos* paintings as aligned with the initiatives started by Pictures Generation artist Gretchen Bender, who focused on corporations. His *Logos* series resembles commercial brands, while some of his *Prototypes* blend elements of the *Simulations* with overpainted sections showcasing prisms of modulated color, creating the illusion of distinct and separate realities. These nonaligned representatives highlight their constructed nature and emphasize the artificiality of each worldview. Other Dorland *Prototypes* appear as monumental collages that juxtapose the artist's use of commercial source imagery with monochromatic areas of blank or colored canvas. If one considers the *Prototypes*, with their layered advertisements and blank monochromes, as dialectical images in the sense that Walter Benjamin intended in *The Arcades Project*, then they do not resolve into meaning but, instead, suspend it. These are not representations of capitalist excess; they are their residual forms—partial, glitchy, abstracted—resisting interpretation even as they demand it. These works' formal fragmentation reflects not only the breakdown of economic systems but also the impossibility of stable subject positions under regimes of constant image circulation.

Instead of assigning the *Prototypes* a fixed political or historical meaning, my theoretical mode of interpretation allows them to remain contingent, open, and conceptually mobile. These works become experiments in visual theory, reframing painting not as a window onto the world but as a medium that theorizes the world's opacity, speed, and recursive logic. Within these dynamics, the aesthetic becomes epistemic: Dorland's layered and overdetermined *Prototypes* serve as sites where knowledge and unknowing coexist.

Painting as Speculative Technology

Through his *Simulations*, *Logos*, and *Prototypes*, Dorland rethinks painting in terms of speculations about new technologies. The resulting work theorizes the visual logic of an era shaped by neoliberal rationality, systemic collapse, and an increasing indistinction between reality and its models. What emerges from this theoretical lens is not an answer but a question: How might painting itself operate as a speculative technology capable not only of reflecting but also of generating thought in a time when image and ideology have become increasingly indistinguishable?

It helps to recall what a difficult transitional time this was for Dorland. After experiencing gratifying critical and commercial success with his early works, he found the Great Recession challenging for some of his fundamental ideas, prompting him to strive to discover ways his art might respond to these dramatic changes. It took him several years to do so. The first step was a turn to video, and Dorland credits his partner, Erin Knutson, with suggesting in 2009 that this medium might enable him to explore aspects of accelerationism in his art. He then started making three- to five-second looped GIFs. By incorporating some of advertising's powerful images into condensed yet appealing sequences, his videos motivated him to create hundreds of scanned drawings, which served as a pathway to his subsequent series: the *Scanners*, *Alumacores*, and *Screenscrapes*.

Around this time [circa 2015], I began working with my current Belgian gallery, Super Dakota. I started to focus on a single body of work, the sewn paintings. I no longer wanted to "simulate" painting, but, rather, felt it was time to fully embrace printing head-on. I bought a large-format printer and began experimenting with in-house printing techniques and stitching the works together into hybrid-like paintings that had no actual paint, only ink.
—Chris Dorland, email to author, April 16, 2023

The *Alumacore* pieces were an evolution of the earlier sewn works. But rather than [creating] something soft and supple like a painting, I wanted these works to have the coldness of a car. Black boxes of technology, these are the only works I have done that [have] been outsourced to a printer as opposed to being made in-house at the studio. The black metal panels were printed onto by a large industrial UV ink printer.
I really look forward to expanding just exactly what machine vision looks like. Machines are increasingly seeing the world—that's really interesting to me.
—Chris Dorland in Pimploy Phongsirivech, "Glitch Artist Chris Dorland Talks Transhumanism with Author Carolyn Kane," *Interview*, 2018

Scanner Aesthetics and the Technical Turn

Chris Dorland's works at the end of 2009 begin to revel in the iconography of digital culture: scanners, screens, mapping technologies, and data infrastructures. These paintings operate within a logic of control, critiquing and reproducing the aesthetics of the technical systems they interrogate. His compositions often resemble interface maps, drone footage, or corrupted blueprints—flattened planes overlaid with mechanical striations and digital noise. These elements echo Jean Baudrillard's theory of simulation, where the map overtakes the territory and representation supersedes reality. Dorland's painterly simulations compel the viewer to confront the seductive yet unstable ground of mediated knowledge.

The *Scanners* and *Alumacores* represent a conceptual intensification in Chris Dorland's practice, shifting the work more decisively toward what could be theorized as an aesthetics of mediation. Rather than interpreting these works as aesthetic expressions or extensions of prior series, I regard them as theoretical objects—artworks that engage in thought. In this manner, they highlight the apparatuses, processes, and perceptual logics that have shaped the postdigital condition, particularly as it intersects with capitalist ideology, technological embodiment, and distributed cognition.

In the *Scanners*, Dorland appropriates the tools of commercial production—scanners, printers, and stitching machines—not merely to simulate painting but to estrange it from its traditional ontology. This shift to "painting without painting" does not signify a retreat from the medium but its critical recalibration. The medium is consequently transformed into a problem space, a field through which the artist theorizes the collapsing distinction between production and reproduction, image and interface, surface and system.

Cognitive Assemblages and Distributed Subjectivity

Rather than viewing the *Scanners* as a critique of advertising or consumerism, a more productive theoretical framework interprets these works as aligned with the ideas promulgated by theorists N. Katherine Hayles and Bernard Stiegler concerning the mutual coevolution of humans and machines. Scanners, printers, collages, and gestures are not separate stages in Dorland's process but interconnected agents within a larger "cognitive assemblage," to use Hayles's apt term. What emerges is not merely a finished image but an enactment of the recursive logic joining technological and human subjectivities.

This approach resonates with Dorland's self-positioning as a "technical painter," an identity that moves beyond the romantic model of the artist as an expressive genius by replacing it with a posthuman figure embedded in systems, flows, and feedback loops. Dorland's pieced, sewn, printed, and fractured compositions during this period do not resolve into coherent wholes. Instead, they operate as aesthetic fields of differential relations, echoing Jean-François Lyotard's notion of the "figural," a realm of affective, non-representational intensity and a vertiginously unknown and vital unconscious force opposed to well-codified, consciously understood, and ultimately representational figuration.

Capitalist Painting

Chris Dorland's *Scanners* series takes the form of scanned-and-copied works on paper, which he began in 2009. These new pieces relied on images appropriated from books and magazines, which he would feed through a printer before stitching them together with Erin Knutson's Bernina sewing machine. At this time, his work benefited from conversations with Knutson, who was then pursuing an MFA in graphic design at Yale University. Dorland was enormously pleased with works in this series, which were 100 percent printed, so that even the apparent gestural movements in them were simulated. One reason for his satisfaction is that the completed works, which often feature a range of ads, seem to be in sync with capitalism and its excesses. Dorland would prepaint canvases slated for the *Scanners* series with emulsion so that the resultant images would exhibit some surface texture, making the works, according to the artist, particularly striking and tactile. He also utilized his scanner's lens by moving selected images across it to create waves and disruptions, thereby guiding viewers to his transformations of the appropriated pictures. The visual sales pitches these selected images originally conveyed as ads were therefore bracketed and objectified to ensure that his art focused on the topic of advertising rather than being subjected to it. Dorland's accordingly playful use of the scanner's lens and its bracketing of information is an approach that the collaborative duo Guyton\Walker [that is, Wade Guyton and Kelley Walker] had initiated a few years before, and Dorland readily acknowledges their work as a positive source.

In his *Scanners*, then, Dorland appropriates and repurposes commercial imagery to support his understanding of accelerationism and its imperative to move capitalism forward, often in ways its practitioners had not anticipated. He has recalled preferring pages of ads found in "junk culture magazines, anything available on the newsstands, including corporate publications, *Vanity Fair*, timely traditional publications, especially corporate ads, pushing images such as sexy advertisements on the public," so that he could create artistic interventions in a range of readily available media.

Advertising and the Anatomy of Desire

When making these works and unpacking some of their mass-media illusions, Dorland became keenly aware of the role of psychoanalytic insights into programming desire through advertising in order to sell merchandise while transforming people's identities so that they might become docile customers. Crucial for capitalism is the idea that individuality should define itself through consumption but not to the extent that potential buyers might comprehend the many ruses advertisers use to manipulate them. Particularly intriguing for Dorland is the role undertaken in the early and mid-twentieth century by Sigmund Freud's nephew Edward Bernays in initiating a new field of public relations in the United States. Dorland had been introduced to Bernays's work through BBC documentary filmmaker Adam Curtis's 2002 award-winning series *The Century of the Self*. In this series, Curtis emphasizes how Bernays began directing the unconscious mind's irrational powers in his campaign to transform females into smokers by branding cigarettes women's "torches of freedom." Among Bernays's many accomplishments were selling Americans on bacon-and-egg breakfasts and convincing shoppers to use germ-free Dixie Cups by implying their usefulness in preventing the spread of venereal diseases. Bernays's pop cultural contributions were especially relevant to Dorland's early work, even though he had been unaware of them at the time because Bernays had overseen the marketing of the 1939 New York World's Fair. Familiarity with the trajectory of Bernays's professional career has enabled Dorland to appreciate the formative role advertising and publicity have assumed in creating models of reality that are then sold to consumers, who regularly buy into these simulated viewpoints, thereby ratifying them as real.

In addition to focusing on advertisements, and, thus, capitalism's roles in the formation of modern consumers, Dorland relied on certain twentieth-century artistic developments when formulating his *Scanners*, especially his resonances with geometric abstraction, Minimalism, and metapainting evident in his reliance on empty pieces of natural or colored canvas, consequently, the *Scanners* assemblages. Thus, Dorland's appropriated images, together with their areas of blank or monochromatically painted canvases, which allude to art history's, embrace the "ideological rubble" Mark Fisher describes as capitalism's political fallout. This debris was to play an important role in Dorland's *Scanners*, his subsequent *Alumacores*, and later *Screenscrapes*, thus becoming a mainstay of his art.

Alumacores:
Machinic Surfaces and Neo-Noir Interfaces

Dorland had only recently begun to think of himself as an "artist-engineer" when he discovered Alumacore, a cutting-edge industrial material that required him to outsource aspects of the production of his work to fabricators with large UV-ink printers. Consisting of corrugated plastic cores wedged between black .013-inch-thick aluminum panels, Alumacore's relatively light yet substantial sheets enabled Dorland to create authoritative and imperturbably mechanical transformations of his formerly soft, sewn-canvas pieces. Choosing this particular medium for his art was a qualitative move that placed his work in an entirely different category, especially since its resilient and mirrorlike darkness, constitute, in the artist's words, a "black screen, . . . [becoming] a kind of abyss—something that's totally impenetrable and also kind of seductive. Like Darth Vader."

The *Alumacores* expand these concerns while amplifying their material and conceptual stakes. Printed on industrial substrates, they literalize the interface. No longer soft or painterly, these objects are transformed into hard-edged emissaries of machinic vision, such as screens, stelae, and black boxes. This shift in material indicates a turn toward Virilio's dromological materiality: one characterized by control and the militarization of vision rather than speed. The *Alumacores*, then, are not paintings of modernity; they are its prosthetic remains.

However, these works do not merely reflect the conditions of late capitalism or postindustrial visuality. Instead, they serve as speculative platforms from which to theorize these conditions. For example, the *Alumacores* draw on Michael Mann's *Heat* and reference Dorland's connection with this American filmmaker's lush yet gritty, high-tech aesthetic, particularly the striking color effects achieved in the acclaimed neo-noir film *Heat* (1995). In this film, violence is filtered through a lyrical lens that blends uncompromising realism with abstract, dystopian perspectives, resulting in stunningly beautiful and dramatically lit night scenes, often featuring blurred backgrounds enveloped in Mann's signature saturated dark blue tones. Sensitive to this intricately layered neo-noir method for depicting a less-than-ideal world, Dorland has found ways to reinterpret aspects of it in his impressively powerful, allusive, and technically adept *Alumacores*, his high-tech abstractions that function less as critiques and more as symptoms, visible manifestations of a visual regime shaped by data, surveillance, and affective saturation.

Civilian's Architectural Field

While some of Dorland's earlier work represented architecture, these imposing sheets of Alumacore enabled him to extend and literalize the architectural spaces in which his new pieces were presented. He designed an installation with steel construction studs that enveloped and sometimes obstructed viewers' access to *Civilian*, his 2018 exhibition at the Manhattan gallery Lyles & King. Dorland's installation defines not only the spaces where his art is displayed but also the ways in which it is observed, as it dictates viewers' movements. Echoes of Gordon Matta-Clark's deconstructed buildings and Michael Asher's 2008 exhibition for the Santa Monica Museum of Art are evident, yet more critically, the work aestheticizes its surroundings. *Civilian* can be understood through the perspective of spatial theory. Rather than serving as a neutral backdrop, the gallery space becomes part of the work's extended field, constructing a semiotic architecture that controls and redirects perception. Furthermore, pioneering video artist Nam June Paik's view of TV screens as new canvases inspired Dorland's short videos and the monitors used to display them. While Paik's videos were formative for Dorland's *Alumacores*, his series *Scanners* also played a significant role, enabling him first to scan mass-media images and then to rescan them repeatedly until they became distorted in the process. He also incorporated transparencies of ads to create enigmatic and layered yet still brash artworks.

Artistic Influences as Semiotic Ghosts

In addition to the previously mentioned artists, Dorland has drawn from Robert Rauschenberg's two-dimensional assemblages, which he readily acknowledges as part of his art's "DNA." Dorland views these, along with traces of other earlier artists' works, particularly Gerhard Richter's abstract paintings, as ghosts that haunt his oeuvre. This relationship is not simply a family tree of traditional art historical lineages but rather a collection of special resonances. Rejecting the conventional art historical focus on stylistic genealogies pertaining to sources and influences, which relegate later artworks to the status of legatees, Dorland adheres to the relatively new theory of hauntology, which he first encountered in Mark Fisher's 2014 book, *Ghosts of My Life: Writings on Depression, Hauntology, and Lost Futures*. Rather than viewing his connection with Fisher's book as a breakthrough revelation, we might more reasonably see it as a reflection of a notable tactic already present in Dorland's early work — its connection with anamorphic strategies and perhaps the "semiotic ghosts" found in William Gibson's "Gernsback Continuum," as suggested earlier. Thus, to be haunted is to be ensnared in the persistence of lost futures, in ideological and aesthetic projections that failed to materialize but continue to shape the present. Dorland's fractured work and recursive processes literalize this condition, making them palimpsests of deferred promises and corrupted codes.

Hauntological Ghosts in the Machine

To appreciate hauntology's far-ranging implications, it helps to connect it to the turn-of-the-twentieth-century Swiss linguist Ferdinand de Saussure, who theorized language as a social construct comprising negative relations between signs, so that a word like *bit* assumes meaning through the conventional usage distinguishing it from such similar-sounding words as *but* and *bat*. "Thus, words construed as sets of signs are haunted by the many negative relations differentiating them from one another, and the same is true of artworks.

In *Specters of Marx: The State of the Debt, the Work of Mourning, and the New International* (1994), French deconstructionist Jacques Derrida is the first to theorize hauntology as a neologistic play on *ontology* and an extension of deconstruction. He suggests that no term or text can stand alone because all are haunted by phantomlike traces. In other words, they are also defined, according to Derrida, by the absences that undermine and constitute a "metaphysics of presence," a theory earlier delineated in twentieth-century philosopher Martin Heidegger's *Being and Time* (1927). In *Specters of Marx*, Derrida playfully refers to the opening statement of Karl Marx and Friedrich Engels's *The Communist Manifesto*, which poetically begins thus: "A specter is haunting Europe — the specter of communism." Fully in compliance with Derrida's hauntology, Fisher writes, "Everything that exists is possible only on the basis of a whole series of absences [ghosts] which precede and surround it, allowing it to possess such consistency and intelligibility that it does." While Marx's capitalist ghost represents communism's foreshadowing phantom, Fisher's is also capital — the spectral yet crucial modus operandi of modern Western society. Derrida's and Fisher's apparitions also serve as the often unrecognized and absent binary on which so much knowledge is based.

Although Fisher cites Derrida as the initiator of hauntology, another source deserves recognition: Jean Baudrillard's simulation, in particular his apparitional models and their descendants that haunt and supplant so-called reality. This concept may have, in fact, impacted Derrida's view of hauntology's pervasiveness. Perhaps thinking of Baudrillard's hyperreality, Derrida asks rhetorically, "Is there *there*, between the thing itself and its simulacrum, an opposition that holds up?" And he responds, "Let us call it a *hauntology*." Baudrillard's radical reevaluation views reality as being superseded by apparitional models, and it correlates well with Dorland's work, beginning with his already discussed early architectural models and continuing with his works on paper as well as his *Prototypes*, *Scanners*, and *Alumacores*, which all include allusive and highly constructed advertisements that bedevil past, present, and future outlooks with their hyperreal specters.

We might extend hauntology into areas Derrida did not contemplate by considering how technical innovations have reframed human vision and transformed the once monolithic understanding of the self, so that a double haunting between humans and machines takes place. It helps to recognize, as visual communications specialist Carolyn Kane points out, that machines and technology can no longer be confined to mere tools and equipment, "but instead [they must embrace] . . . history, infrastructure, memory, knowledge, and cultural convention," thereby becoming "a system and context of innovation, application, awareness, and use." According to history-of-consciousness specialist Teresa de Lauretis, "Technology is now, not only in a distinct, science fictional future, an extension of our sensory capacities; it shapes our perceptions and cognitive processes, mediates our relationship with objects of the material and physical world, and our relations with our own or other bodies." De Lauretis's view is fully in compliance with literary specialist Claire Sponsler's conclusion that "technology has shaped new modes of consciousness and behavior," and literary critic N. Katherine Hayles's assessment that situations in which the human body is allied with nonorganic materials outside itself is a posthuman one: "[T]he posthuman view thinks of the body as the original prosthesis we all learn to manipulate, so that extending or replacing the body with other prostheses becomes a continuation of a process that began before we were born." This state of affairs, as Hayles cogently reminds her readers, is now one of "distributed cognition."

The Posthuman Eye and the Ghost in the Machine

Early posthuman inroads into the Italian Renaissance liberal-humanist view of fully autonomous individuals were made by linear perspective paintings, which retrained aspects of the human sensorium, thereby defining a new and revelatory way for people to look at the world, so that it appeared to be a rational and empirical construct in which each element has its mathematically and geometrically assigned place as well as its specified relation to everything else deemed worthy of representation. In this way, linear perspective transformed human understanding both aesthetically and historically. In doing so, it set up new power and knowledge relationships tantamount to seeing life afresh. In addition to one-point perspective, we might consider such transformative prosthetic inventions as eyeglasses (circa 1290), microscopes (1590), and telescopes (1608), which have impacted peoples' views of themselves and their enhanced roles, even though such seventeenth- and eighteenth-century philosophers as René Descartes and Immanuel Kant persisted in viewing humans as autonomous subjects. In hauntology, we might conclude that our mutable definitions of ourselves are vulnerable to different technologies, which act as changing panoplies to become the internalized phantoms that haunt and transform our lives.

Throughout the nineteenth and twentieth centuries, the subjugation of humans to concepts and media outside themselves has taken far too many meaningful steps to be recounted in this discussion, but I can point to German literary and media specialist Friedrich Kittler's twentieth-century reversal of Canadian philosopher Marshall McLuhan's belief in human beings' extraordinary ability to extend themselves through various media while maintaining their integrity. Kittler does so by pointing out that while people may have innovated their mechanical knowledge, by an ironic turnabout, they ultimately become extensions of this knowledge. In this way, technology serves contradictorily as humanity's a priori. Fully in agreement with this diminution of human beings while still empowering them through collaborations with outside media, Stiegler has proposed the term *technogenesis* to underscore humans' and machines' reciprocal dependence and related development over time. Given Stiegler's premise, we might well conclude that differences among humans and machines have become so interconnected that one shadows or haunts the other. Stiegler's technogenesis depends on the landmark redefinition of humanity in 1947, coming soon after the first workable computer in 1944, when MIT mathematician Norbert Wiener originated the new science of cybernetics by studying flows of information among humans, animals, and machines as cognitive communicative patterns. In this way, Wiener posits a new equity between them, thus initiating a major break in which the patterning of thought ceases to be comprehended as only a human trait. Understood in this manner, humans are cybernetic organisms and so are machines and animals.

According to Hayles, "Henceforth, humans were to be seen primarily as information-processing entities who are essentially similar to intelligent machines." On another occasion, she points to the "rapidly escalating complexities created by the interpenetration of cognitive technologies with human systems," in other words, "the exteriorization of cognitive abilities," so that "human subjects are no longer contained—or even defined—by the boundaries of their skins." We might expand on Hayles's view of cognition as comprising informational patterns by pointing to the ongoing mutuality in which humans shadow machines and vice versa, so that each haunts the other to a certain degree. Because technology and perception go far beyond mere tools and human vision by participating in the overarching systems of knowledge giving rise to them, it helps to acknowledge the reciprocity among these different cognitive modes. We might also recognize the blurred lines among them so that intelligences involve a new hauntology in which one is neither fully present nor absent from the others, even though they are all cognitively implicated with one another.

This approach is fully consistent with Dorland's observation, "I'm into modernity. In the ways modern technologies affect the way we see the world." This view is compatible with his acknowledgment, "I really look forward to expand[ing] just exactly what machine vision looks like. Machines are increasingly seeing the world—that's really interesting to me." Among these machines, we might include such computer technologies as flight simulators, AI smart glasses, computer animation, and magnetic resonance imaging, in addition to image classification, detection, tracking, and retrieval devices, among others. While some of these prostheses appear to be external, others can be internalized as immersive experiences. Dorland recognizes the impact of this cybernetic turn. "My generation," he has elaborated, "those of us who were kids in the eighties, all tend to be concerned, in some way or another, with the blurring of reality and virtuality. I've been conscious of this blur since I was very young." Dorland's outlook helps to explain his long-term fascination with fellow Canadian David Cronenberg and the schizophrenic human bodies in his films that unite, interconnect, and propagate with inanimate substances. This necessary downgrading and consequent leveling of humanity also entails questioning the veracity of its presumed empirical abilities. According to physicist David Deutsch, even empiricism should be put on notice because the human sensorium has been retooled and redirected by its immersion in virtual reality, so that people may think they are experiencing life when they are actually seeing through the virtual-reality lens technology has provided them. At this point, I would add that not only individuals but also to individuals and entire societies have been profoundly affected by simulation's virtual reality lens.

Dorland's *Scanners* and *Alumacores* function not only as media-specific inquiries but also as theoretical models for examining the entangled relationships among machines, perception, subjectivity, and history. Rather than decoding them for meaning, we might better approach them as theoretical engines, objects that do not merely represent but enact the processes they question. They ask not "what is the image of?" but "how is this image produced, circulated, and inhabited?" They enact, in other words, a theory of vision in which seeing is always already technologized, ideologically framed, and recursively haunted.

Created in 2017, the year Dorland began his *Alumacores* series, *Untitled (Memory Cortex)*, his thirty-three-second single-channel loop video, may be interpreted personally as his "prime object," a term coined by art historian George Kubler for preeminent artworks so innovative that they can initiate paradigmatic, stylistic shifts. Representing a fusion of mind and machine, this compact video, with its fluctuating, glimmering, and interwoven sequences, celebrates both human and mechanical memory through online programs that have been pirated and collected into a grand, yet brief and intense, viewing experience that reflects on the *Simulations* while anticipating the *Alumacores* and *Screenscrapes*. It references architecture, machines, body parts such as a cervical spine, materials sourced from online sites, and the potent words *shift* and *reckless emotion*. Dorland's short video is an exciting and intentionally overloaded work that fulfills the artist's desire to incorporate iconographic elements from both his early architectural models and his latest creations.

Untitled (Memory Cortex) and Dorland's related *Alumacores* and *Screenscrapes* are fully conversant with his life in New York City, where he has lived since graduating from Purchase College in 2002. These works may also hark back to the artist's early and enthusiastic reading of Italian author Italo Calvino's *Invisible Cities*, in which the Venetian merchant Marco Polo conjures up stories for the elderly Chinese emperor Kublai Khan during the late thirteenth century, when the Italian explorer was in the far east. Fantasizing about distant cities in Khan's empire, Calvino gives them the improbable names of captivating women and presents such preposterous types of municipalities as cities of desire, towns touched with regrets, thin centers, failing settlements, and vibrant metropolises. In retrospect, there is not a huge qualitative difference between Dorland's childhood writing of graffiti on Montreal's city walls and his decades-later creation of a video in which fragments of machinery, architecture, language, and body parts come together in the piece appropriately subtitled *Memory Cortex*.

CHAPTER FOUR
Screenscrapes and Their Whiteouts (2020–Present), Digital Fragments, and Semiotic Ghosts

> The specter of twentieth-century abstraction haunts these works like ghosts in the machine. With this latest iteration, I have increasingly been collaborating with text-to-image AI tools to generate large sections of the paintings. Images and structures are stitched and spliced together using a variety of different softwares in order to arrive at a final image. My process is a form of postdigital bricolage, whereby data is scraped, collected, and glitched from a variety of sources and then assembled and retransmitted onto canvas [to create] new forms of machinic abstractions.
> —Chris Dorland, text for Liste Art Fair Basel, 2023

> I already feel like my role is that of a facilitator. I think of the event being the scan, and how can I set it up so that the machine is doing its own thing and takes more and more of my own agency out of it?
> —Chris Dorland in Pimploy Phongsirivech, "Glitch Artist Chris Dorland Talks Transhumanism with Author Carolyne Kane," *Interview*, 2018

> My current work consists of really dense and thick fossilized surfaces that are built up and almost bone-like or archaeological. And then there's this infra-thin digital membrane fused into it. They're very Cronenbergian in the sense of flesh and machine collapsing into one.
> —Chris Dorland in Willa Koerner, "Hidden Gems: Chris Dorland on the Transformation of Reality," *Static 1*, 2023

The Studio as Laboratory

Developed within a self-described "laboratory" of both obsolete and current hardware, Chris Dorland's process underscores the recursive, iterative, and machinic logic of contemporary image-making. Each of his *Screenscrape* paintings begins with digital detritus—fragments scraped from various visual environments, processed through scanners, distorted by filters, and broken down before being reconstituted into new composites. The resulting images are not mere representations but events: painterly sites where informational systems collide, glitch, and mutate. Consequently, the *Screenscrapes* may be viewed as cognitive clusters, distributed fields of agency that blur the distinctions between human and nonhuman forms of cognition.

Dorland's *Screenscrapes* emerged from the overlapping crises of the early 2020s, a time shaped by a global pandemic, rising automation, and intensified digital culture. Instead of positioning these works as responses to a specific historical rupture, my theoretical approach treats them as contingent enactments of a broader epistemic shift: the breakdown of traditional distinctions between digital and analog worlds, human and machinic realms, and aesthetic and infrastructural domains. In this context, Dorland's paintings do not merely depict a postdigital precinct; they theorize it.

Glitches

In Dorland's practice, glitches are aesthetic devices for manifesting conceptual rupture.
As we will see, his recurring use of scraping, overprinting, and digital layering in the
Screenscrapes disrupts lingering illusions of seamless control. These glitches can be
conceived through the mixed metaphor of visual stutters—instances when a system mis-
fires, revealing something beneath or beyond its surface. In this way, paintings in the
Screenscrapes series align with those artists and theorists who view the glitch as a systemic
failure and site of potential critical resistance. However, these works reveal such errors
to be revelations rather than mere accidental breakdowns: they represent moments when
the repeated workings of digital equipment become visible.

In early 2020, at the onset of the Covid-19 pandemic, Chris Dorland cloistered
himself in his New Jersey studio with the expressed goal of figuring out how to transform
the imagery of his 2017 *Untitled (Memory Cortex)* video into a new type of screen-based
painting. He was often the only person taking the PATH train from his Lower Manhattan
home, and he wore three masks to protect himself. It was an apocalyptic time calling
for radically new solutions, and Dorland wanted to mine this particular video's complex
and layered digital iconography for his reproduced-and-painted canvases. Because of
the pandemic, he intended to make his art entirely by himself, thereby obviating the need
for industrial suppliers and commercial printers while hopefully avoiding occasions for con-
tracting Covid. He began utilizing a range of this equipment, including obsolete computers,
scanners, and printers, when experimenting with ways to fuse ink-jet-printed images on film
with plastic-polymer-and-gesso-prepared grounds that he had shaped into ridges. He then
articulated these bonded-film-and-lenticular-shaped substrates with discrete passages of
gestural painting, thereby melding together these techniques and leaving viewers unable to
easily differentiate painted from printed passages and incapable of effectively discriminat-
ing real from simulated components. Dorland has named these works *Screenscrapes* to refer
to the technique of data scraping, which involves extracting information from various web-
sites and importing it into spreadsheets or files. They resonate with N. Katherine Hayles's
cybernetic views about "what it means to be human in [contemporary] developed societies."

Whiteouts and the Breakdown of Representation

Dorland forged a view of the cybernetic reciprocity between himself and his array of
machines to arrive at a fecund yet ultimately mysterious exchange tantamount to a cognitive assemblage, involving a productive type of disorder. "I actually get inspiration and
ideas from the chaos and instability in the world," Dorland has acknowledged. "It feeds my
work, and it inspires me." This visual bedlam is evident in the jostling and interpenetrating
fragments of codes and images populating his *Screenscrapes*, in addition to the anomalies
stemming from slippages that occur when scraped data is filtered through multiple programs
and machines, resulting in the ghostly white passages—the captivating semiotic breaks
I am calling "whiteouts"—that he then enhances with glowing paint.

These white voids resist simple classification. They may resemble accidents or
glitches, but a theoretical reading insists they are symptomatic of deeper structural ruptures,

moments when translations between systems fail and meanings collapse under the
weight of excessive data. Dorland's whiteouts operate less as visual mistakes and more
as epistemological breaks—points of interruption where the ideological architectures
of images become visible through their own breakdown.

These whiteouts may be understood, in the terms of philosopher Jean-Luc Nancy,
as excriptions—not simply absences but sites where incompatible systems of inscription
reach their limit and fail to converge. Rather than unifying the rational codes of digital
imaging, scanner errors, or AI renderings into a coherent symbolic order, Dorland leaves
their incongruities exposed, allowing whiteouts to appear where meaning cannot be
synthesized. These are not mere voids or breakdowns; they are traces of the Real, marks
of what exceeds symbolic capture. As such, the whiteouts act as default excriptions—
formal interruptions where socially ratified codes collide and collapse, leaving a space
that is not empty but saturated with unrepresentable presence. Dorland does not erase or
conceal these failures; he amplifies them, accentuating the disjunctive remnants left by
incompatible rationalities. In doing so, he refuses the seamlessness of simulation and foregrounds the *hauntological* dimension of technological life: where fragments do not align,
the ghost appears. These excriptive gaps become not only aesthetic breaks but ethical
ones—inviting viewers to reflect on what remains unrenderable in a world governed by
systems of image-control.

Ghosts in the Archive:
Hauntology and the Loss of Memory

In his recent works enunciated with whiteouts, Dorland's long-standing interest in simulation gives way to an exploration of memory loss, pointing to the fragility of the archive.
The ghostliness of digital culture—its endless duplication, erasure, and overwriting—
becomes apparent in works that seem to be haunted by their own instability. Drawing on
hauntological theory, Dorland's images flicker between presence and absence. Here, the
glitch is no longer an interruption; it serves as a trace of loss, a spectral residue that disrupts
the very notion of permanence.

Dorland's whiteouts also engage with the longer tradition of visual estrangement
I discussed earlier. From Hans Holbein's anamorphic skull in *The Ambassadors* to William
Gibson's "semiotic ghosts" in "The Gernsback Continuum," these figures create ruptures
in representational space. They provoke rather than resolve, thereby highlighting the
productive failures of machinic and human vision as well as cognition. In other words,
in Dorland's work, these ghosts are both machinic and cultural: they delineate the entangled
processes through which algorithms, scanners, and AI-generated fragments reshape human
perception from the inside out.

Instead of treating glitch aesthetics as expressive or symbolic, Dorland's work
encourages a theoretical reading of the glitch as systemic, an index of the collapse of
legibility in a culture of relentless mediation. While Carolyn Kane has usefully defined
glitch art as a dialectic of "control and its renunciation; a flirtation with breakdown,
chaos, and total immersion in technology, followed by a level-headed bait and switch,"
Dorland's interventions surpass these binaries. His works do not merely relinquish control;

they problematize it, staging a recursive field where agency, authorship, and perception are profoundly unsettled.

Dorland's *Screenscrapes* examine the concept of cloning a repository—a process aimed at replicating and preserving digital content—as a metaphor for the futility of reproduction itself. Works in this series envision a collapsed network of digital ruins, the material residues of technological decay revealing a landscape of decayed servers, lost transmissions, and corrupted archives. While earlier works allude to simulation and control systems at the peak of their functioning or dysfunction, the *Screenscrapes* immerse us in a world where the network has already failed. With their thick layers of polymer and ink, the paintings resemble drone-captured stills from a glitched, fractured, and somewhat unreadable system. These distorted images evoke archival trauma: fragments from servers that no longer transmit, repositories cloned too late. The archive becomes spectral rather than stable; its assumed preservation function gives way to destruction and loss. If Dorland's earlier works grappled with the violence of systems, his *Screenscrapes* mourn their futility. As imperfect clones, which have been overwritten, corrupted, and rendered unstable, these paintings evoke a sublime archaeology of failure, where memory is no longer preserved but disintegrated, creating confusion rather than clarity through duplication. These works are haunted by the very systems they invoke, revealing surveillance, storage, and simulation to all be fragile, fallible, and ultimately impermanent. What remains in Dorland's most recent works is not the power of simulation, but its ruin, a record of technologies once imagined as omniscient, now exposed in their failure to preserve, transmit, or even remember. These works represent a shift in tone to something much quieter, more poignant, and undeniably elegiac.

Painting as Interface:
Toward a Hybrid Vision

The various disturbances comprising the *Screenscrapes* extend to the genre of painting itself. Dorland's fusion of gestural marks with printed overlays, lenticular ridges, and AI-generated imagery renders the distinction between painted and digital passages irrelevant. Painting here becomes a hybrid surface, an interface where different systems or realities converge and interconnect, a palimpsest of human and machinic visions, affective residues, and technical manipulations. It is no longer a window onto the world or merely a mirror of it but a volatile interface that stages the collapse of older categories of medium, subjectivity, and authenticity while loosely uniting them into a new form of cybernetic cognition.

Sensation and the Diagram:
Deleuze, Lyotard, and the Logic of Collapse

The *Screenscrapes* are profoundly informed by the theories of French philosopher Gilles Deleuze, particularly his engagement with sensation, which in part is based on the forces Jean-François Lyotard calls "figural." Dorland's whiteouts participate in a vertiginously unknown and vital unconscious force opposed to well-codified, consciously understood, and ultimately representational figuration. Deleuze has advanced Lyotard's differentiation of these two artistic modes in his book subtitled *The Logic of Sensation*, which focuses on British expressionist Francis Bacon's painting and the condition Deleuze calls "sensation," which is not representational but affective, constituting a force that acts directly on the nervous system. He defines *sensation* as a moment of anarchy generated by such improvisational marks as stains and painterly traits in order to differentiate painting from illustrative work. He eloquently describes these eminently generative yet chaotic moments in the following statement:

> It is like the emergence of another world. For these marks, these traits, are irrational, involuntary, accidental, free, random. They are nonrepresentative, nonillustrative, nonnarrative. They are no longer either significant or signifiers: they are a-signifying traits. . . . The painter's hand intervenes in order to shake its own independence and break up the sovereign optical organizations: one can no longer see anything, as if in a catastrophe, a chaos. This is the act of painting, or the turning point of the painting.

Because it is unable to communicate direct and unequivocal meanings, the role of painterly sensation, which Deleuze calls "the diagram," is allusive. Dorland's whiteouts and dense compositional fragments similarly bypass conventional cognition, enacting the diagrammatic, a zone of indeterminacy that precedes form and meaning. These diagrams do not illustrate: they convulse, destabilize, and mutate. As an initial improvisatory tactic, the "diagram" supposedly touches the nerves directly rather than being channeled through acculturated perception, which Deleuze equates with the conscious mind. He also connects these a-signifying painterly sensations with the waves flowing through his and his co-author Felix Guattari's "body without organs," as discussed in their two-volume study *Capitalism and Schizophrenia*."

In his enlightening introduction to Deleuze's *Francis Bacon: The Logic of Sensation*, philosopher Daniel W. Smith points to the early twentieth-century German psychologist Marius von Senden's analyses of the painful visual encounters congenitally blind individuals face when their cataracts are removed. Although able to see, they initially experience vision in terms of painfully disparate sensations before acquiring, through trial and error, the schemata necessary to structure what they are perceiving, thereby enabling them to learn how to make sense of it. Smith connects this initially overwhelming experience of sight facing blind individuals with Paul Cézanne's positive remarks about immersing himself in his environs in order to come to terms with their foundational potencies and dynamisms. As Smith relates:

> Cézanne said that the painter must look beyond a landscape to its chaos:
> he spoke of the need to always paint at close range, to no longer see the wheatfield, to be too close to it, to lose oneself in the landscape, without landmarks, to the point where one no longer sees forms or even matters, but only forces, densities, intensities. This is what Cézanne called the world before humanity, "dawn of ourselves," "iridescent chaos," "virginity of the world"—a complete collapse of visual coordinates in a universal variation or interaction. Afterward, in the act of painting, the earth can emerge, with its "stubborn geometry," its "geological foundations" as "the measure of the world."

This emphasis on the primacy of seeing, with all its confusing anomalies and powerful energies, has its aesthetic counterpart in the ghostlike passages haunting Dorland's *Screenscrapes*. However, Cézanne's chaos differs substantially from the jostling and competing representational fragments in Dorland's art, since the latter's whiteouts provide an even more basic and dynamic way to apprehend a hybridized cybernetic vision's primacy anew so that light and color are at times liberated, thereby enabling these intensities to be seen for themselves rather than as adjuncts endorsing traditional socially sanctioned modes of looking.

Surprisingly, neither Lyotard nor Deleuze point to primal vision's antecedents in Surrealism's psychic automatism and Abstract Expressionism's more plastic emendation of this improvisatory practice, which begin with spontaneous smudges, strokes, and absent-minded scribbling, with the expressed objective of tapping into artists' unconscious reserves that are only later cohered into compositions, often with recognizable yet highly abstract figuration. This Surrealist and Abstract Expressionist exploration of art's potency and its connections to the unconscious mind constitutes yet another example of painting's necessary reliance on concentrated dynamisms to underscore its inscrutable otherness rather than stressing any representational imagery it might suggest. Differing from psychic automatism, Dorland's self-reflexive, hauntological, and cybernetic inscriptions come near the end rather than the beginning of his creative process.

The Cybernetic Sublime:
Goldstein, Heidegger, and Broken Tools

While Dorland's apparitional passages may have a formal antecedent in the streaks of light signaling the pathways of fighter jets, bolts of lightning, showers of fireworks, and bomb explosions in paintings by fellow-Canadian-expatriate artist Jack Goldstein, a key member of the Pictures Group, whom Dorland has cited as a respected source, the meaning of his whiteouts differs substantially from Goldstein's depictions. In other words, Dorland's art—particularly his glowing, ghostlike concentrations that I'm calling "whiteouts"— are much more attuned to the random patterns, openness, contingency, and unpredictability connecting his work with a human-machine alliance. These breaks, tantamount to Jacques Lacan's Real, which cannot be symbolized, conjure up a cybernetic sublime.

By viewing these puzzling whiteouts in Dorland's *Screenscrapes* as breaks in the digital world of amassed fragments composing his works, we can rethink his cybernetic views in terms of their poignant and obviously intended ineffectuality. Similar to Martin Heidegger's well-known section in *Being and Time* pertaining to the broken hammer that suddenly appears un-ready-to-hand (rather than in its former ready-to-hand position where it was taken for granted), Dorland's art enables us to view technology from a new perspective by imagining possibilities extending far beyond the digital world's utilitarian functions. In other words, Dorland's apparitional forces permit us to consider their role in cybernetic thinking as an unknowable other so that his dystopic characterization of this new human and machine hybridized aesthetic underscores both its status as sets of fragmented ruins and their captivating mystery.

33

Technogenesis and Recursive Creation

Such theoretical frameworks as I have discussed also resonate with Dorland's use of
AI and machine learning. His increasing reliance on text-to-image generators signals a
shift not toward the posthuman as spectacle but toward Bernard Stiegler's technogenesis:
the cybernetic co-evolution of human and technical systems. Within this framework,
the artist becomes less a sovereign subject and more a facilitator of cognitive and recursive
exchanges among machines, images, and their cultural substrates. Dorland's often-stated
desire to reduce his own agency and "let the machine do its own thing" connotes a recon-
figuration of artistic labor as distributed, networked, and entangled rather than artistic
passivity.

The *Screenscrapes* can thus be theorized in hauntological terms. Their formal
language of layered glitches, broken sequences, and residual fragments bears the trace
of lost technological promises and utopian futures. These works are not nostalgic; they
are spectral. They engage with Mark Fisher's "slow cancellation of the future," presenting
aesthetic terrains where obsolescence and innovation cohabitate, and they might also be
considered potential denizens of William Gibson's *Neuromancer*. When viewed in this manner, Dorland's paintings can be interpreted as diagnostic, reflecting the anxiety, volatility,
and excess of a culture that has stopped believing in progress while remaining addicted
to its many overlapping and conflated images of change.

The Ethics of Representation After Technological Failure

A theoretical approach to these works does not close them down; instead, it opens them
to a multiplicity of readings: media-theoretical, deconstructive, and posthuman. Dorland's
Screenscrapes are not so much solutions to a visual problem as sites of inquiry. They
are image-thoughts and theoretical objects that reflect the recursive conditions of their
own making. In them, painting becomes not just an aesthetic practice but a speculative act
that asks how art might appear to think in the aftermath of traditional representational goals.

In his *Screenscrapes*, Dorland confronts the endpoint of simulation—not its peak,
but its entropy. Their strong hyperreal implications no longer function critically because
these allusions add up to an archaeological site, comprising layers of superannuated models.
The *Screenscrapes*'s all-important glitch is structural and deconstructive so that the archive,
once imagined as a stable repository, disintegrates under its own duplications. What remains
is the discomfiting question: What kind of knowledge—and what kind of responsibility—
can be extracted from systems that fail to preserve the so-called realities they claim to
portend? Dorland's *Screenscrapes*, which point to broken servers and fractured screens,
do not just mourn the loss of reality; they implicate the very systems that claimed to
preserve it. In revealing the violence embedded in mediation itself, his work invites us
to confront the ethics of representation after technological failure.

CODA
Dorland's Eloquent Ruins as Semiotic Phantoms,
Theorizing His Aesthetic Interventions

"If you want a classier explanation," Merv Kihn explained, "I'd say you saw a
semiotic ghost. All these contactee stories, for instance, are framed in a kind of
sci-fi imagery that permeates our culture. . . . They're semiotic phantoms, bits
of deep cultural imagery that have split off and taken on a life of their own."
—William Gibson, "The Gernsback Continuum," 1981

Recognizing the extent to which the world is a social and historical construct, Dorland
has found art's highly contrived means an excellent way to focus on the simulated worlds
that have been ratified as reality in the late twentieth and early twenty-first centuries.
His art appropriates a number of wonderfully eloquent ruins that haunt his work, start-
ing with the world's fair sites that are antiquated modern-era relics, the "semiotic ghosts"
found in William Gibson's "Gernsback Continuum." Other phantoms appear in Dorland's
works incorporating scanned ads, which serve as models of consumption, and they
culminate, in his latest works, the *Screenscrapes*, with their whiteout passages that haunt
an advanced and diminished view of humans by observing them as informational patterns
on a par with those exhibited by machines. In this way, they provide nonliteral, anamorphic
perspectives that upend traditional theories about humanity's autonomy. While Dorland's
art might appear to be simply the latest advances of the early twentieth-century utopian
machine aesthetic, his dystopian attitude provides a perspective for assessing the present
and future, albeit through an informed and definitely skeptical lens. His most recent works
embody the ghostly archive he has always hinted at, albeit in a now more materialized
and mournful manner.

From the speculative architectures of Dorland's *Memoryscapes* to the digital-material
intensity of his *Screenscrapes*, I have been involved in a consistent desire to interrogate the
conditions under which his images are made, circulated, and perceived. These are not paintings in search of stable interpretations; they are inquiries into the instability of language
itself, including visual, historical, ideological, and technological vernaculars. Interpreting
such works requires an approach that does not presume mastery over meaning but, instead,
theorizes how meaning becomes contingent, recursive, and haunted by the very systems
that attempt to contain it.

In this situation, my role has not been to extract hidden content or to impose
coherence, but to situate Dorland's work within overlapping discursive fields such as
semiotics, simulation theory, cybernetics, hauntology, and media archaeology, while tracing
the theoretical problems his art proposes. To me, interpretation is a mode of theorization:
a sustained engagement with the philosophical, technological, and affective structures
that inform Dorland's art without determining it.

In conclusion, I would like to reaffirm that Dorland's work does not provide singular
messages; it resists illustration, disavows aesthetic comfort, and disorients perception.
Its surfaces, particularly those in his *Screenscrapes*, shimmer with painterly density
and machinic estrangement. These works thrust viewers into the new terrain of questioning
what seeing means when vision is no longer a purely human function, when cognition

is distributed across networks, and when the future can no longer be imagined outside its recursive entanglement with the past. In such conditions, theory becomes a manner of understanding that does not stabilize meaning but acknowledges its fragmentation, its spectral returns, and its structural deferrals.

Dorland's *Screenscrapes* invite us to contemplate the meaning of failing digital systems. Although his glitches—or whiteouts—constitute modes of critique, and his aesthetic practice confronts technology's ideological claims, his response to these failures is not simply analytical, as his recent works do not merely diagnose collapse: they provide opportunities for us to lament its occurrence. While his critique exposes the fragility of technological memory, his elegiac *Screenscrapes* bear witness to its aftermath. This shift marks Dorland's movement from systemic deconstruction to emotional and philosophical reckoning. While the art is plaintive, it is not accusatory.

ENDNOTES

1   Dorland's mother has published work under the names of Anna Alexander as well as A. A. and Alexander Antonopoulos. A notable publication is the collection of essays, edited by Anna Alexander and Mark S. Roberts, titled *High Culture: Reflections on Addiction and Modernity* (Albany: State University of New York Press, 2002). Antonopoulos has been recognized for their work at the Simone de Beauvoir Institute.

2   Jean Baudrillard, "The Evil Demon of Images," (The Inauguration of the Mari Kuttna Memorial Lecture on Film, Power Institute of Fine Arts, University of Sydney, July 25, 1984), https://monoskop.org/images/4/47/Baudrillard_Jean_The_evil_demon_of_images_1987.pdf, consulted April 19, 2024.

3   Baudrillard, "Evil Demon of Images," 42.

4   Chris Dorland, email to author, May 2, 2023.

5   Dorland, email to author, May 2, 2023.

6   Two of Michael Dorland's scholarly works are *So Close to the State/s: The Emergence of Canadian Feature Film Policy, 1952–1976* (Toronto: University of Toronto Press, 1998) and *Cadaverland: Inventing a Pathology of Catastrophe for Holocaust Survival*, Tauber Institute for the Study of European Jewry Series (Waltham, MA: Brandeis University Press, 2009), representing sixty years of psychiatric research on Holocaust survival. Dorland also wrote a novel called *The Double-Cross Circuit* (New York: Signet, 1980). He was a professor in the School of Journalism and Communication at Carleton University in Ottawa, Canada, and was working on a book about Michel Foucault's *The Order of Things*, which he was investigating from the perspective of visual communication when he died.

Willa Koerner, "Hidden Gems: Chris Dorland on the Transformation of Reality," *Static 1* (November 17, 2023), https://static1.squarespace.com/static/5f9cd0ec2020 532d6b5ece0a/t/6557e85734047a4f63f00801/1700259929258/Chris+Dorland+-+Hidden+Gems+-+2023.pdf, consulted April 20, 2024.

7   Koerner, "Hidden Gems."

8   Chris Dorland, Zoom interview by author, January 18, 2024.

9   Chris Dorland, untitled talk (School of Visual Arts, New York City, January 30, 2024).

10   Darko Suvin, "Estrangement and Cognition," *Strange Horizons* (November 24, 2014): n.p.f5

11   The trilogy begins with *Neuromancer* (1984) and ends with *Mona Lisa Overdrive* (1988).

12   Istvan Csicsery-Ronay, "Cyberpunk and Neuromanticism," *Mississippi Review* 16, no. 2/3 (1988): 274, 275.

13   Csicsery-Ronay, "Cyberpunk and Neuromanticism," 269.

14   Chris Dorland, email to author, July 5, 2024.

15   "Interview with Painter Chris Dorland—Part 1," *Modern Art Obsession* (blog) November 30, 2006, n.p., https://modernartobsession.blogs.com/modern_art_obsession/2006/11/catching_up_wit.html, consulted April 10, 2024.

16   "Interview with Painter Chris Dorland—Part 1," n.p.

17   Koerner, "Hidden Gems."

18   Thomas Lawson, "Last Exit: Painting" in *Art After Modernism: Rethinking Representation*, ed. Brian Wallis (New York: New Museum of Contemporary Art; Boston: David R. Godine, 1984), 160.

19   This is the conclusion drawn by art critic Peio Aguirre, "Semiotic Ghosts: Science Fiction and Historicism," *Afterall: A Journal of Art, Context and Enquiry* 28 (Autumn–Winter, 2011): 125.

20   Because this short story was published multiple times in notable publications and has consequently been read and widely discussed. Dorland may have been aware of its contents even if he had not actually read it. "The Gernsback Continuum" was first published in 1981 in *Universe 11*, edited by Terry Carr; later it was reprinted in Bruce Sterling's widely heralded edition of science-fiction stories *Mirrorshades* (1986); that same year it was included in Gibson's collection of short stories *Burning Chrome*. I suggested the relevance of this story to Dorland; soon thereafter, he read it and was convinced of its uncanny relevance to his work.

21   Chris Dorland, email to author, April 16, 2023.

22   William Gibson, "The Gernsback Continuum," in *Burning Chrome* (New York: Eos, an imprint of HarperCollins Publishers, 2003), 25–26, 28.

23   Gibson, "Gernsback Continuum," 35.

24   Gibson, "Gernsback Continuum," 31.

25   This is essentially American philosopher and cultural critic Steven Shaviro's overall view of science fiction, which "is not about the actual future, but about the *futurity* that haunts the present." Steven Shaviro, *No Speed Limit: Three Essays on Accelerationism* (Minneapolis: University of Minnesota Press, 2015), 2.

26   Mark Fisher, "What Is Hauntology?," *Film Quarterly* 66, no. 1 (Fall 2012): 16.

27   Chris Dorland, Zoom interview by author, June 8, 2023.

28   Klaus Kertess, "Malcolm Morley: Talking about Seeing," *Artforum* 18, no. 10 (Summer 1980): 48.

29   Dorland, untitled talk, School of Visual Arts, New York City, January 30, 2024.

30   Dorland, Zoom interview by author, June 8, 2023.

31   Chris Dorland, Zoom interview by author, May 18, 2023.

32   Saul Appelbaum, "What Progress: Chris Dorland," *Curator Guide* (blog), n.p., https://curator.guide/chris-dorland, consulted May 11, 2024.

33   David Smith, "'He's a Financial Serial Killer': How Bernie Madoff Became the Monster of Wall Street," *The Guardian* (January 4, 2023), n.p., https://www.theguardian.com/tv-and-radio/2023/jan/04/netflix-bernie-madoff-monster-of-wall-street, consulted May 12, 2024.

34   Scott Tobias, "American Psycho at 20: A Vicious Satire That Remains as Sharp as Ever," *The Guardian* (April 14, 2020), n.p. https://www.theguardian.com/film/2020/apr/14/american-psycho-bret-easton-ellis-christian-bale, consulted May 12, 2024.

35   Steven Shaviro, *No Speed Limit: Three Essays on Accelerationism* (Minneapolis: University of Minnesota Press, 2015), 2.

36   Andy Beckett, "Accelerationism: How a Fringe Philosophy Predicted the Future We Live In," *The Guardian* (May 11, 2017), n.p., https://www.theguardian.com/world/2017/may/11/accelerationism-how-a-fringe-philosophy-predicted-the-future-we-live-in, consulted April 19, 2024.

37   Shaviro, *No Speed Limit*, ix.

38   Benjamin Noys, *Malign Velocities: Accelerationism and Capitalism* (Winchester, UK: Zer0 Books, 2014), 33.

39   According to media commentator Steve Redhead, "Virilio is the theorist closest to Baudrillard's ideas (though they differ in subtle ways), and Virilio is the one person Baudrillard has engaged with most over the years. . . . Virilio worked with Baudrillard on the journal *Traverses* between 1975 and 1990." Steve Redhead, "The Art of the Accident: Paul Virilio and Accelerated Modernity," *Fast Capitalism* 2, no. 1 (2006): 24, https://fastcapitalism.journal.library.uta.edu/index.php/fastcapitalism/article/view/60, consulted April 20, 2024.

40   Mark Fisher, *Capitalist Realism: Is There No Alternative?* (Winchester, UK: Zer0 Books, 2014): 1.

41   Fisher, *Capitalist Realism*, 18.

42   Gilbert Ryle, *The Concept of Mind* (London: Hutchinson, 1949).

43   Dorland, email to author, April 16, 2023.

44   Walter Benjamin, *The Arcades Project*, trans. Howard Eiland and Kevin McLaughlin (Cambridge: Bellknap Press, Imprint of Harvard University Press, 2002).

45   A GIF is a Graphics Interchange Format that supports both static and animated images.

46   N. Katherine Hayles, *Unthought: The Power of the Cognitive Nonconscious* (Chicago: University of Chicago Press, 2017), 116-120.

47   Dorland, Zoom conversation with author, September 14, 2023.

48   Jean-François Lyotard, *Discourse, Figure*, trans. Antony Hudek and Mary Lydon (Minneapolis: University of Minnesota Press, 2011), 3.

49   Chris Dorland, Zoom conversation with author, September 14, 2023.

50   Dorland, Zoom conversation with author, September 14, 2023.

51   Dorland, Zoom conversation with author, September 14, 2023.

52   Fisher, *Capitalist Realism*, 78.

53   Dorland, Zoom conversation with author, September 14, 2023.

54   Pimploy Phongsirivech, "Glitch Artist Chris Dorland Talks Transhumanism with author Carolyn Kane," *Interview* (January 19, 2018), n.p., https://www.interview

magazine.com/art/glitch-artist-chris-dorland-talks-transhumanism-author-carolyn-kane, consulted April 19, 2024.

55 Chris Dorland, Zoom interview by author, January 25, 2024. Dorland has pointed out that at the beginning of his career, he was obsessed with Rauschenberg's art; he especially liked the earlier artist's use of representational elements to make his *Combines*, but for his own works he prefers to remain on the edge of recognizability.

56 Mark Fisher, *Ghosts of My Life: Writings on Depression, Hauntology, and Lost Futures* (Winchester, UK: Zer0 Books, 2014).

57 Karl Marx and Friedrich Engels, *The Communist Manifesto* (New York: Bantam Classic, an imprint of Random House, 1992), 13.

58 Fisher, *Ghosts of My Life*, n.p.

59 Jacques Derrida, *Specters of Marx: The State of the Debt, the Work of Mourning, and the New International* (New York: Routledge, 1994), 10.

60 Carolyn L. Kane, *Chromatic Algorithms: Synthetic Color, Computer Art, and Aesthetics after Code* (Chicago: University of Chicago Press, 2014), 91, 13.

61 Teresa de Lauretis, "Signs of Wo/ander," in *The Technological Imagination*, ed. Teresa de Lauretis, Andreas Huyssen, and Kathleen Woodward (Madison, WI: Coda, 1980), 167.

62 Claire Sponsler, "Cyberpunk and the Dilemmas of Postmodern Narrative: The Example of William Gibson," *Contemporary Literature* 33, no. 4 (Winter 1992): 626.

63 N. Katherine Hayles, *How We Became Posthuman: Virtual Bodies in Cybernetics, Literature, and Informatics* (Chicago: University of Chicago Press, 1999), 3.

64 Hayles, *How We Became Posthuman*, ix.

65 Friedrich A. Kittler, *Gramophone, Film, Typewriter*, trans. Geoffrey Winthrop-Young and Michael Wutz (Stanford: Stanford University Press, 1999), xxxix. Kittler rethinks the historical a priori in terms of a media a priori, so that "media determine our situation."

66 Eva Horn in Geoffrey Winthrop-Younk and Eva Horn, "Machine Learning: Friedrich Kittler," *Artforum* 51, no. 1 (September 2012): 477. I greatly appreciate Carolyn Kane's role in directing me to this essay. Cf. Kane, *Chromatic Algorithms*, 14.

67 Kane, *Chromatic Algorithms*, 3.

68 Bernard Stiegler, *Technics and Time, 1: The Fault of Epimetheus*, trans. Richard Beardsworth and George Collins (1994; repr., Stanford: Stanford University Press, 1998), ix.

69 Hayles, *How We Became Posthuman*, 7.

70 Hayles, *Unthought*, 19, 3, 2.

71 "Interview with Painter Chris Dorland—Part 1," n.p.

72 Phongsirivech, "Glitch Artist Chris Dorland Talks Transhumanism with author Carolyn Kane," n.p.

73 "Interview with Painter Chris Dorland—Part 1," n.p.

74 David Deutsch, *The Fabric of Reality: The Science of Parallel Universes—and Its Implications* (City of Westminster, London: Viking Books UK, 1997).

75 George Kubler, *The Shape of Time: Remarks on the History of Things* (New Haven: Yale University Press, 1962).

76 Hayles, *Unthought*, 120.

77   Paige Silveria, "Conversation with Chris Dorland," *Hearts* no. 4 (Spring–Summer 2018): 28.

78   Jean-Luc Nancy, "Exscription," trans. Katherine Lydon, *Yale French Studies* No. 78 "On Bataille" (1990), 64 and 65. Nancy explains, "But this 'outside'—entirely exscribed into the text—is the infinite retreat of meaning by which each existence exists. Not the brute datum, material, concrete, reputed to be outside meaning and which meaning represents but the 'empty freedom' through which the living being comes to presence—and absence."

79   Carolyn L. Kane, *High-Tech Trash: Glitch, Noise, and Aesthetic Failure* (Oakland: University of California Press, 2019), 16.

80   Jean-François Lyotard, *Discourse, Figure*, trans. Antony Hudek and Mary Lydon (Minneapolis: University of Minnesota Press, 2011), 3.

81   Gilles Deleuze, *Francis Bacon: The Logic of Sensation*, trans. and intro. Daniel W. Smith (Minneapolis: University of Minnesota Press, 2003), 82–83.

82   Deleuze, *Francis Bacon*, 83.

83   Gilles Deleuze and Félix Guattari, *Capitalism and Schizophrenia*, vol. 1, *Anti-Oedipus*, trans. Robert Hurley, Mark Seem, and Helen R. Lane; and vol. 2, *A Thousand Plateaus*, trans. Brian Massumi (London: Continuum, 2004).

84   Daniel W. Smith, "Translator's Introduction: Deleuze on Bacon: Three Conceptual Trajectories in *The Logic of Sensation*," in Gilles Deleuze, *Francis Bacon: The Logic of Sensation*, trans. and intro. Daniel W. Smith (Minneapolis: University of Minnesota Press, 2003), xxiv. Marius von Senden, *Space and Sight: The Perception of Space and Shape in the Congenitally Blind Before and After Operation*, trans. Peter Heath (Glencoe, IL: The Free Press, 1960).

85   Smith, "Translator's Introduction," in Deleuze, *Francis Bacon*, xxi.

86   Hayles, *How We Became Posthuman*, 285–86.

87   Critical theorist Warwick Mules provides a lucid discussion of the insufficiency of technology in relation to Heidegger's theories. Warwick Mules, "The Limits of Heidegger's Earth," *Colloquy: Text, Theory, Critique* 30 (2015): n.p.

88   Dorland, Zoom interview by author, January 25, 2024.

89   Fisher, *Ghosts of My Life*, n.p.

INDEX

Abstract Expressionism   33
accelerationism   12, 16–19, 21
The Airstream Futuropolis: The Tomorrow That Never Was   10
Alumacores   1–3, 11, 19–20, 22–23, 25, 27
Amazing Stories   10
American Psycho (Ellis)   16
Animal Farm (Orwell)   40
The Ambassadors (Holbein)   4, 30
Alexander, Anna   36

Anamorphism   6
Antonopoulos, Alexander   36, 120
Art After Modernism: Rethinking Representation (ed. Wallis)   8
The Art of the Deal (Trump)   16
Art Deco   10
Art Moderne   10
Asher, Michael   23
Ballard, J.G.   3, 5–7
Bateman, Patrick   16
Baudrillard, Jean   3–6, 10, 12–14, 17, 20, 25
"Beautiful Inside My Head Forever"   15
Beckett, Andy   16
Being and Time (Heidegger)   24, 33
Bender, Gretchen   19
Berlin Wall   16
Bernina sewing machine   21
Bernays, Edward   22
Biosphere   11
Blade Runner   6
Body without organs   32
Borden Pavilion   7, 11
Braque, Georges   17
Burning Chrome (Gibson)   37
Calvino, Italo   27
capitalism   3, 6–8, 13, 15–18, 21–23, 32
Capitalism and Schizophrenia (Deleuze and Guattari)   32
Capitalist Realism: Is There No Alternative? (Virilio)   17–18
Carr, Terry   37
The Century of the Self (Curtis)   22
Cézanne, Paul   32
Civilian (1918)   1, 23
cognitive assemblage (Hayles)   2, 21, 29
cognitive estrangement (Suvin)   6
Cold War   14
Combines (Rauschenberg)   16
The Communist Manifesto (Marx and Engels)   24
Concrete Island (Gibson)   3, 5–7
Connor, Sarah   5
Covid-19   29
Count Zero (Gibson)   6
Cronenberg, David   27
Csicsery-Ronay, Istvan   6
Curtis, Adam   22
Cybernetic Culture Research Unit (CCRU)   17
cybernetics   3, 6, 26, 35

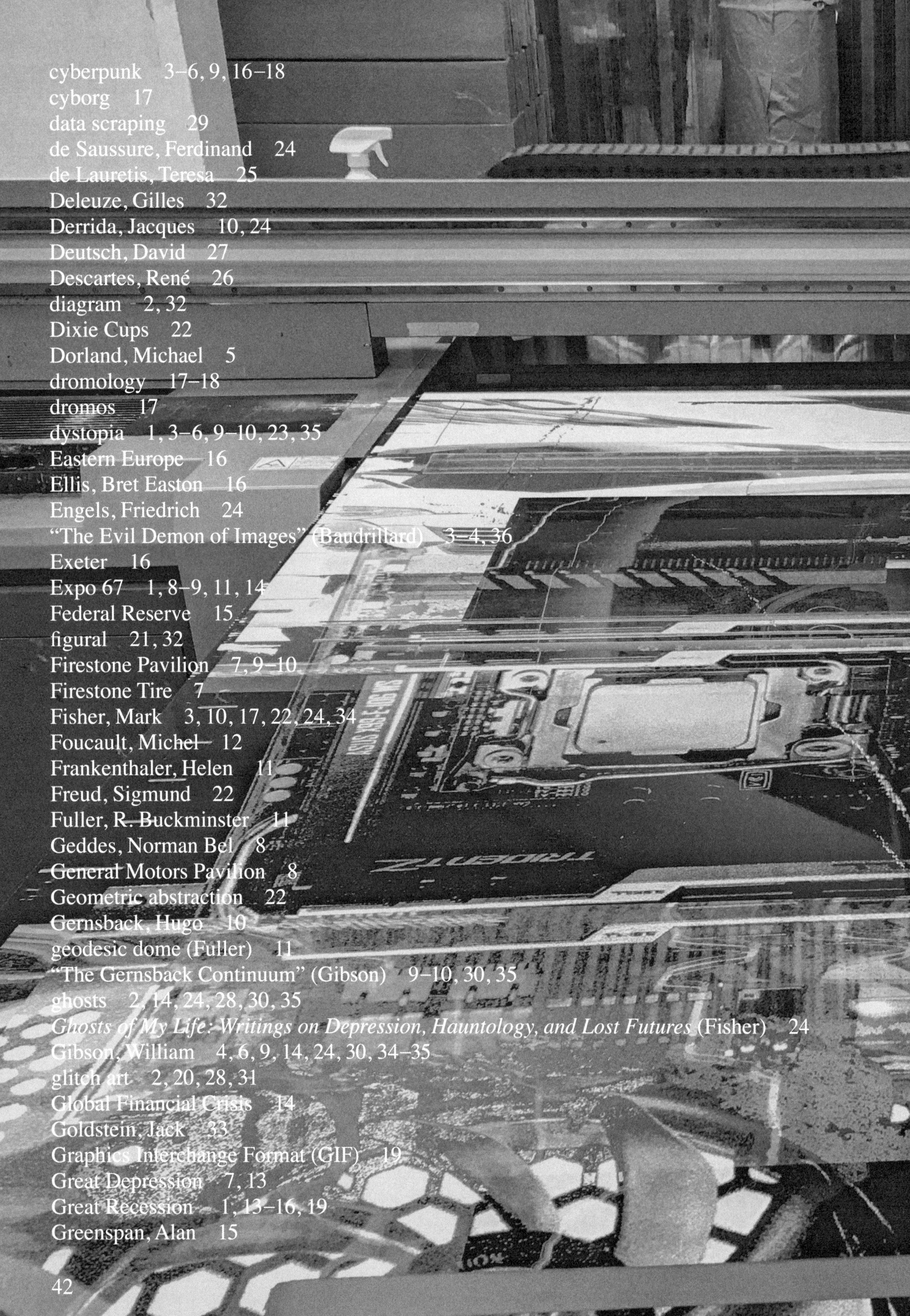

cyberpunk   3–6, 9, 16–18
cyborg   17
data scraping   29
de Saussure, Ferdinand   24
de Lauretis, Teresa   25
Deleuze, Gilles   32
Derrida, Jacques   10, 24
Deutsch, David   27
Descartes, René   26
diagram   2, 32
Dixie Cups   22
Dorland, Michael   5
dromology   17–18
dromos   17
dystopia   1, 3–6, 9–10, 23, 35
Eastern Europe   16
Ellis, Bret Easton   16
Engels, Friedrich   24
"The Evil Demon of Images" (Baudrillard)   3–4, 36
Exeter   16
Expo 67   1, 8–9, 11, 14
Federal Reserve   15
figural   21, 32
Firestone Pavilion   7, 9–10
Firestone Tire   7
Fisher, Mark   3, 10, 17, 22, 24, 34
Foucault, Michel   12
Frankenthaler, Helen   11
Freud, Sigmund   22
Fuller, R. Buckminster   11
Geddes, Norman Bel   8
General Motors Pavilion   8
Geometric abstraction   22
Gernsback, Hugo   10
geodesic dome (Fuller)   11
"The Gernsback Continuum" (Gibson)   9–10, 30, 35
ghosts   2, 14, 24, 28, 30, 35
Ghosts of My Life: Writings on Depression, Hauntology, and Lost Futures (Fisher)   24
Gibson, William   4, 6, 9, 14, 24, 30, 34–35
glitch art   2, 20, 28, 31
Global Financial Crisis   14
Goldstein, Jack   33
Graphics Interchange Format (GIF)   19
Great Depression   7, 13
Great Recession   1, 13–16, 19
Greenspan, Alan   15

Guattari, Félix   32
Guyton, Wade   13, 21
Guyton\Walker   21
Harvard   16
hauntology   2, 24–26, 30, 35
Hayles, N. Katherine   21, 25, 29, 38–39
Heat (Mann)   23
hedge funds   15
Heidegger, Martin   24, 33
highbrow   14, 16
Hirst, Damien   15
Holbein the Younger, Hans   4
hyperreality   1, 6, 13, 25
illudere   4
Indiana, Robert   11
infrared   14, 53–54
Invisible Cities (Calvino)   27
Jameson, Fredric   18
Johns, Jasper   11
Kane, Carolyn L.   39–40
Kant, Immanuel   26
Khan, Kublai   27
Khrushchev, Nikita   14
Kihn, Merv   10, 35
Kittler, Friedrich   26, 39
Knutson, Erin   19, 21
Kubler, George   27, 39
Lacan, Jacques   18, 33
laser printing   13
Lawson, Thomas   37
Land, Nick   16
"Last Exit: Painting" (Lawson)   8, 37
Lehman Brothers   15
Lichtenstein, Roy   11
Liste Art Fair Basel   28
The Logic of Sensation (Deleuze)   32, 40, 43
Logos [series, 2010–14]   1, 3, 12–13, 18–19, 43, 53, 57
lowbrow   10
Lyles & King   23
Lyotard, Jean-François   21, 31, 38, 40
Madoff, Bernie   15, 38
Manichaeism; Manichean   4
Mann, Michael   23
Maitland, Robert   5
Marx, Karl   16, 24, 39
Matisse, Henri   17

The Matrix   6
Matta-Clark, Gordon   23
Mass-media   22–23
McLuhan, Marshall   26
meta: metapainting   22
Memoryscapes [series, 2001–7]   1, 3–4, 8–9, 11, 16, 35
metapainting   22
Minimalism   22
Mona Lisa Overdrive (Gibson)   37
Morley, Malcolm   11, 37
Mules, Warwick   40
neoliberalism   12–13, 15–16
neo-noir   1, 22–23
Neuromancer (Gibson)   6, 34, 37
New York World's Fair (1939; 1964)   7–9, 11, 22
Nexus 4   6
Newman, Barnett   11
No Speed Limit: Three Essays on Accelerationism (Shaviro)   12, 37–38
Noys, Benjamin   17, 38
October Revolution   14
Omni Consumer Products   6
on-site   10
Orwell, George   40
Paik, Nam June   23
PATH train   29
phantom ruins   3
photomechanical   13
Pictures Generation   19
Plant, Sadie   16
Polo, Marco   27
Post: posthuman; postindustrial   5–6, 23
prime object   27
Prototypes [series 2010–14]   1, 3, 12–13, 18–19, 25
psychic automatism   33
Purchase College   27
Rauschenberg, Robert   11, 24
Reagan, Ronald   15
Redhead, Steve   38
Richter, Gerhard   24
RoboCop   6
Rotolactor   7
S&P 500   15
Salle, David   8
Santa Monica Museum of Art   23
Scanners [series. 2009–16]   1, 3, 19–23, 25, 27–30

science fiction   6, 10, 25, 37
Screenscrapes [series 2020–present]   1–3, 6, 11, 18–19, 22, 27–29, 31, 33–36
Semiotext(e)   3
semiotic ghost (Gibson)   2, 10, 14, 24, 28, 30, 35, 37
Shaviro, Steven   12, 16, 37–38
Simulacra and Simulation (Baudrillard)   12
Simulations [series, 2007–14]   1, 3, 11–14, 16, 18–20, 27
Skynet   5
Smith, Daniel W.   32, 40
Sotheby's   15
Soviet Pavilion   1, 14
*Specters of Marx: The State of the Debt, the Work of Mourning,
    and the New International* (Derrida)   24, 39
Sponsler, Claire   4, 25, 39
Sprawl trilogy (Gibson)   6
Sterling, Bruce   37
Stiegler, Bernard   21, 34, 39
subprime mortgage   14
Surrealism   33
Super Dakota   20
Suvin, Darko   6, 37
T-1000   5, 17
Tansey, Mark   8
technogenesis   2, 26, 34
The Terminator   5
Terminator 2: Judgment Day   5
Thatcher, Margaret   15, 17
Tobias, Scott   16, 38
Total Recall   6
The Truman Show   15
Trump, Donald   16
Untitled (Memory Cortex) (2017)   27, 29
University of Warwick   16–17
U.S. Constitution's fourteenth amendment   16
U.S. Federal Reserve   15
U.S. Pavilion   11
Vader, Darth   23
Vanity Fair   21
Verne, Jules   10
Virilio, Paul   3, 17, 38
virtual reality   27
von Senden, Marius   32, 40
Voorhees, Gmelin and Walker   7
Walker, Kelley   13, 21
Warhol, Andy   13

whiteouts   2, 18, 28–33, 36
Wiener, Norbert   26, 46
Wool, Christopher   13
World Fairs   2, 6–11, 14, 22, 35
Xerox   2, 4, 12–13

GLOSSARY OF TERMS

Accelerationism
A political and aesthetic theory that advocates intensifying or exacerbating capitalist
or technological processes to achieve systemic change or collapse. In Dorland's work,
accelerationism is first reflected in the overload of visual information and later in the
hyper-circulation of corrupted digital imagery.

Anamorphism
A perceptual condition in which images are distorted or fragmented so that they cohere only
from an oblique or partial vantage point. Dorland's work enacts a conceptual anamorphism,
where meaning emerges through layered distortion, delay, and obfuscation.

Assemblage
A method of composition that juxtaposes diverse elements like found objects and industrial materials within a single structure. Dorland's paintings consist of assemblages of ruin,
debris, and code, presenting nonlinear temporalities and fractured spatialities.

Cognitive Assemblage
A term coined by N. Katherine Hayles that describes distributed cognitive systems involving both humans and machines. This framework articulates how Dorland's paintings register
the logic of ambient machinic vision, digital feedback, and nonhuman perception.

Cybernetics
A theory examining information flows between humans, animals, and machines as cognitive
communication patterns. Focusing on systems, feedback loops, and control, cybernetics
was developed in the mid-20th century by Norbert Wiener and others. Bernard Stiegler's
related term, *technogenesis*, highlights a reciprocal dependence and co-development
of humans and machines over time. In Dorland's work, cybernetic thinking underpins
his recursive processes and painterly emulation of feedback mechanisms, where glitches,
corrections, and errors become part of an iterative cycle of production and breakdown.

Cybernetic Sublime
An update to the Kantian sublime in which the imagination collapses under the weight
of digital feedback mechanisms and the resulting gaps between non-aligned systems.
This represents a fertile area of investigation in Dorland's most recent works, where his
whiteouts signal these glitches.

Cyberpunk
A dystopian literary and film genre, originating in the 1980s and continuing into the '90s, emphasizing ruins, hyper-urbanism, and blurred distinctions between humans and machines, along with digital decay. This genre informs Dorland's aesthetic, extending it into the realm of painterly expression.

Data Scraping
The automated extraction of data from digital platforms. Data scraping often occurs without consent or context. Dorland's practice aesthetically mirrors this technique, as he collects and metabolizes digital detritus—found images, corrupted files, algorithmic textures— transforming acts of scraping into gestures of critical transformation.

Diagram
A non-mimetic visual system that organizes relationships, flows, and concepts rather than representing likeness. Dorland's paintings often function as diagrams of collapse by mapping networks of digital decay, affective residue, and painterly intervention. His images reject traditional spatial coherence in favor of a layered schematic tension.

Glitch Aesthetics
An aesthetic mode that foregrounds errors, bugs, and malfunctions in digital media. In Dorland's case, glitch becomes a form of painterly sublimation, where the foundering of the image serves as a generative act.

Hauntology
A neologism developed by Jacques Derrida to describe the persistence of lost futures. Dorland's haunted screens evoke spectral residues from both analog and digital epochs, layered with obsolescence and nostalgia.

Hyperreality
A condition described by Jean Baudrillard in which simulated models overtake the real, creating a world of signs without referents. Dorland's work portrays hyperreality as a collapse of image and world, where digital simulacra cannibalize meaning.

Interface
The threshold or point of contact between systems—both human and machine—as well as between image and viewer. Dorland's luminous canvases function as haunted interfaces, drawing attention to the porous and glitching membrane that exists between surface and data, painting and screen. They illustrate the collapse of a seamless culture of interfaces into sites of noise, abrasion, and spectral return.

Media Archaeology
A method for studying past media forms (e.g., analog video, CRT monitors, outdated software) to understand contemporary visual culture. Dorland's frequent use of obsolete forms engages media archaeology as both critique and homage.

Neoliberalism
A political and economic logic first theorized in the 1930s, which gained traction in the 1970s and '80s, prioritized deregulation, privatization, and hyper-competitive individualism. Neoliberalism has influenced both the content and circulation of some contemporary artworks. Dorland's aesthetics of ruin, which include oversaturation, collapse, and burnout, reflect the conditions of life under neoliberalism, where excess becomes indistinguishable from waste, and speed from exhaustion.

Opacity (Visual and Ethical)
The resistance of an image or form to complete transparency or interpretation. Dorland's reliance on literal and conceptual opacity compels viewers into spaces of ethical delay, where recognition is postponed and affect becomes ambient.

Postdigital
A cultural condition where digital technologies are no longer novel but are fully integrated into everyday life. Dorland's postdigital work combines traditional painting with algorithmic debris and digital excess.

Semiotic Phantoms
A poetic term describing signifiers that no longer refer to or stabilize meaning. Dorland's glitch-ridden figures and vaporous forms resemble semiotic phantoms, ghost-images flickering with past significance. These forms hover between presence and obsolescence, evoking trauma's refusal to fully signify.

Virtual Reality
An immersive digital simulation of reality. Dorland's work does not depict VR directly but thematizes *aesthetic virtuality* as the suspended, immersive state in which viewers engage with fragmented realities, corrupted visions, and post-analog residues. His paintings simulate a world where the virtual seeps into the real as visual hauntings.

Whiteouts
Visual obliterations—whether of detail, meaning, or surface—are often achieved through literal whiteness or pixelic erasure. In Dorland's work, whiteouts serve as zones of forgetting, erasure, or signal loss. These ghostlike placeholders mark the limits of visibility, both aesthetic and ethical, and become critical sites of resistance to total legibility.

MEMORYSCAPES

Untitled (firestone), 2000
Oil on linen, 14 inches × 18 inches

Untitled (red skies), 2002
Ink, watercolor, gouache on paper, 38 inches × 50 inches

Untitled (human potential), 2002
Oil on linen, 32 inches × 78 inches

Untitled (memory dome), 2003
Ink, watercolor, gouache on paper, 30 inches × 40 inches

Untitled (US pavilion), 2003
Oil on linen, 28 inches × 32 inches

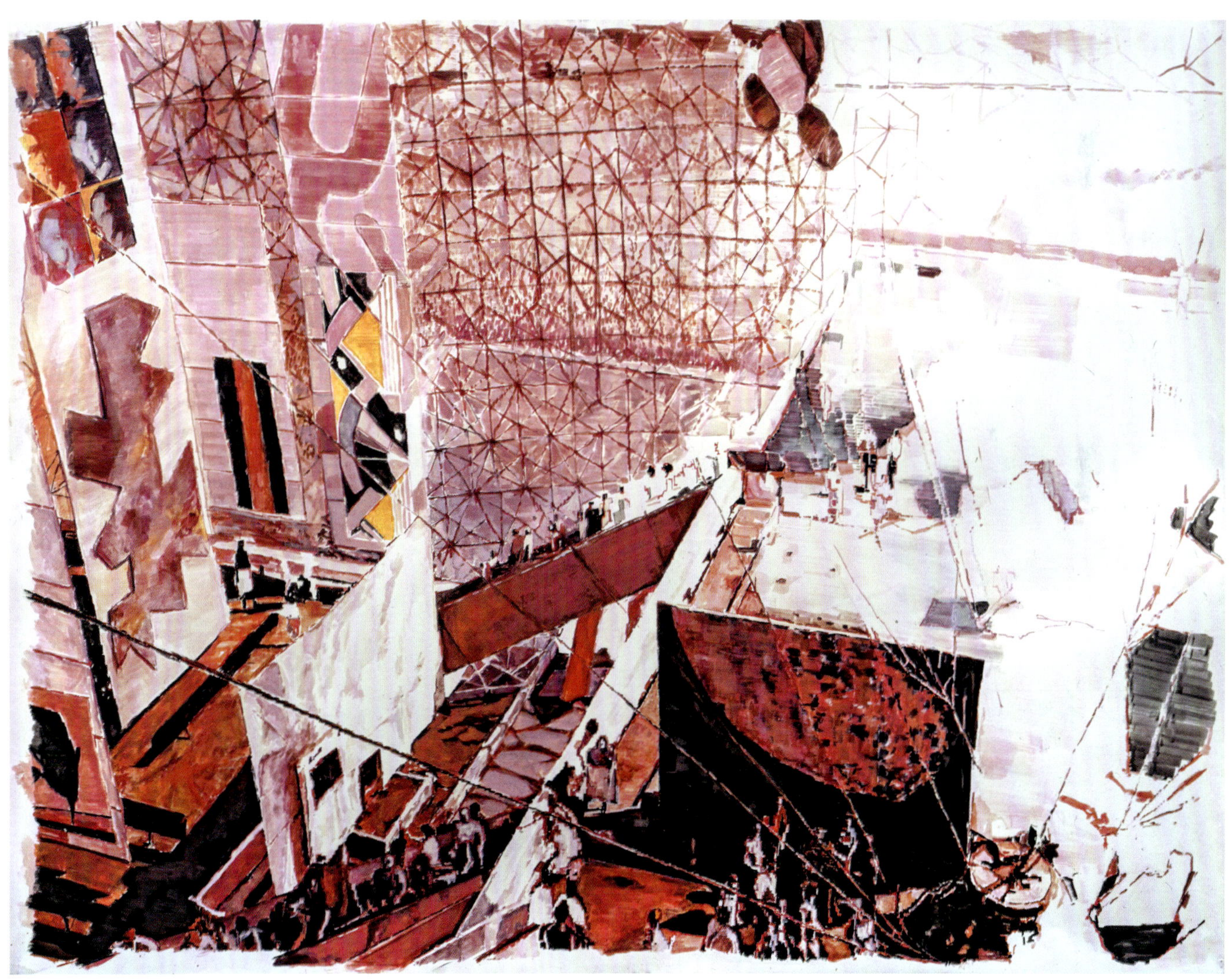

Untitled (analog dream), 2003
Ink, watercolor, gouache on paper, 50 inches × 65 inches

Untitled (festival of gas), 2003
Oil on linen, 16 inches × 24 inches

Untitled (the crystal world), 2004
Oil on canvas, 50 inches × 84 inches

Untitled, 2004
Ink, watercolor on paper, 38 inches × 50 inches

Untitled (two figures), 2004
Acrylic on linen, 14 inches × 16 inches

Untitled (american century), 2005
Oil on linen, 19 inches × 44 inches

Untitled (memory park), 2005
Oil on canvas, 34 inches × 54 inches

Untitled (november beach), 2005
Oil on canvas, 21 inches × 27.75 inches

Untitled (century city), 2005
Oil on canvas, 54 inches × 72 inches

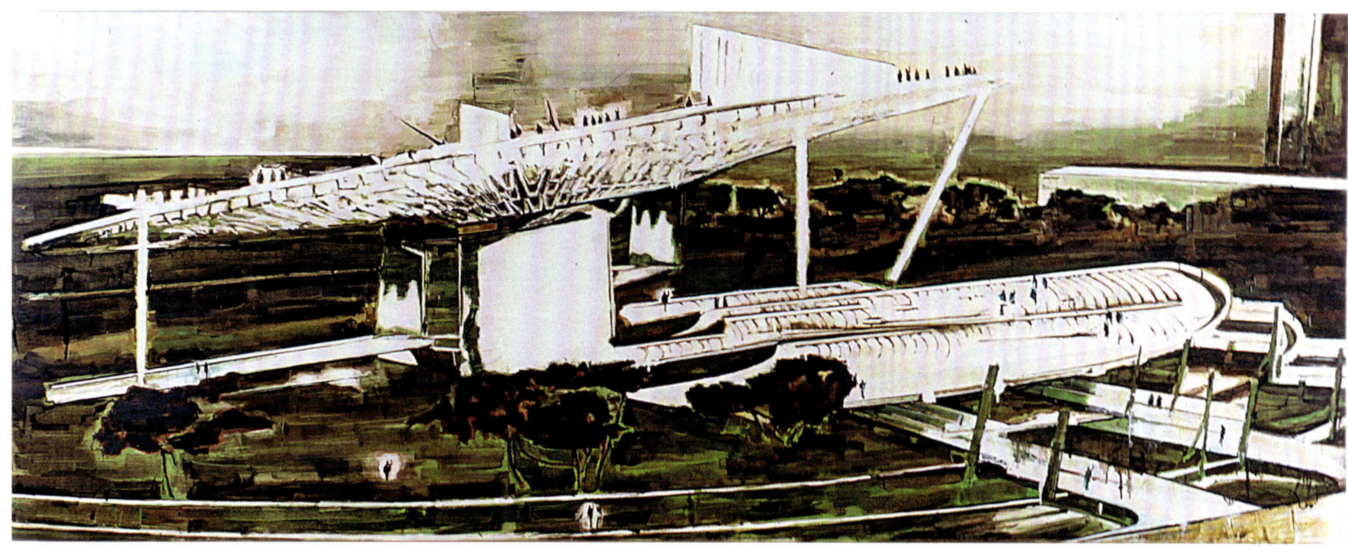

Untitled (event horizon), 2006
Oil on canvas, 36 inches × 84 inches

Untitled (future perfect), 2006
Oil on linen, 30 inches × 40 inches

Untitled (green), 2006
Oil on linen, 32 inches × 48 inches

Untitled (symposium), 2006
Acrylic on linen, 20 inches × 20 inches

Untitled (What Dies for Me to Live), 2006
Oil on linen, 60 inches × 72 inches

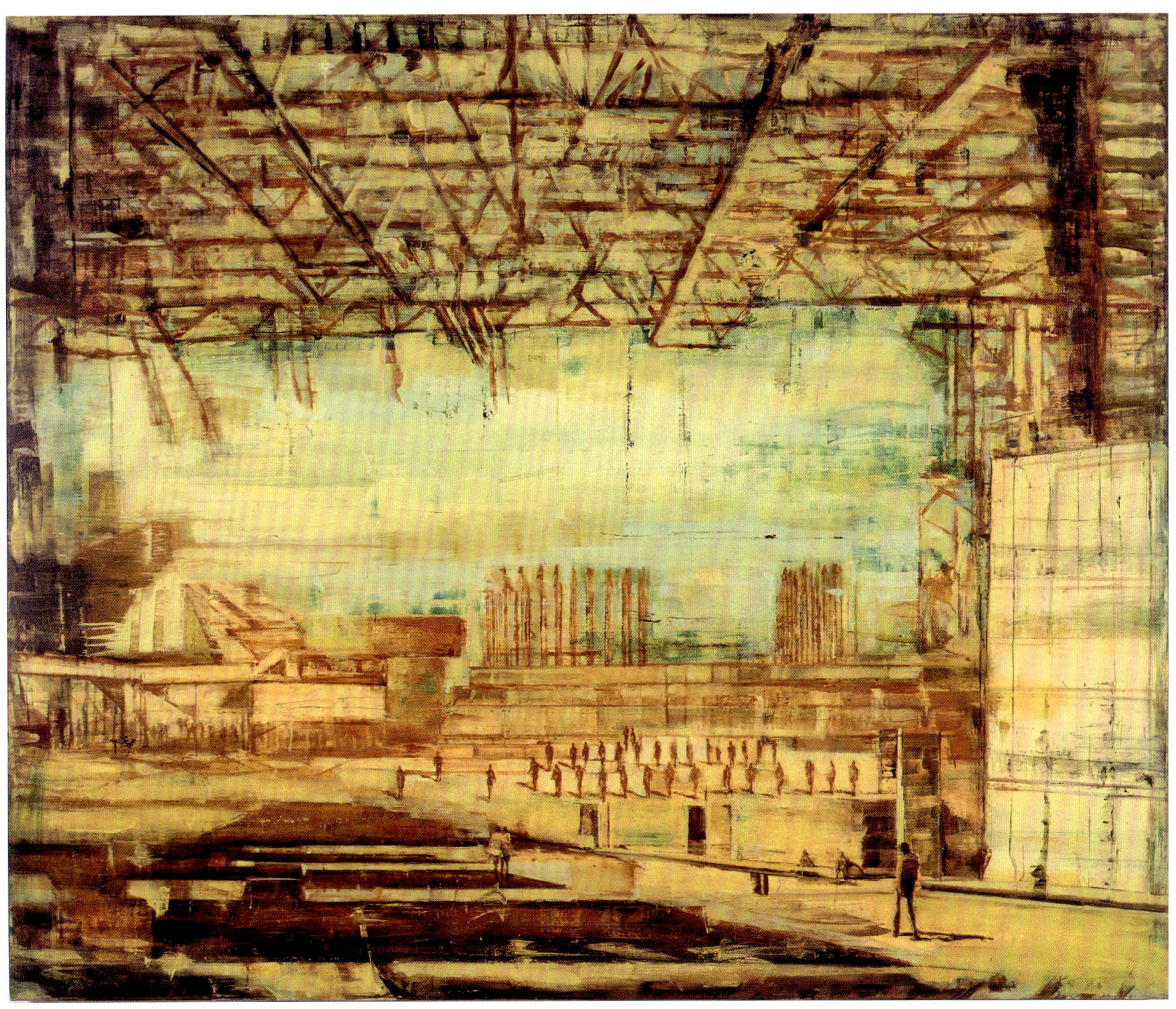

Untitled (walkway), 2006
Oil on linen, 60 inches × 72 inches

Untitled (vermilion sands), 2006
Oil on linen, 30 inches × 40 inches

Untitled (sunspot), 2006
Oil on canvas, 16 inches × 20 inches

Untitled (acid), 2006
Oil on linen, 44 inches × 66 inches

51

Untitled (white heat), 2006
Oil on canvas, 44 inches × 66 inches

Untitled (PI-IV), 2006
Oil on linen, 20 inches × 32 inches

Untitled (flare), 2006
Oil on linen, 30 inches × 40 inches

Untitled (plaza), 2006
Oil on canvas, 48 inches × 60 inches

Untitled (indian summer), 2006
Oil on canvas, 40 inches × 50 inches

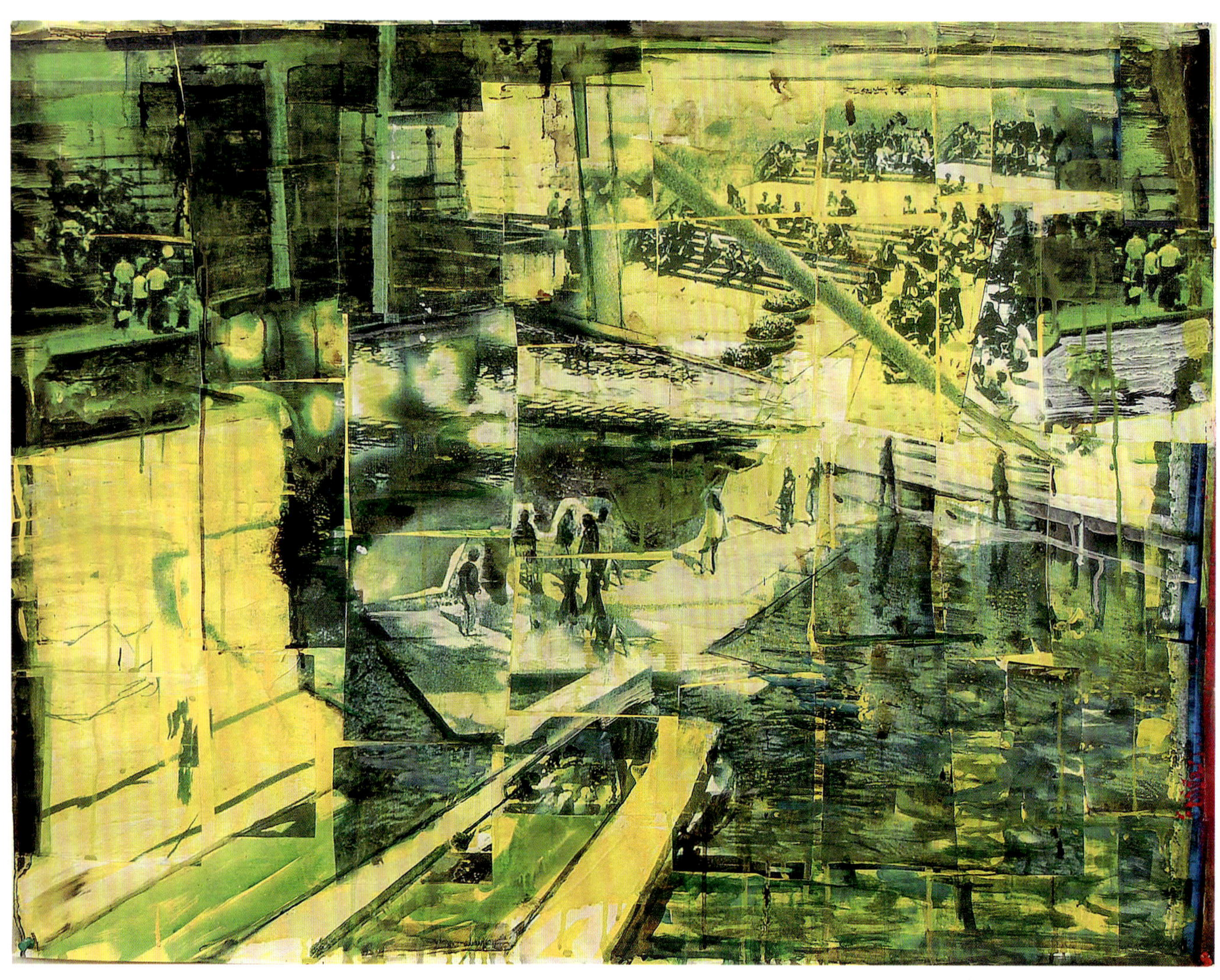

Untitled, 2006
Photocollage, enamel on paper, 30 inches × 40 inches

Untitled (deconstruction II), 2007
Photocollage, enamel on paper, 30 inches × 40 inches

SIMULATIONS, LOGOS, AND PROTOTYPES

Untitled (infrared), 2007
Oil on linen, 54 inches × 66 inches

Untitled (black ice), 2007
Oil on linen, 20 inches × 26 inches

Untitled (deconstruction II), 2007
Photocollage, enamel on paper, 38 inches × 50 inches

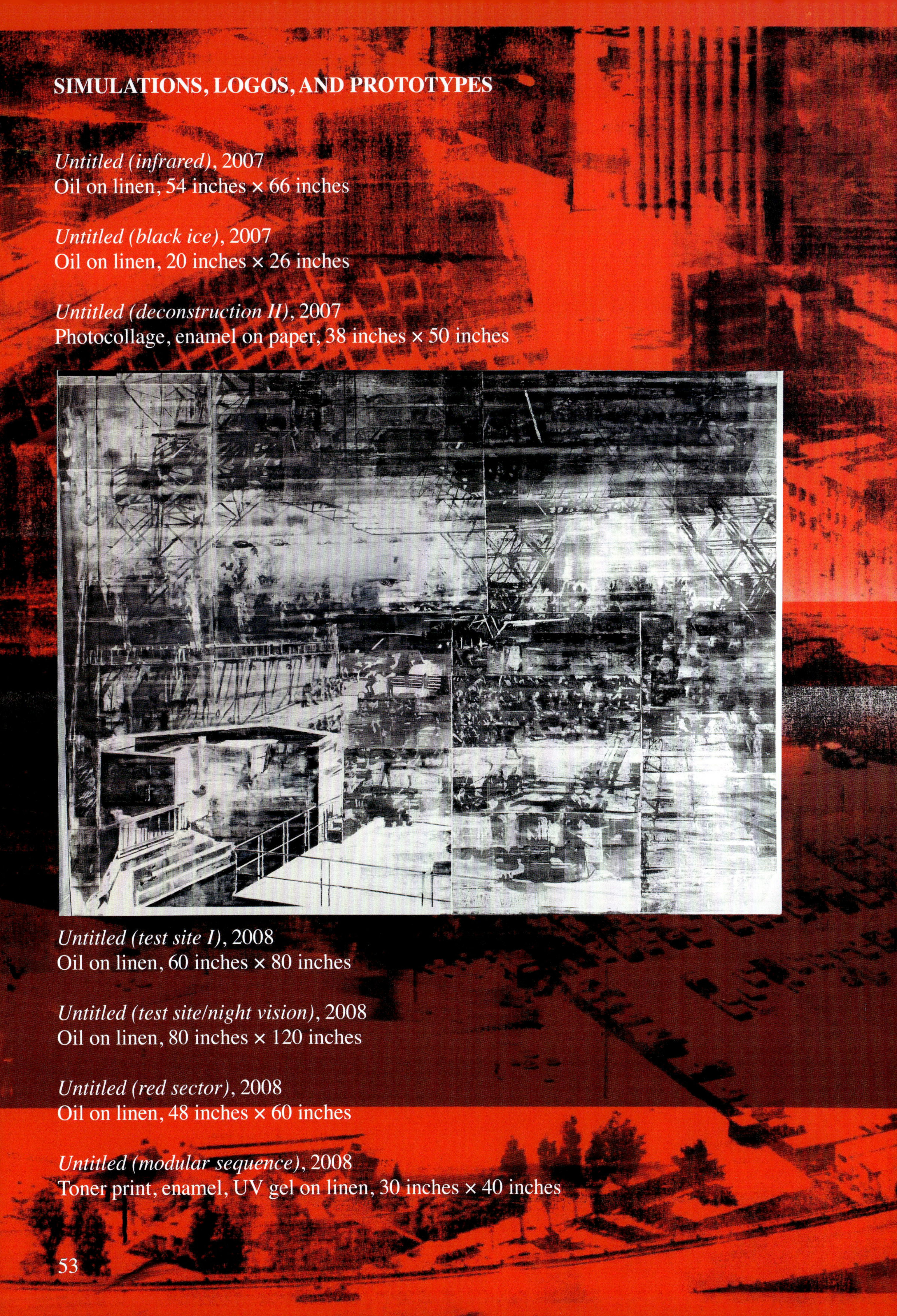

Untitled (test site I), 2008
Oil on linen, 60 inches × 80 inches

Untitled (test site/night vision), 2008
Oil on linen, 80 inches × 120 inches

Untitled (red sector), 2008
Oil on linen, 48 inches × 60 inches

Untitled (modular sequence), 2008
Toner print, enamel, UV gel on linen, 30 inches × 40 inches

Untitled (modular sequence), 2008
Toner print, enamel, UV gel on linen, 30 inches × 40 inches

Untitled (infrared III), 2008
Oil on linen, 54 inches × 74 inches

Untitled (plaza), 2008
Oil on linen, 30 inches × 40 inches

Untitled (green screen), 2008
Oil on linen, 60 inches × 80 inches

Untitled (infrared IV), 2008
Oil on linen, 54 inches × 76 inches

Untitled (infrared V), 2008
Oil on linen, 54 inches × 76 inches

Untitled (bladerunners), 2008
Oil on linen, 52 inches × 72 inches

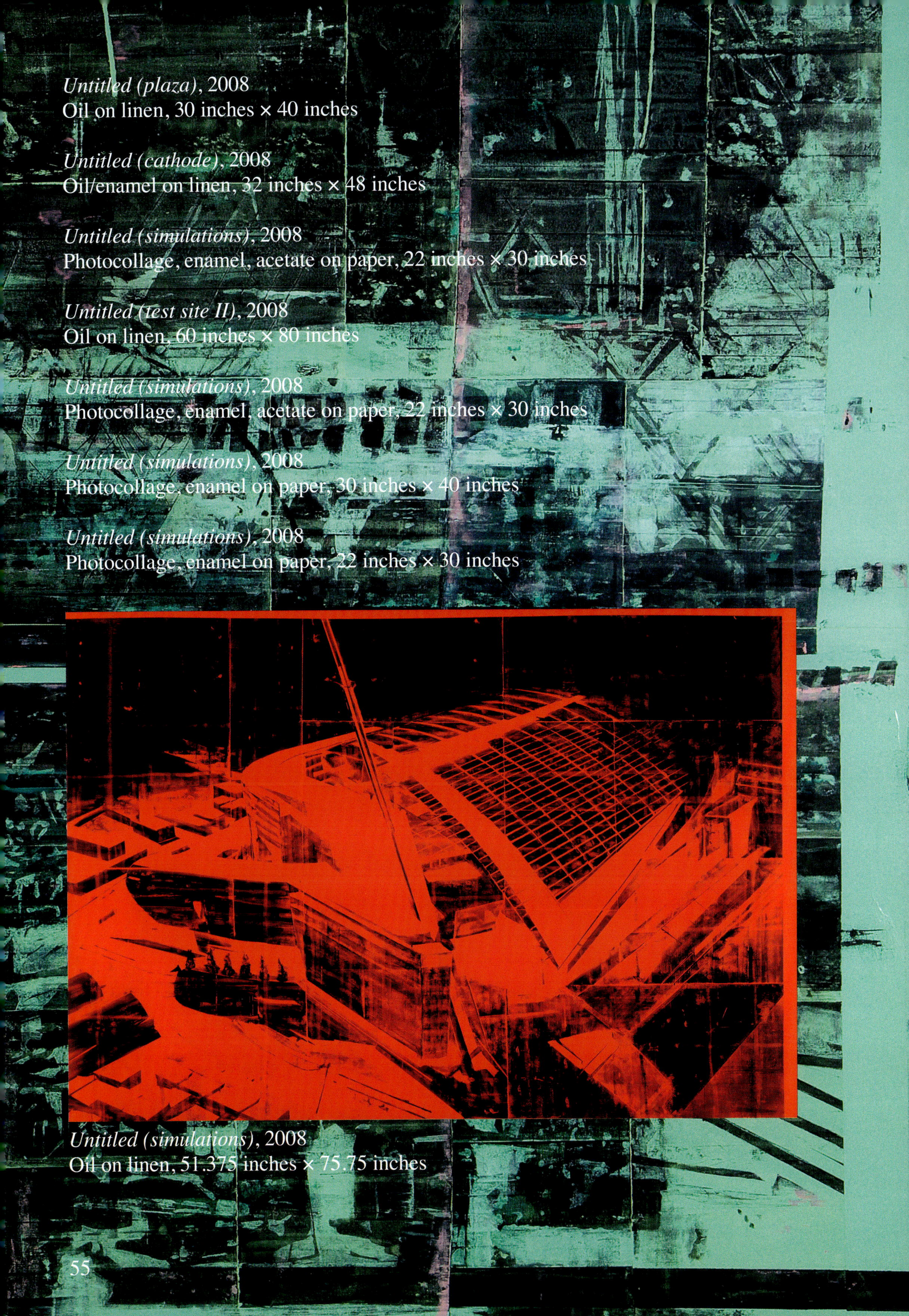

Untitled (plaza), 2008
Oil on linen, 30 inches × 40 inches

Untitled (cathode), 2008
Oil/enamel on linen, 32 inches × 48 inches

Untitled (simulations), 2008
Photocollage, enamel, acetate on paper, 22 inches × 30 inches

Untitled (test site II), 2008
Oil on linen, 60 inches × 80 inches

Untitled (simulations), 2008
Photocollage, enamel, acetate on paper, 22 inches × 30 inches

Untitled (simulations), 2008
Photocollage, enamel on paper, 30 inches × 40 inches

Untitled (simulations), 2008
Photocollage, enamel on paper, 22 inches × 30 inches

Untitled (simulations), 2008
Oil on linen, 51.375 inches × 75.75 inches

55

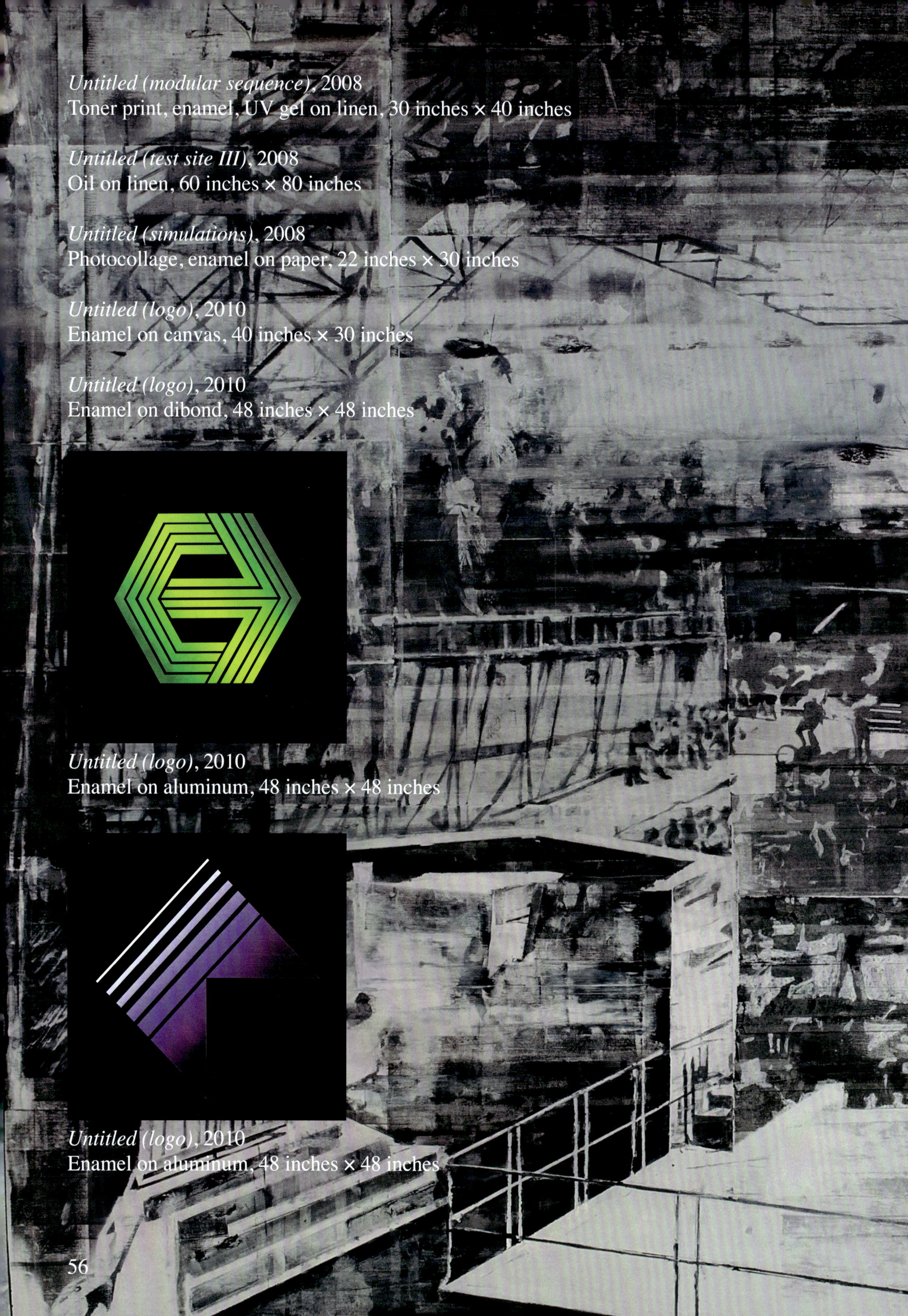

Untitled (modular sequence), 2008
Toner print, enamel, UV gel on linen, 30 inches × 40 inches

Untitled (test site III), 2008
Oil on linen, 60 inches × 80 inches

Untitled (simulations), 2008
Photocollage, enamel on paper, 22 inches × 30 inches

Untitled (logo), 2010
Enamel on canvas, 40 inches × 30 inches

Untitled (logo), 2010
Enamel on dibond, 48 inches × 48 inches

Untitled (logo), 2010
Enamel on aluminum, 48 inches × 48 inches

Untitled (logo), 2010
Enamel on aluminum, 48 inches × 48 inches

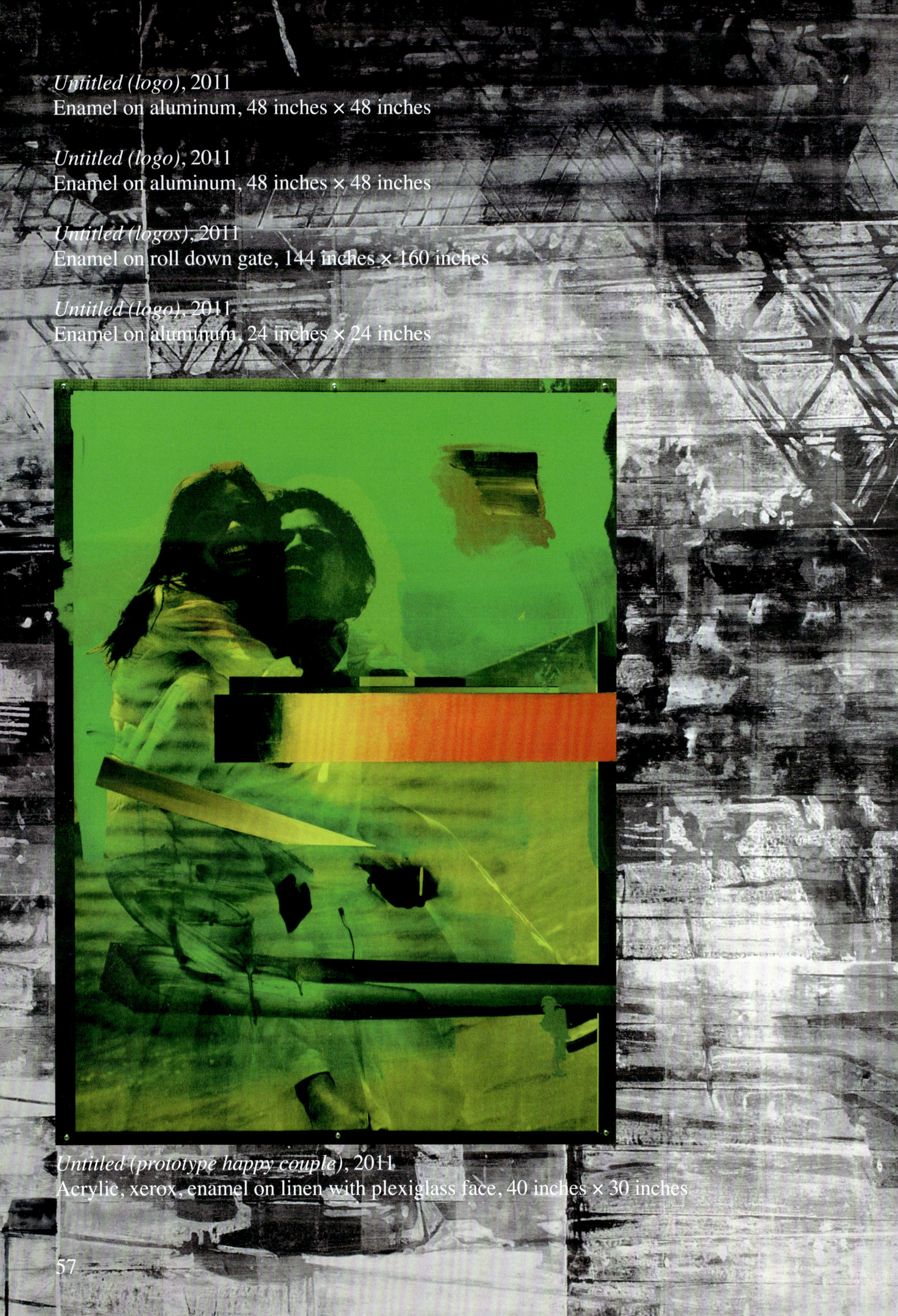

Untitled (logo), 2011
Enamel on aluminum, 48 inches × 48 inches

Untitled (logo), 2011
Enamel on aluminum, 48 inches × 48 inches

Untitled (logos), 2011
Enamel on roll down gate, 144 inches × 160 inches

Untitled (logo), 2011
Enamel on aluminum, 24 inches × 24 inches

Untitled (prototype happy couple), 2011
Acrylic, xerox, enamel on linen with plexiglass face, 40 inches × 30 inches

Untitled (body invader), 2011
Enamel on aluminum, 24 inches × 24 inches

Untitled (prototype), 2011
Acrylic, xerox, enamel on linen with plexiglass face, 40 inches × 30 inches

Untitled (prototype), 2011
Enamel on aluminum, 23.5 inches × 23.5 inches

Untitled (prototype), 2011
Photocollage, plexi, hardware with stretcher bars, 60 inches × 48 inches

Untitled (prototype), 2011
Photocollage, plexi, hardware with stretcher bars, 60 inches × 48 inches

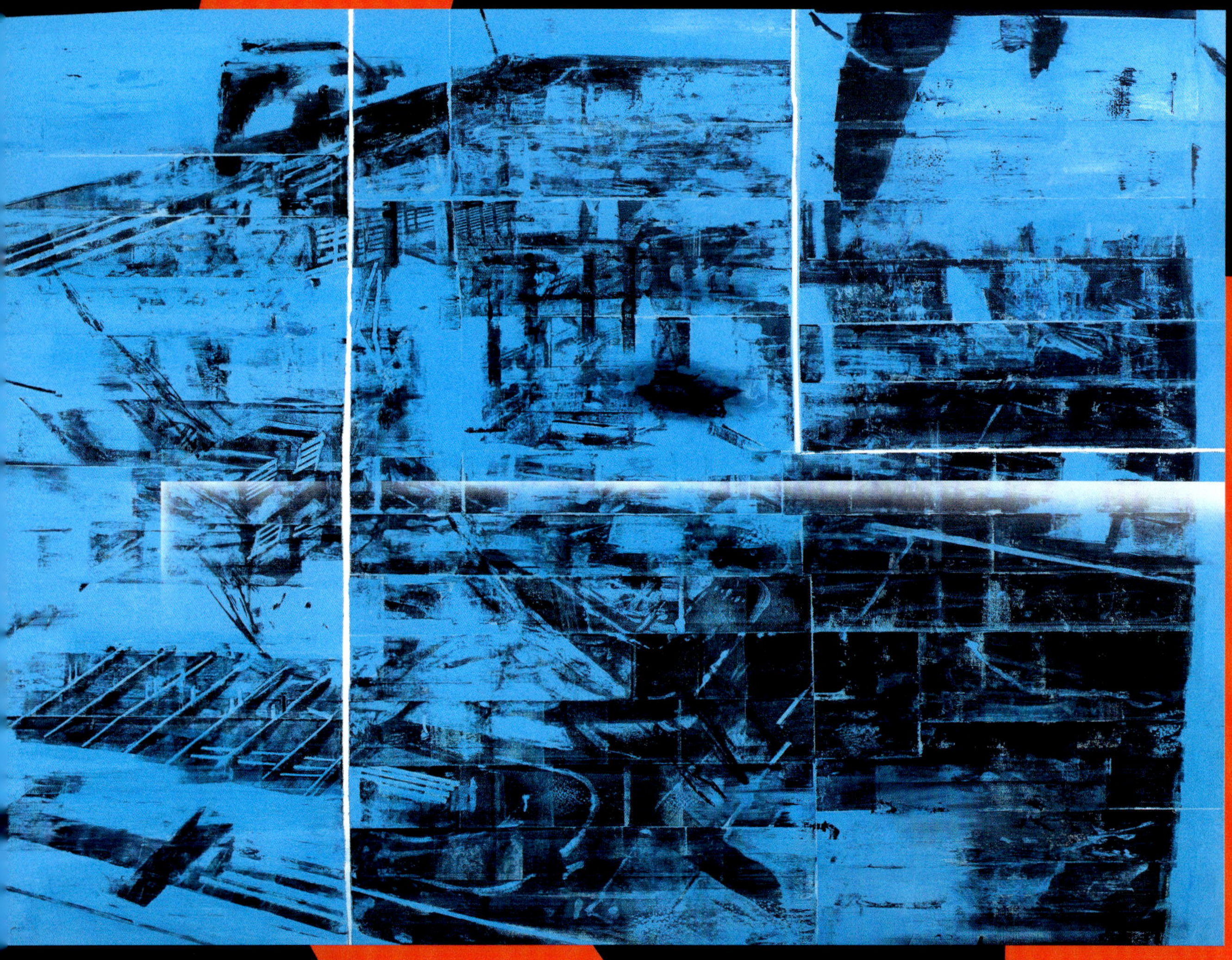

Untitled (landscape), 2012
Oil on linen, 58 inches × 80 inches

Untitled (gradient fall), 2012
Enamel on canvas, 48 inches × 48 inches

Untitled (wild dead), 2012
Enamel on canvas, 48 inches × 48 inches

Untitled (fanstreaks), 2012
Oil on linen, 64 inches × 72 inches

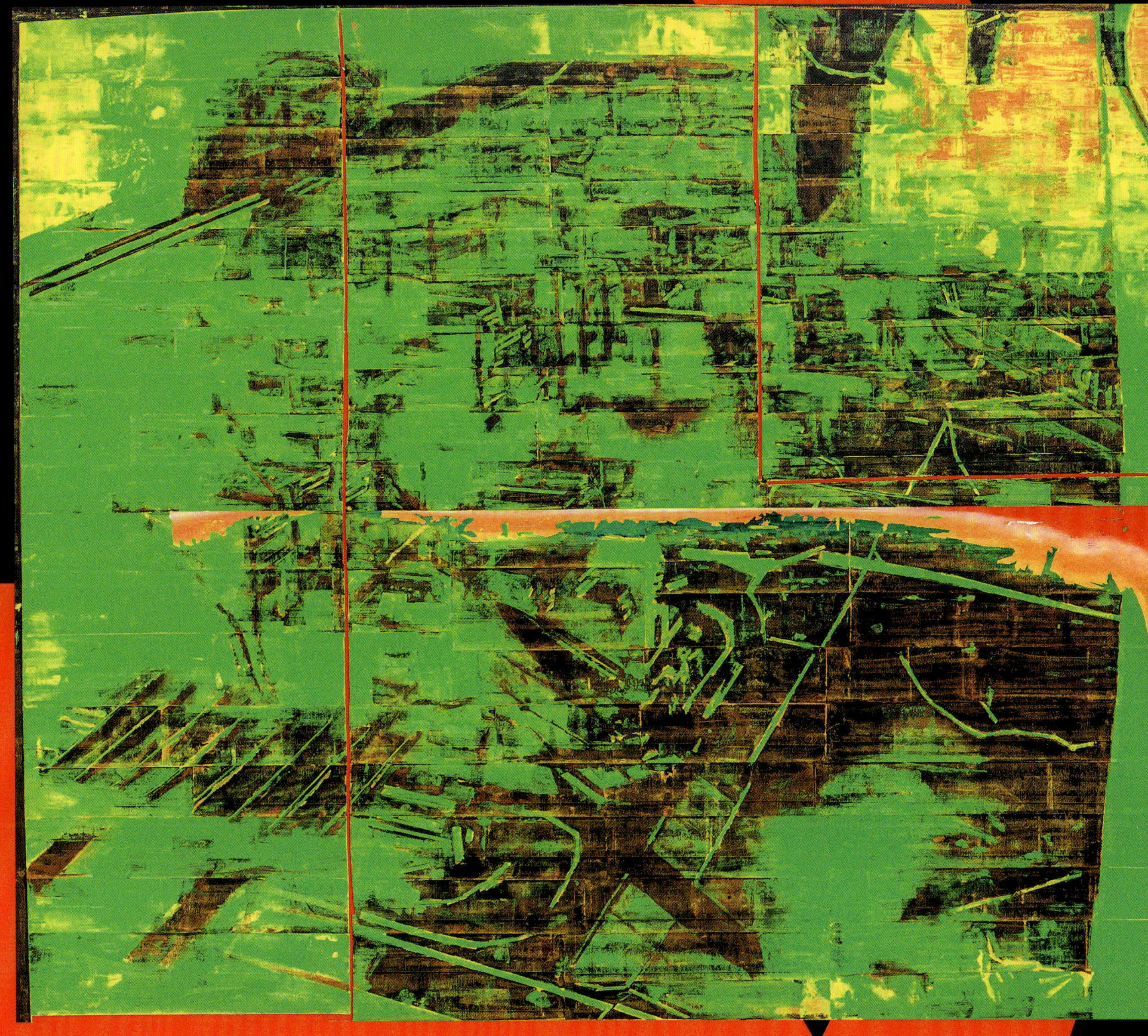

Untitled (dumping core—after GB), 2012
Oil on canvas, 72 inches × 84 inches

Untitled (entertainment hardware), 2012
Single-channel video, 00:02:31

Untitled (hyatt), 2012
Oil on canvas, 66 inches × 88 inches

Untitled (prototype), 2012
Photocollage, later, plexiglass on canvas, 14 inches × 12 inches

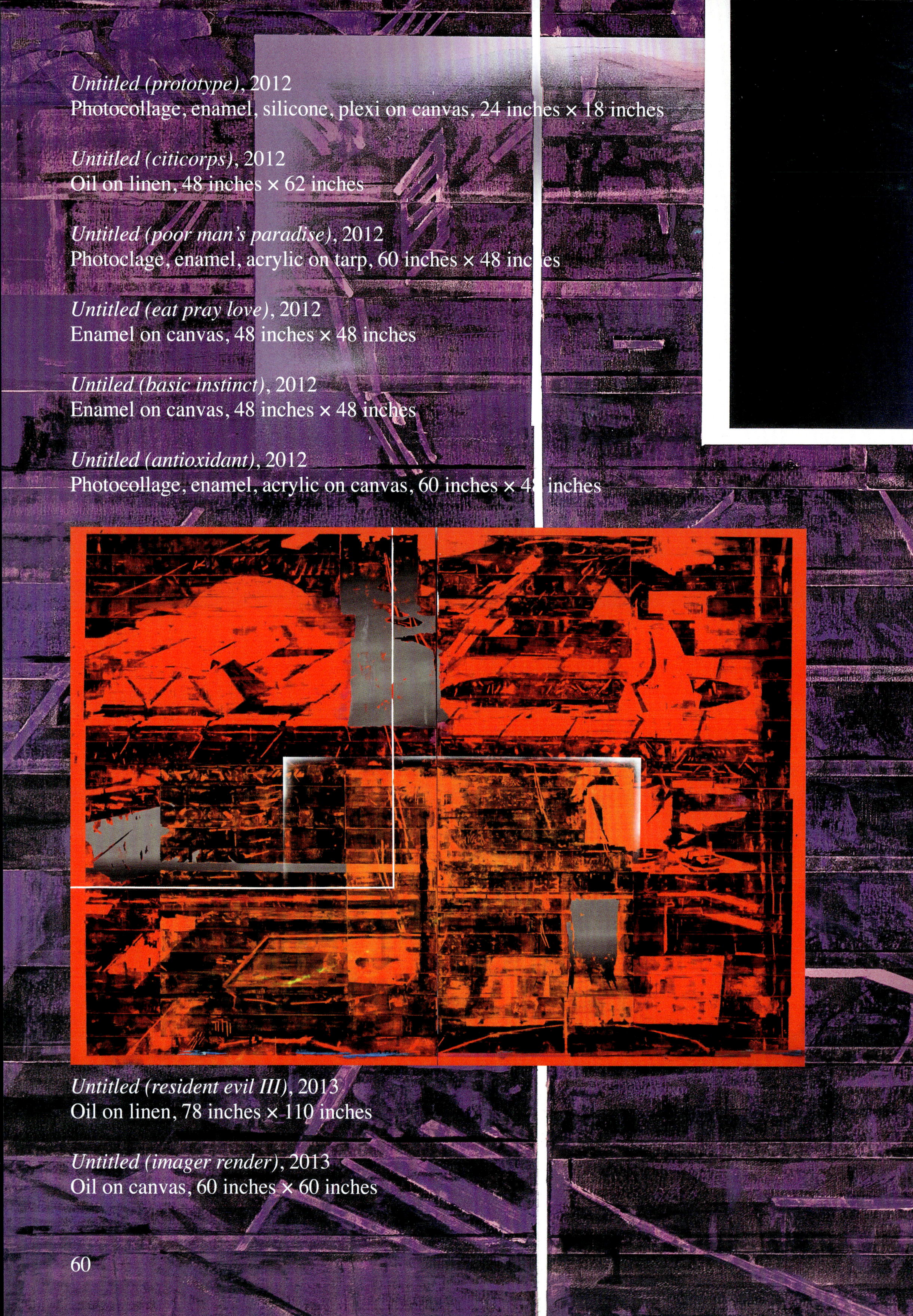

Untitled (prototype), 2012
Photocollage, enamel, silicone, plexi on canvas, 24 inches × 18 inches

Untitled (citicorps), 2012
Oil on linen, 48 inches × 62 inches

Untitled (poor man's paradise), 2012
Photoclage, enamel, acrylic on tarp, 60 inches × 48 inches

Untitled (eat pray love), 2012
Enamel on canvas, 48 inches × 48 inches

Untiled (basic instinct), 2012
Enamel on canvas, 48 inches × 48 inches

Untitled (antioxidant), 2012
Photocollage, enamel, acrylic on canvas, 60 inches × 48 inches

Untitled (resident evil III), 2013
Oil on linen, 78 inches × 110 inches

Untitled (imager render), 2013
Oil on canvas, 60 inches × 60 inches

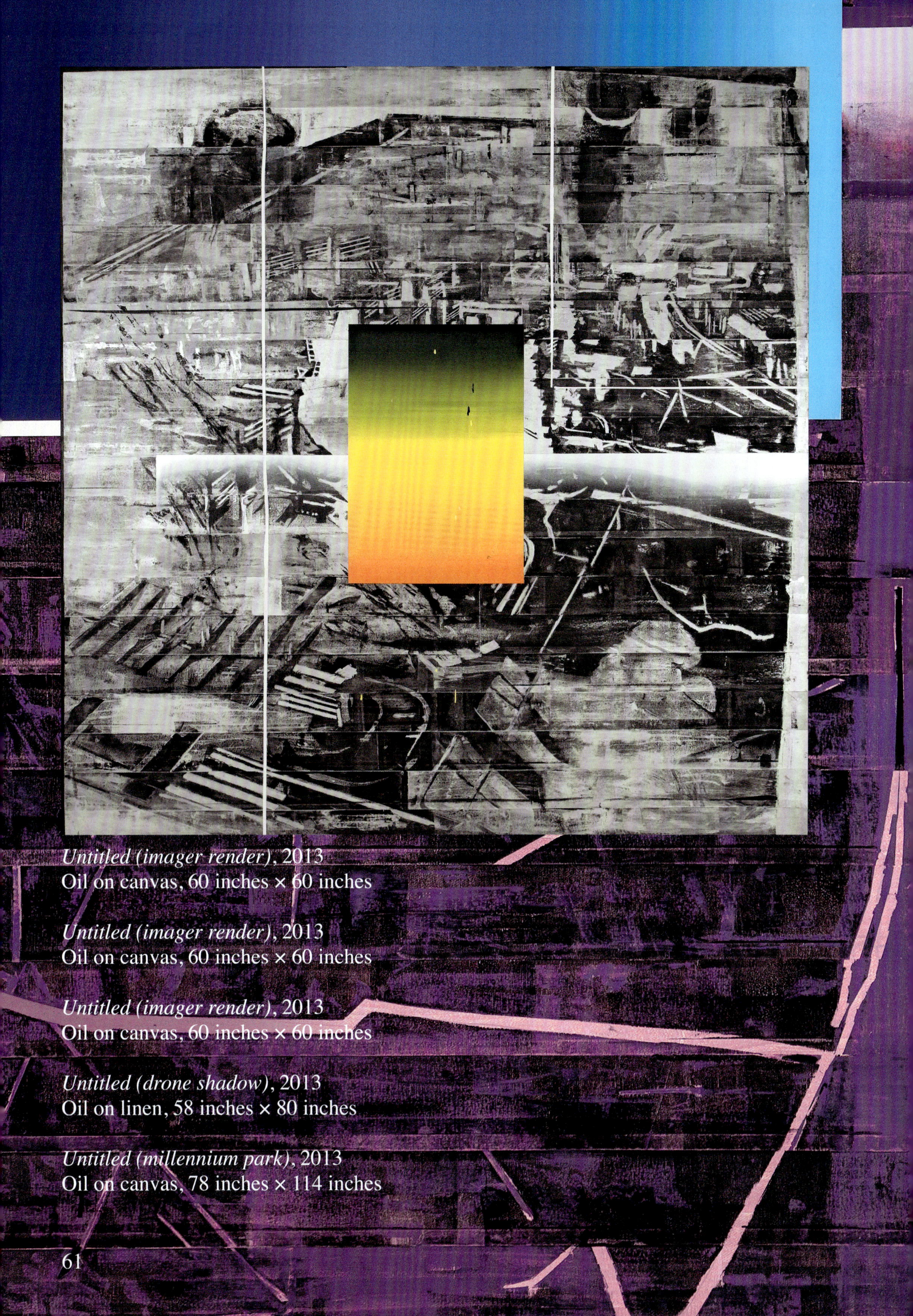

Untitled (imager render), 2013
Oil on canvas, 60 inches × 60 inches

Untitled (imager render), 2013
Oil on canvas, 60 inches × 60 inches

Untitled (imager render), 2013
Oil on canvas, 60 inches × 60 inches

Untitled (drone shadow), 2013
Oil on linen, 58 inches × 80 inches

Untitled (millennium park), 2013
Oil on canvas, 78 inches × 114 inches

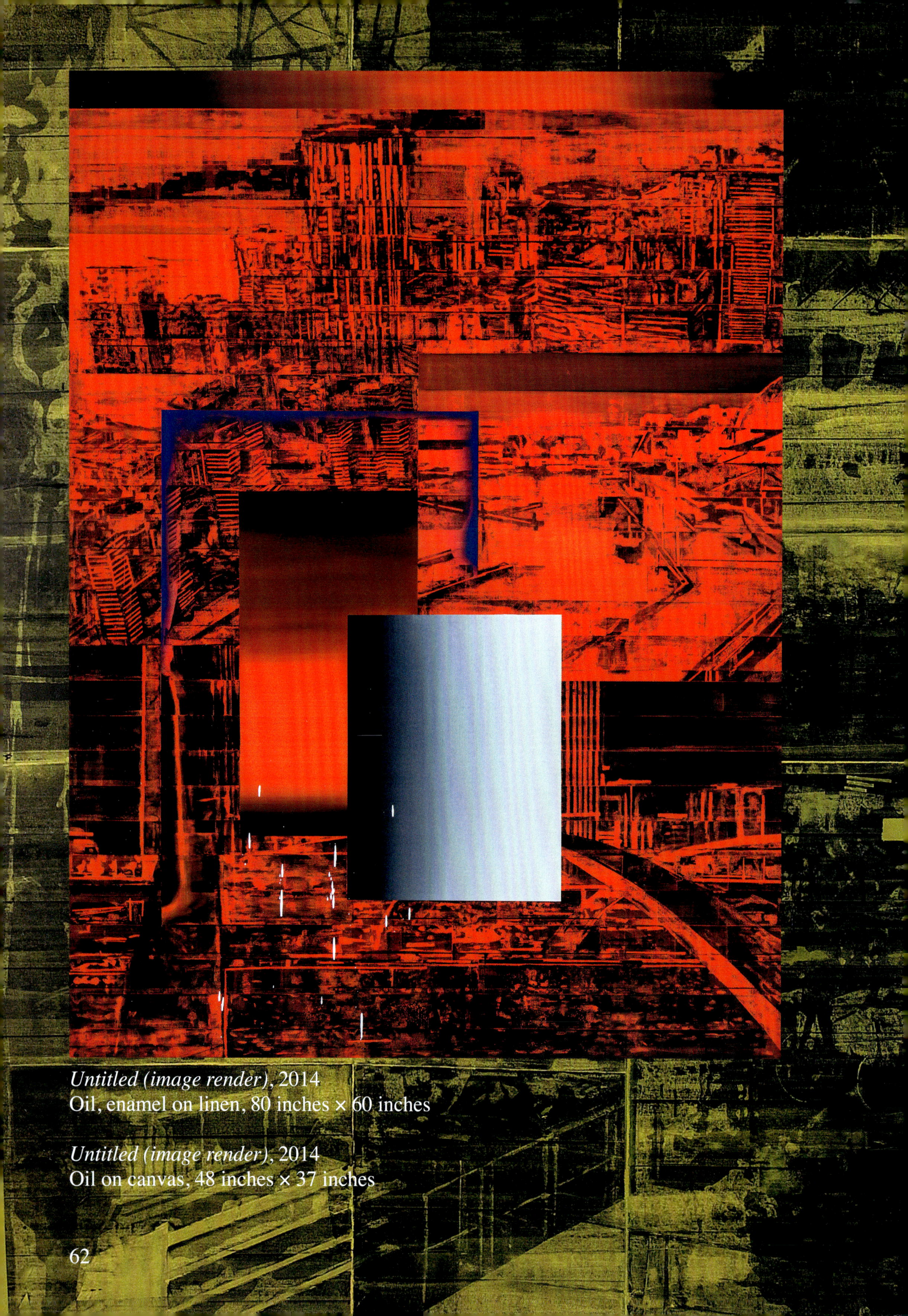

Untitled (image render), 2014
Oil, enamel on linen, 80 inches × 60 inches

Untitled (image render), 2014
Oil on canvas, 48 inches × 37 inches

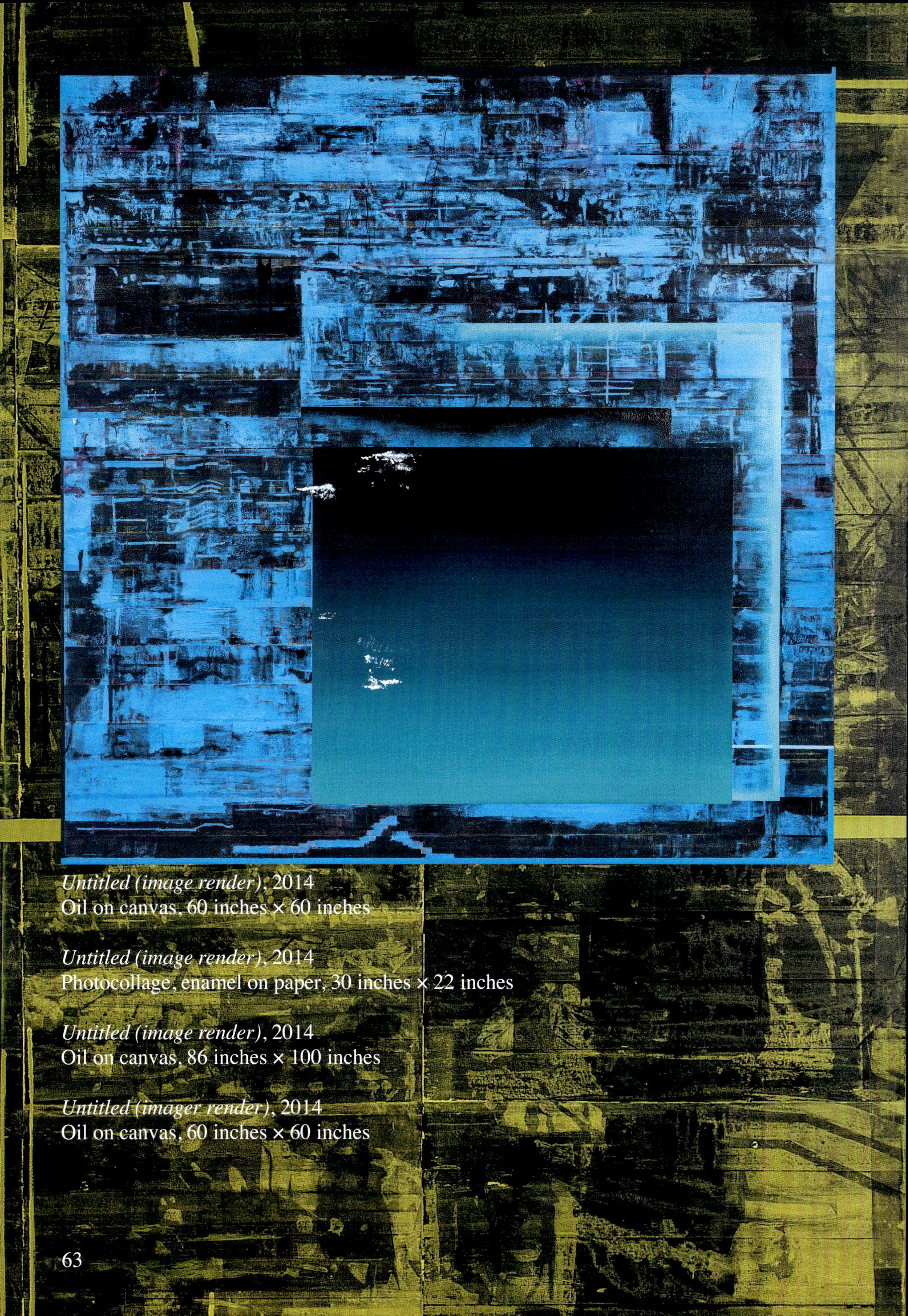

Untitled (image render), 2014
Oil on canvas, 60 inches × 60 inches

Untitled (image render), 2014
Photocollage, enamel on paper, 30 inches × 22 inches

Untitled (image render), 2014
Oil on canvas, 86 inches × 100 inches

Untitled (imager render), 2014
Oil on canvas, 60 inches × 60 inches

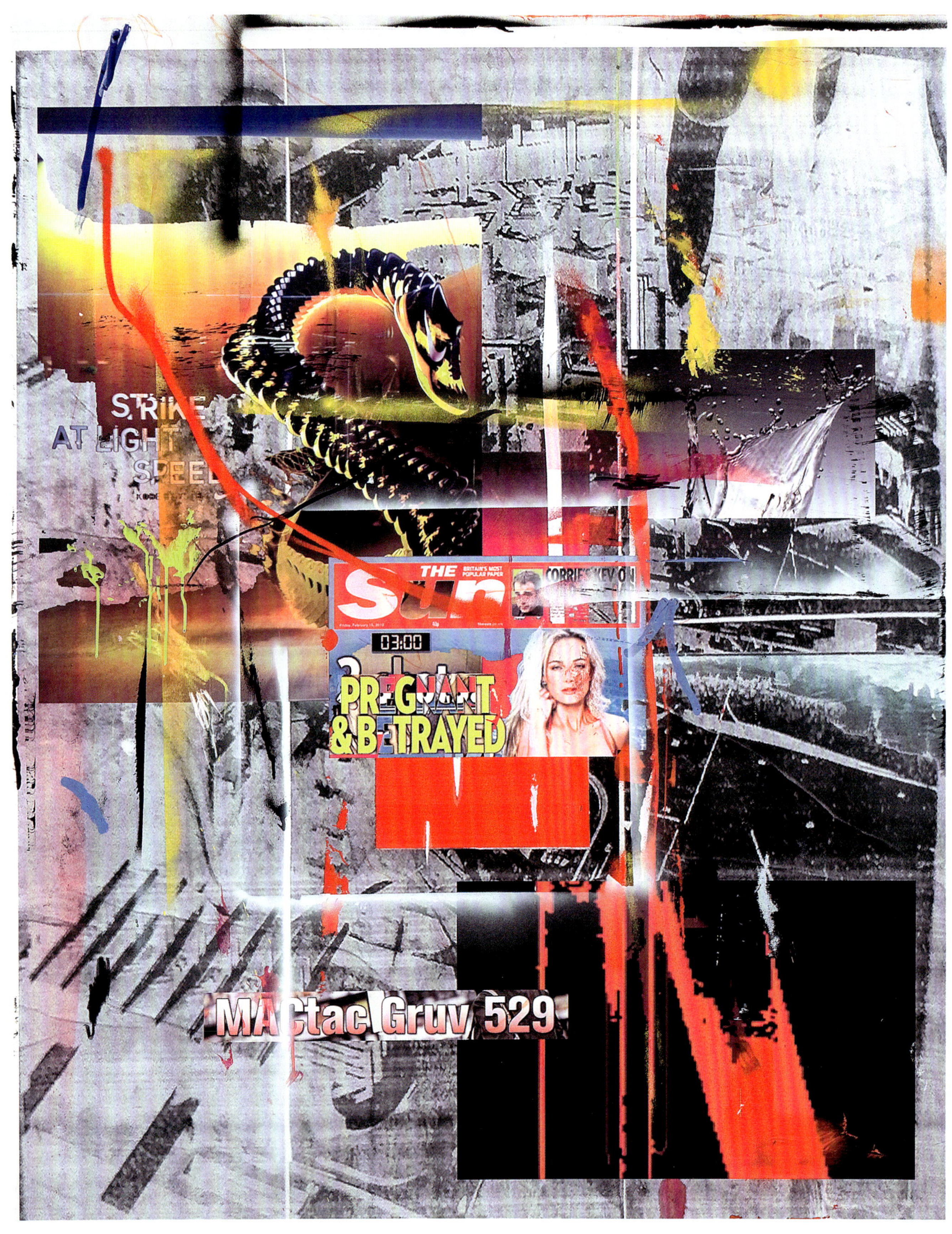

Untitled (mactac), 2014
Photocollage, enamel on canvas, 60 inches × 48 inches

Untitled (tilt/shift), 2014
Oil, enamel on linen, 72 inches × 64 inches

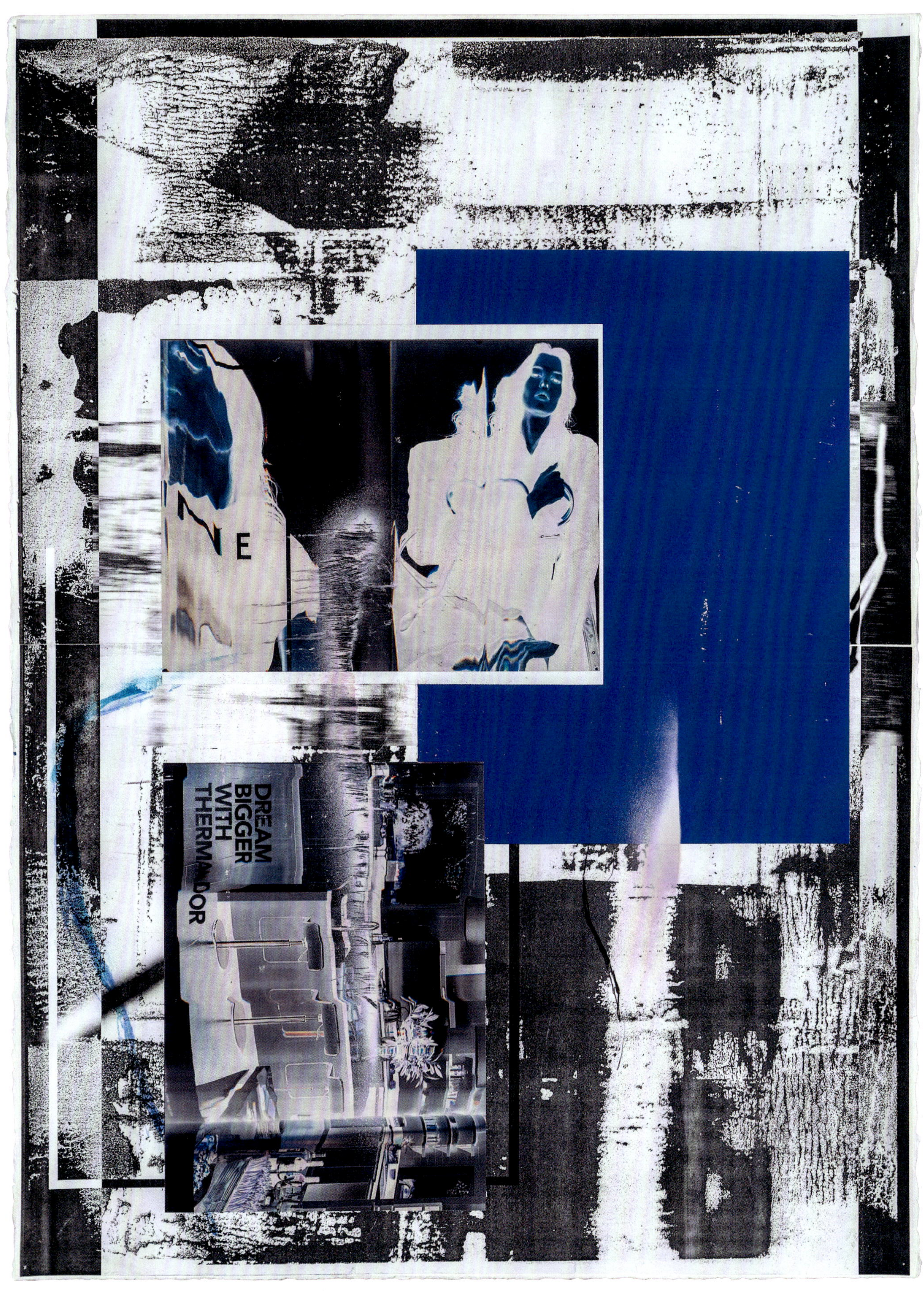

Untitled (image render), 2014
Photocollage, enamel on paper, 30 inches × 22 inches

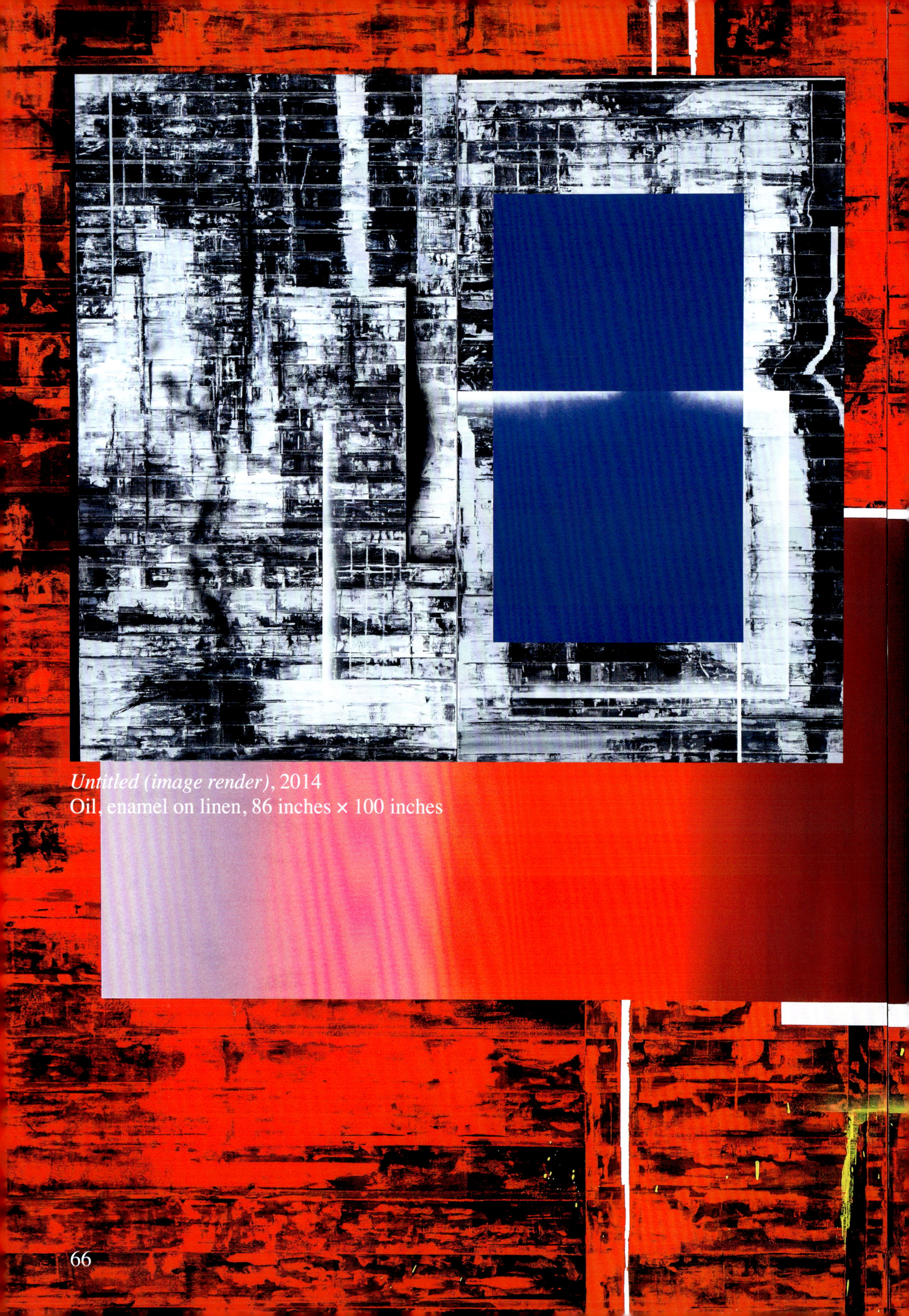

Untitled (image render), 2014
Oil, enamel on linen, 86 inches × 100 inches

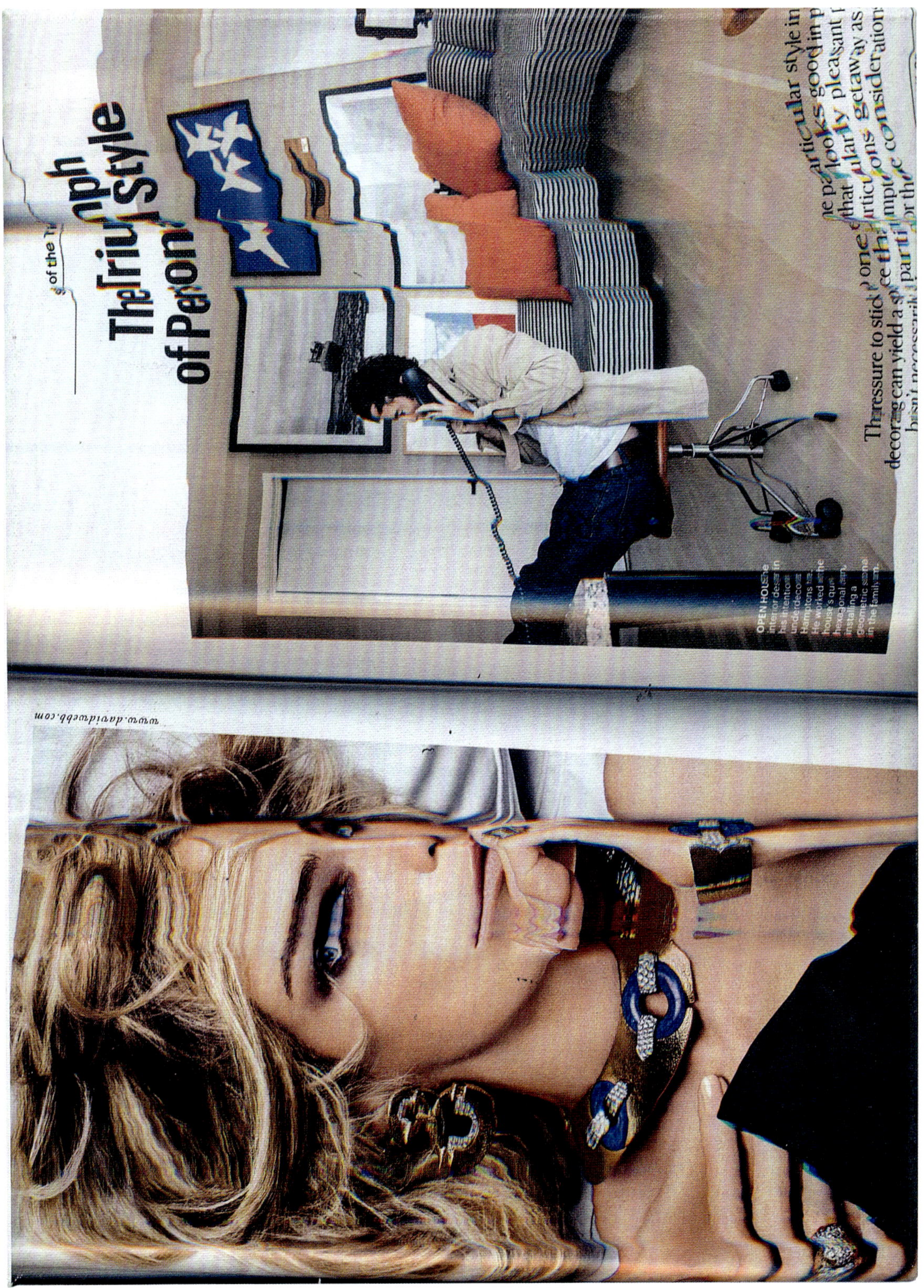

Untitled (scanners), 2015
Durabrite ink, UV gel on canvas with aluminum stretcher bars, 18 inches × 14 inches

Untitled (leviathan), 2015
Durabrite ink, vinyl, linen, canvas, gesso, UV gel with aluminum stretcher bars
86 inches × 100 inches

Untitled (debt economy/ratchet strap), 2015
Durabrite ink, gesso, canvas, linen, cotton, UV gel with aluminum stretcher bars
60 inches × 80 inches

Untitled (lake vermillion), 2015
Durabrite ink, canvas, gesso, UV gel with aluminum stretcher bars, 80 inches × 60 inches

Untitled (t602200), 2015
Durabrite ink, canvas, gesso, UV gel with aluminum stretcher bars, 60 inches × 48 inches

Untitled (efficient frontier), 2015
Durabrite ink, canvas, linen, gesso, UV gel with aluminum stretcher bars
80 inches × 60 inches

Untitled (today's man), 2015
Durabrite ink, canvas, gesso, UV gel with aluminum stretcher bars, 40 inches × 30 inches

Untitled (broad new rules), 2015
Durabrite ink, canvas, gesso, UV gel with aluminum stretcher bars, 40 inches × 30 inches

Untitled (scanners), 2015
Durabrite ink, vinyl, tarp, gesso with stretcher bars, 60 inches × 48 inches

Untitled (scanners), 2015
Durabrite ink, canvas, gesso, UV gel with aluminum stretcher bars, 60 inches × 48 inches

Untitled (scanners), 2015
Durabrite ink, canvas, gesso, UV gel with aluminum stretcher bars, 60 inches × 48 inches

Untitled (catch me if i fall), 2015
Durabrite ink, gesso, linen, canvas with stretcher bars, 60 inches × 48 inches

Untitled (extraction), 2015
Durabrite ink, uv gel on canvas, 60 inches × 48 inches

Untitled (image render), 2015
Oil on canvas, 80 inches × 60 inches

Untitled (heliotrope), 2015
Durabrite ink, gesso, canvas, UV gel with aluminum stretcher bars, 72 inches × 48 inches

Untitled (scanners), 2015
Durabrite ink, gesso, canvas, UV gel with aluminum stretcher bars, 60 inches × 48 inches

Untitled (scanners), 2015
Ink on paper, 11 inches × 8.5 inches

Untitled (infinity pools ss series above ground swimming pool), 2015
Ink on paper, 11 inches × 8.5 inches

Untitled (soft power, franz kline, tommy hilfiger), 2015
Ink on paper, 11 inches × 8.5 inches

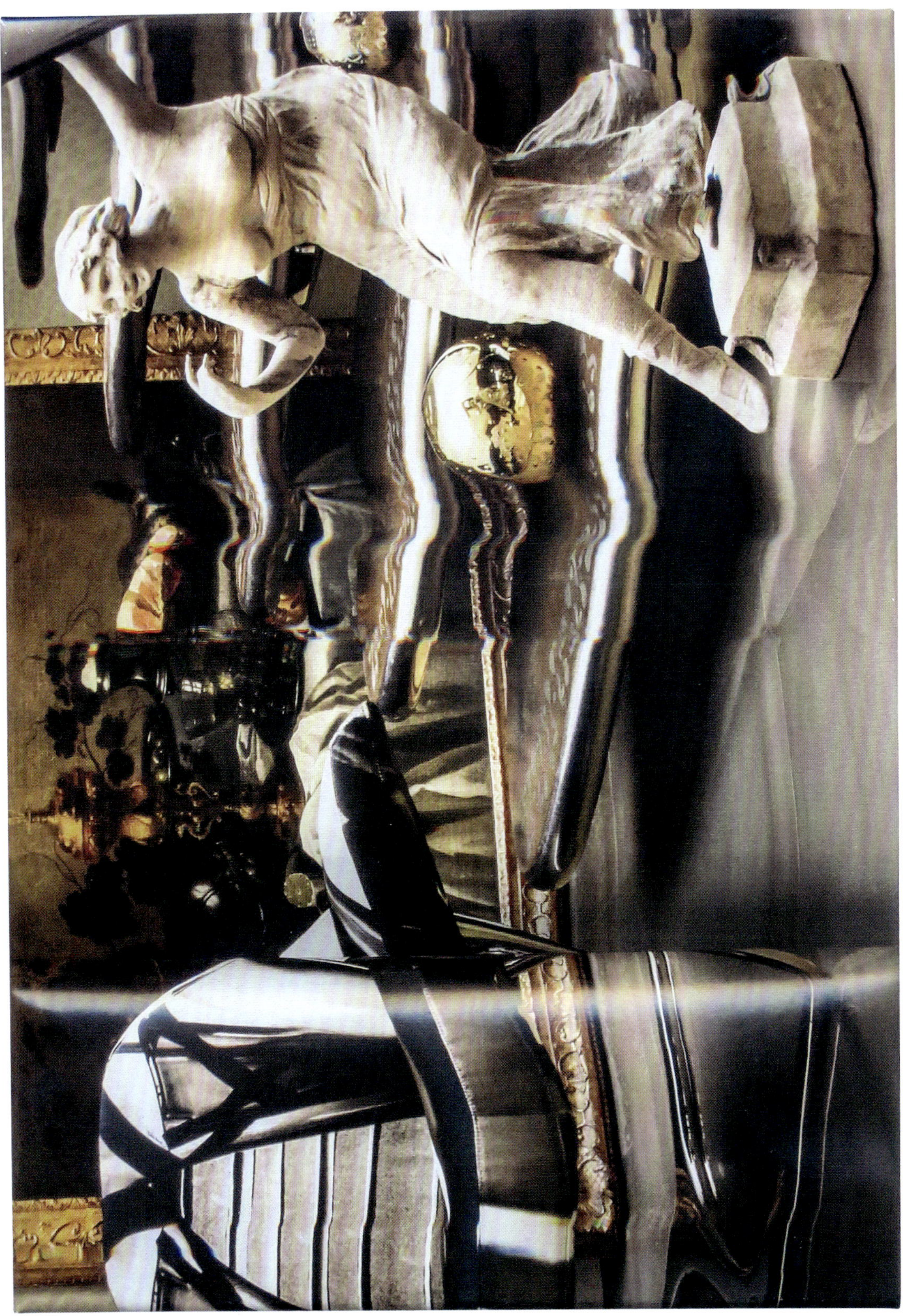

Untitled (scanners), 2015
Durabrite ink, canvas, gesso, UV gel with aluminum stretcher bars, 18 inches × 14 inches

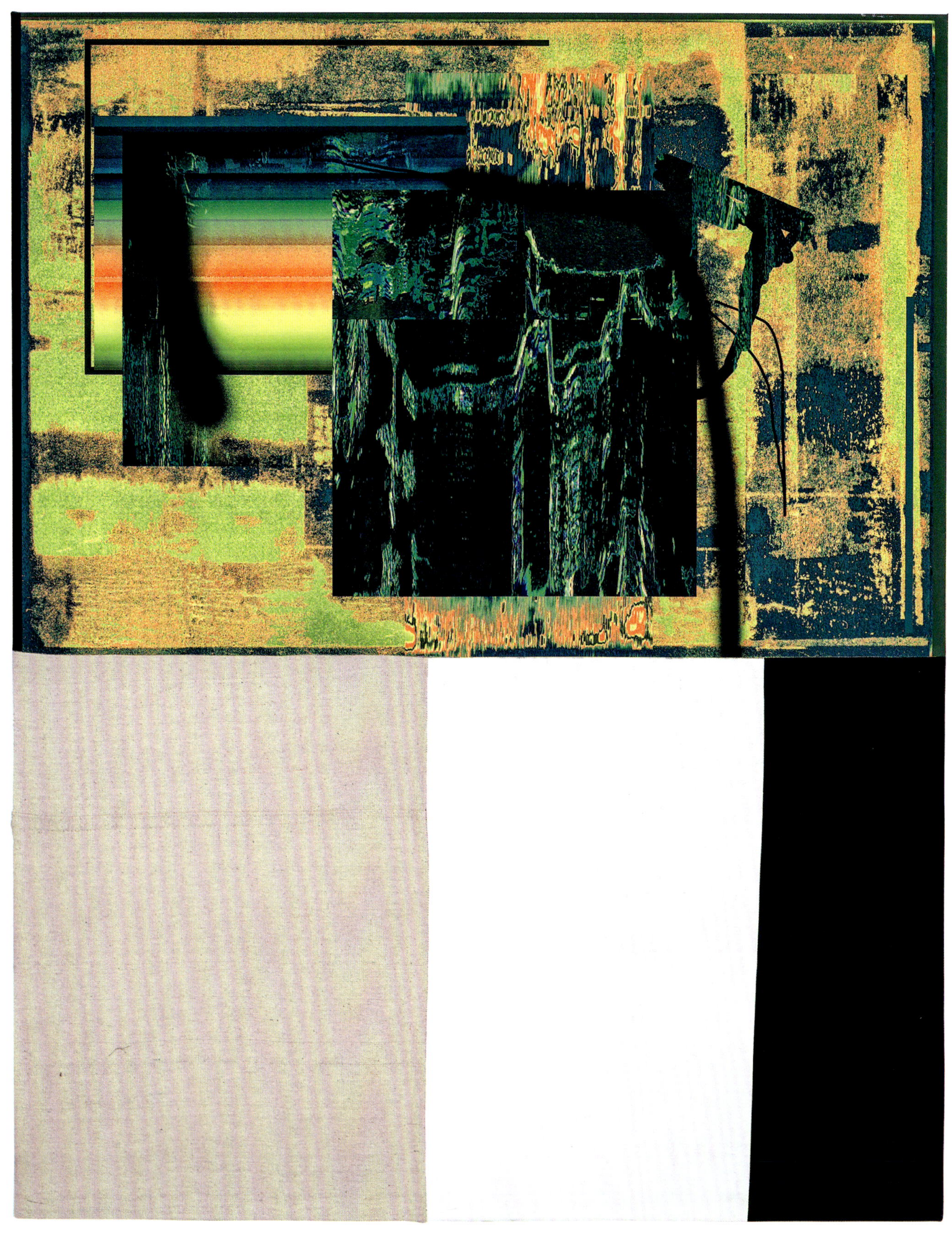

Untitled (scanners), 2015
Durabrite ink, vinyl, tarp, gesso with stretcher bars, 60 inches × 48 inches

Untitled (today's man), 2015
Durabrite ink, vinyl, gesso, cotton with stretcher bars, 80 inches × 60 inches

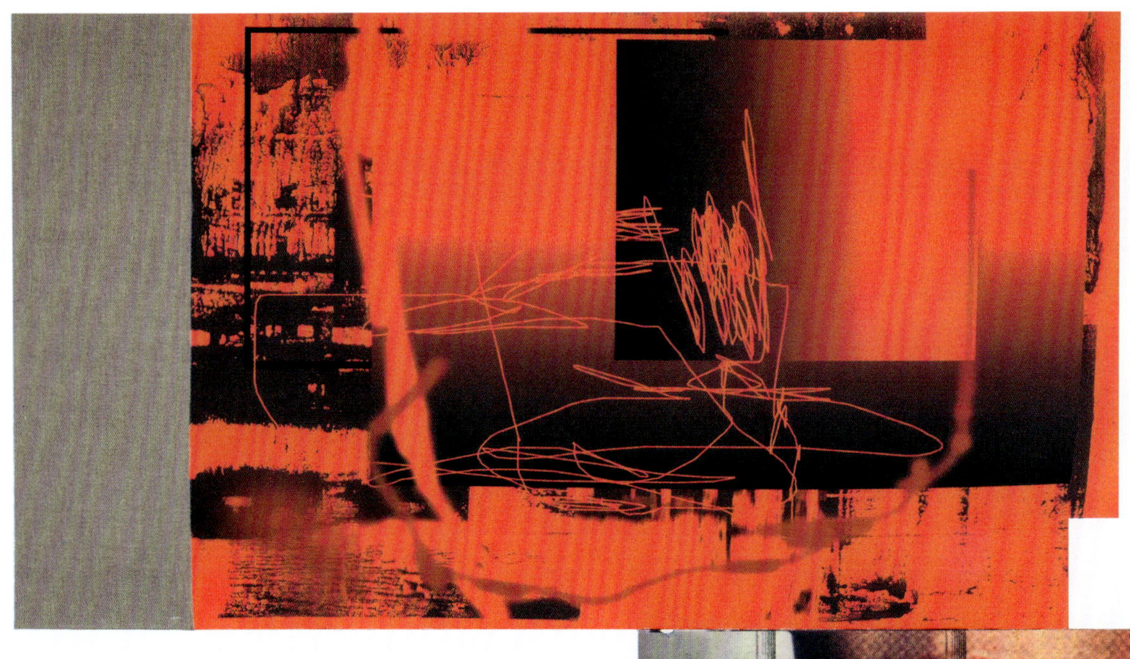

Untitled (soft power), 2015
Durabrite ink, linen, canvas, gesso, UV gel with aluminum stretcher bars
78 inches × 78 inches

Untitled (silicon violence), 2016
UV ink on alumacore, 46 inches × 32 inches

Untitled (corporate cannibal), 2016
UV ink on alumacore, 94 inches × 46 inches

Untitled (body degree zero), 2016
UV ink on dibond with aluminum support, 26 inches × 18 inches

Untitled (dangerous emotions, ultra black), 2016
UV ink on dibond with aluminum support, 26 inches × 18 inches

Untitled (factory reconditioned), 2016
UV ink on alumacore, 94 inches × 46 inches

Untitled (scanners), 2016
Ink on paper, 11 inches × 8.5 inches

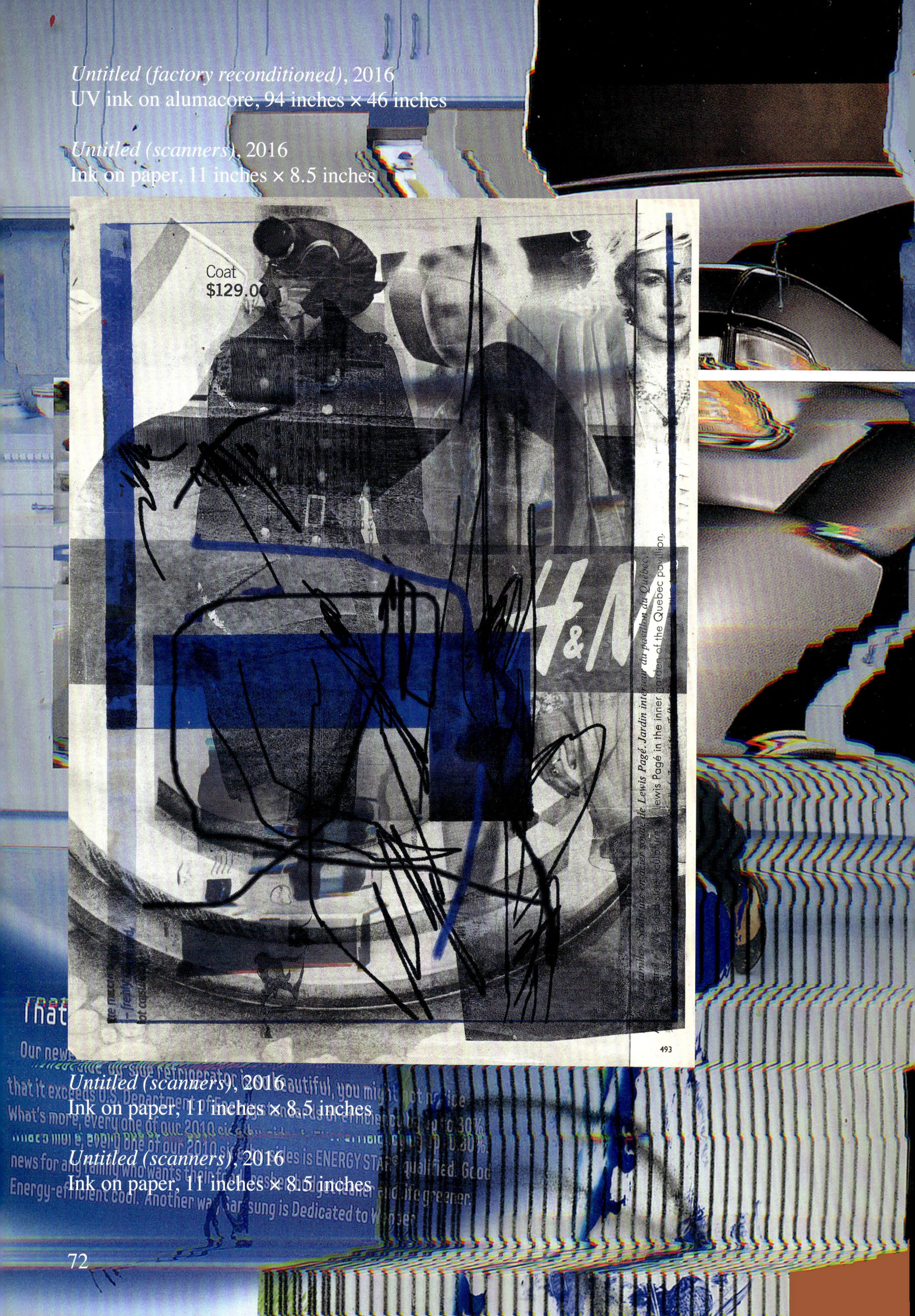

Coat
$129.00
H&M
493

Untitled (scanners), 2016
Ink on paper, 11 inches × 8.5 inches

Untitled (scanners), 2016
Ink on paper, 11 inches × 8.5 inches

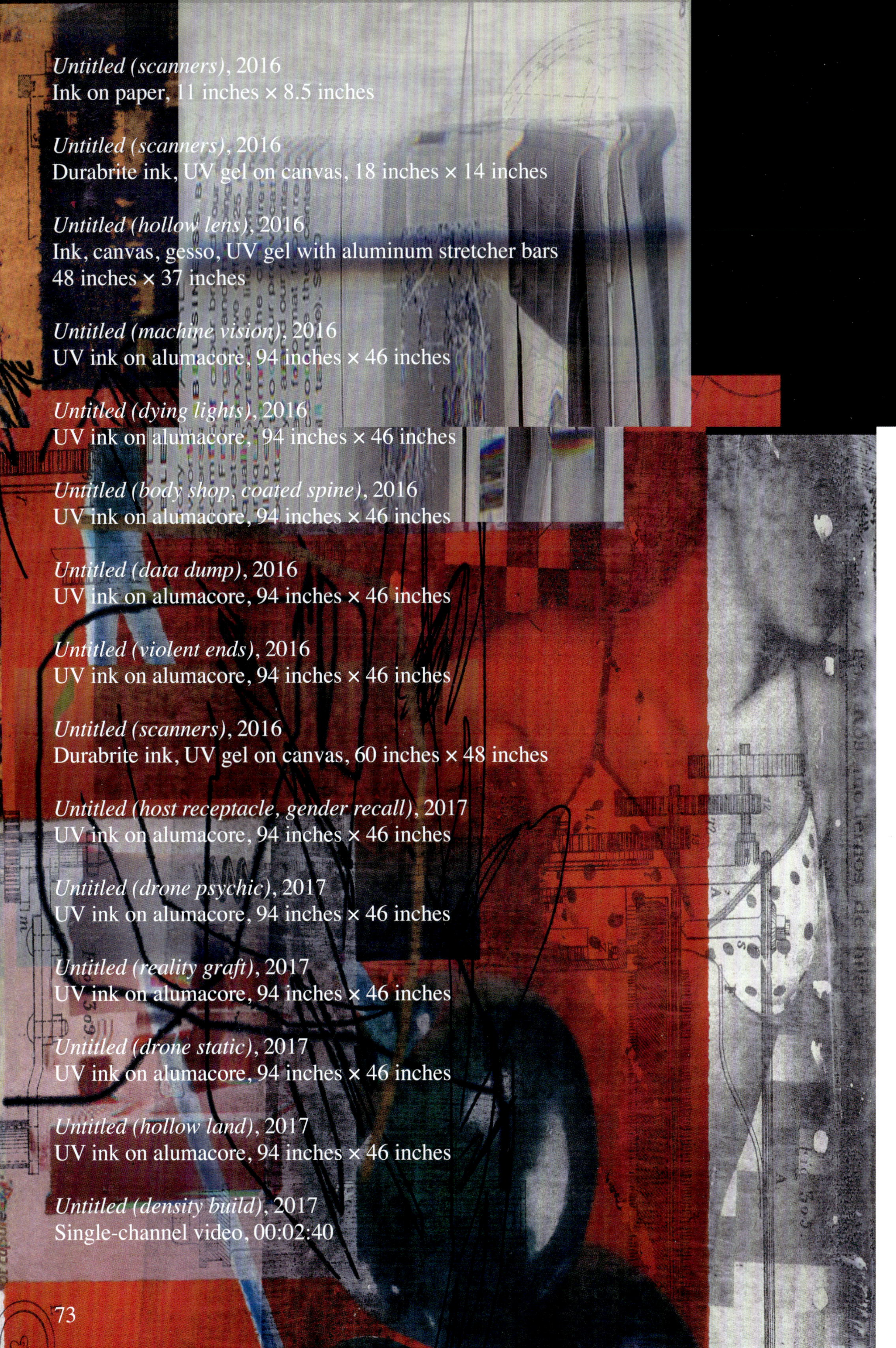

Untitled (scanners), 2016
Ink on paper, 11 inches × 8.5 inches

Untitled (scanners), 2016
Durabrite ink, UV gel on canvas, 18 inches × 14 inches

Untitled (hollow lens), 2016
Ink, canvas, gesso, UV gel with aluminum stretcher bars
48 inches × 37 inches

Untitled (machine vision), 2016
UV ink on alumacore, 94 inches × 46 inches

Untitled (dying lights), 2016
UV ink on alumacore, 94 inches × 46 inches

Untitled (body shop, coated spine), 2016
UV ink on alumacore, 94 inches × 46 inches

Untitled (data dump), 2016
UV ink on alumacore, 94 inches × 46 inches

Untitled (violent ends), 2016
UV ink on alumacore, 94 inches × 46 inches

Untitled (scanners), 2016
Durabrite ink, UV gel on canvas, 60 inches × 48 inches

Untitled (host receptacle, gender recall), 2017
UV ink on alumacore, 94 inches × 46 inches

Untitled (drone psychic), 2017
UV ink on alumacore, 94 inches × 46 inches

Untitled (reality graft), 2017
UV ink on alumacore, 94 inches × 46 inches

Untitled (drone static), 2017
UV ink on alumacore, 94 inches × 46 inches

Untitled (hollow land), 2017
UV ink on alumacore, 94 inches × 46 inches

Untitled (density build), 2017
Single-channel video, 00:02:40

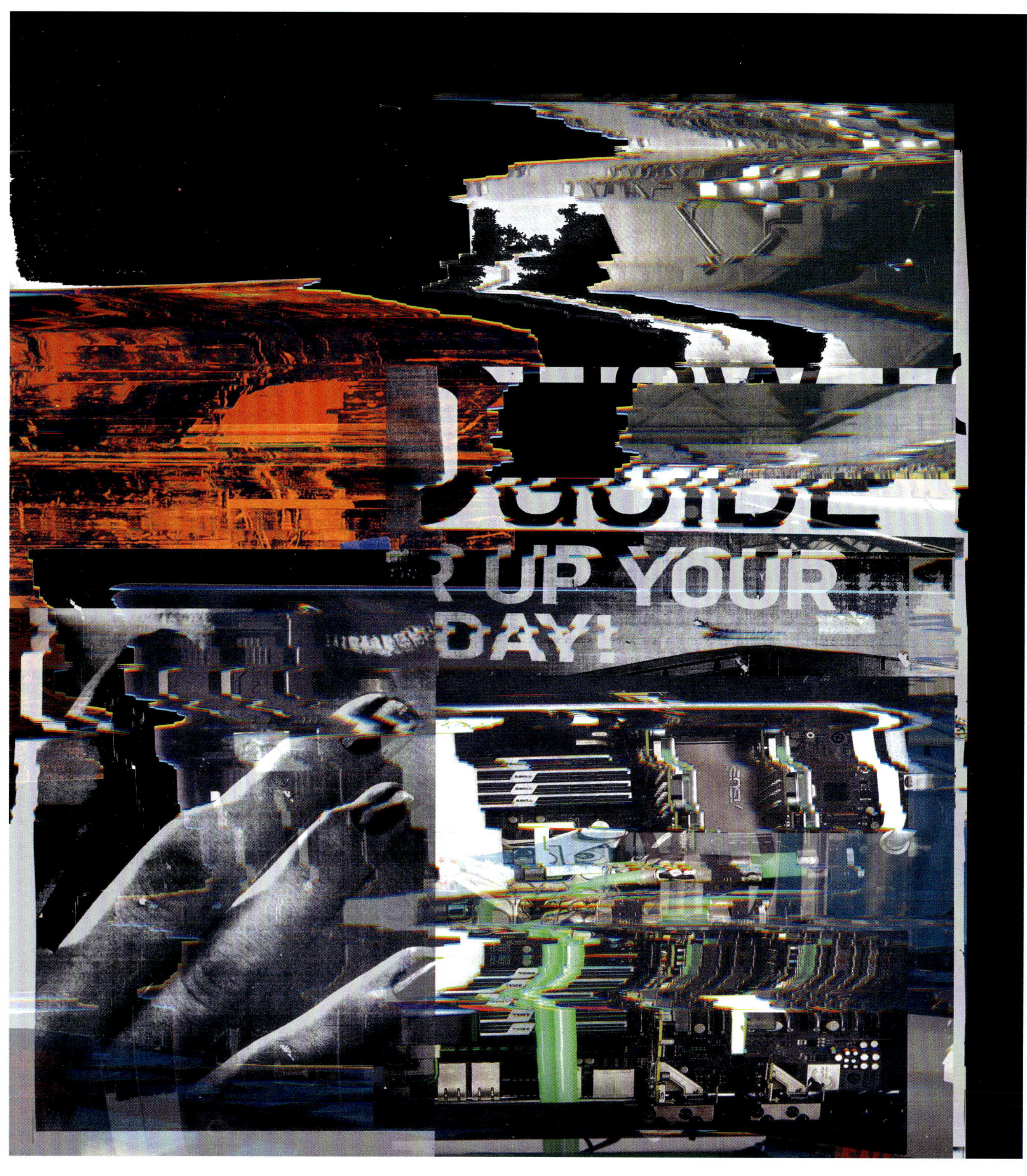

Untitled (coil whine), 2017
UV ink on alumacore, 88 inches × 78 inches

Untitled (anthracite), 2017
UV ink on alumacore, 94 inches × 46 inches

Untitled (touchscreen), 2017
Single-channel video, 00:00:09

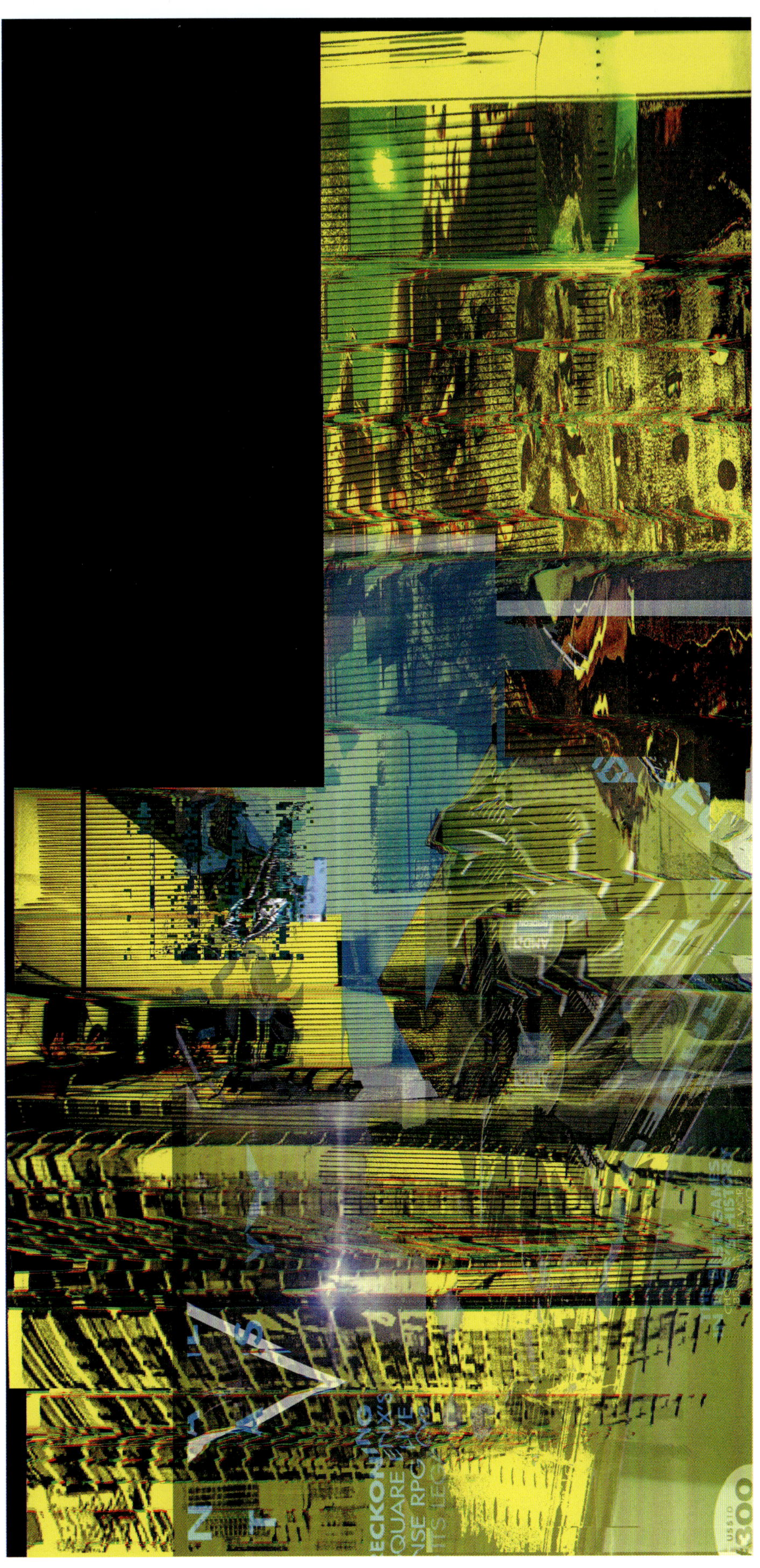

Untitled (apache struts), 2017
UV ink on alumacore, 94 inches × 46 inches

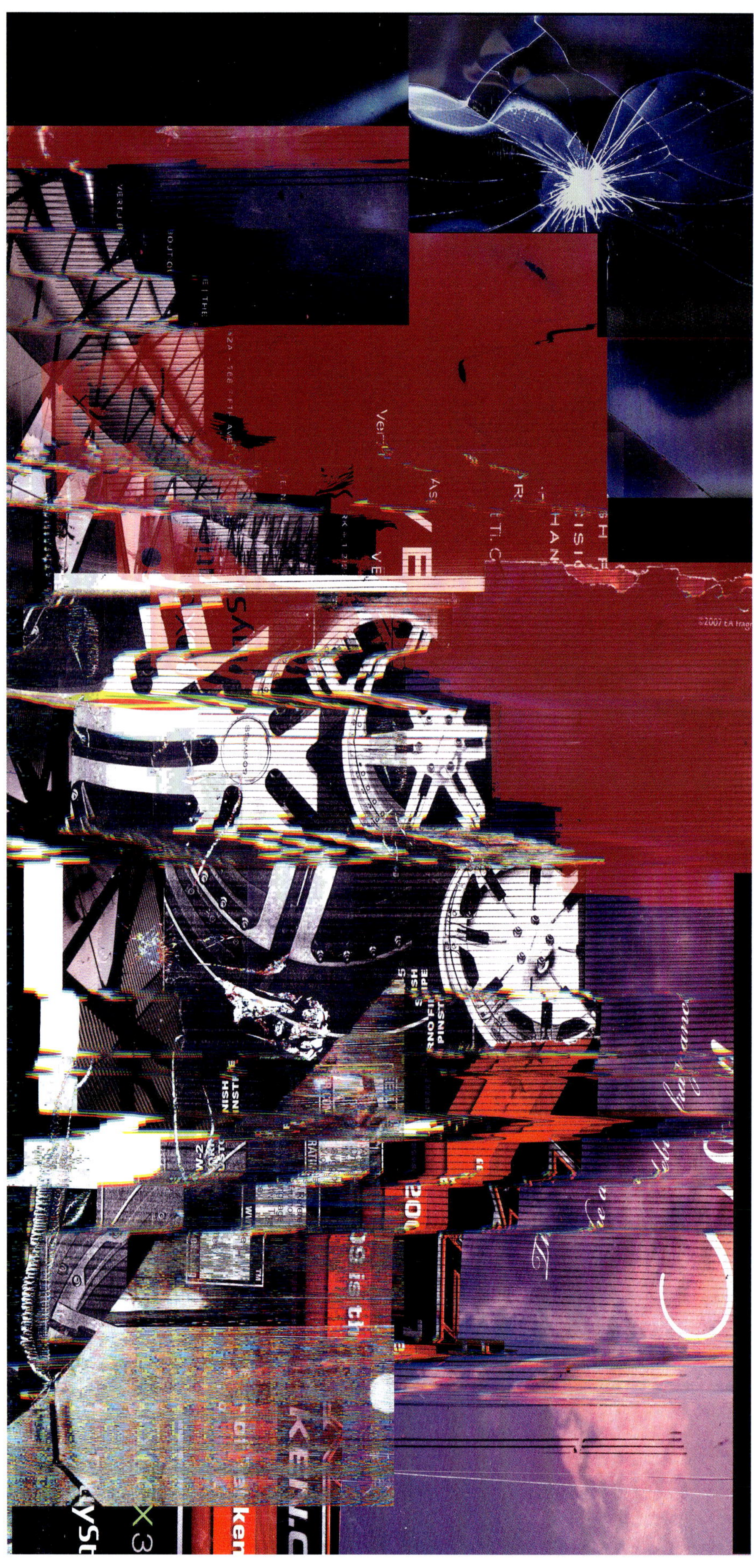

Untitled (drift upload), 2017
UV ink on alumacore, 94 inches × 46 inches

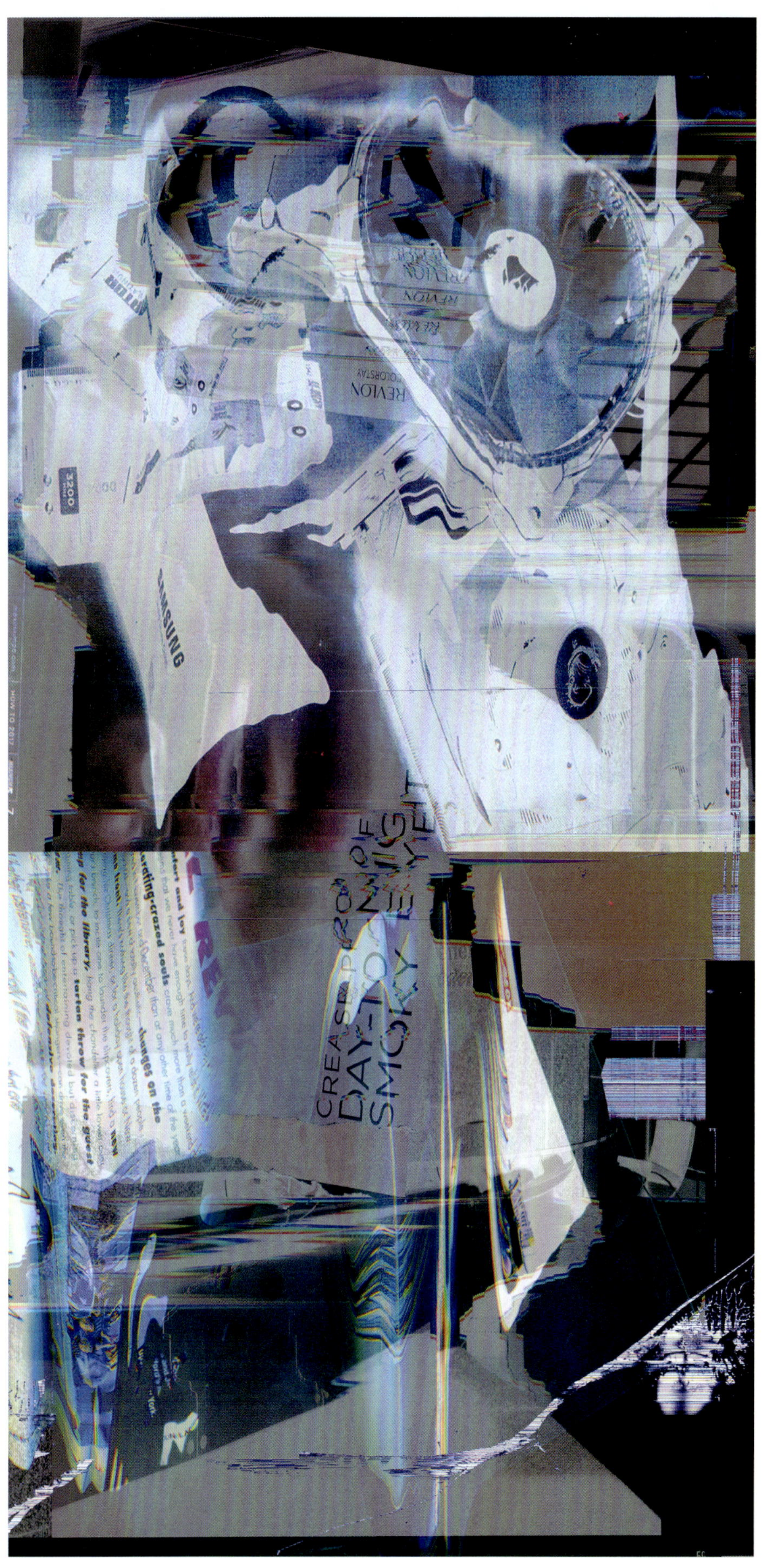

Untitled (skin crawler), 2018
UV ink on alumacore, 94 inches × 46 inches

Untitled (blade server), 2017
UV ink on acrylic panel with mounting hardware
32 inches × 18 inches

Untitled (SATA II, hard drive, HD103UJ), 2017
UV ink on acrylic panel with mounting hardware
32 inches × 18 inches

Untitled (core dump), 2017
UV ink on acrylic panel with mounting hardware
32 inches × 18 inches

Untitled (density build), 2017
UV ink on acrylic panel with mounting hardware
32 inches × 18 inches

Untitled (synthetic membrane), 2018
UV ink on alumacore, 78 inches × 44 inches

Untitled (colony), 2018
UV ink on alumacore, 78 inches × 44 inches

Untitled (heat stamp), 2018
UV ink on alumacore, 32 inches × 20 inches

Untitled (deep mind), 2018
UV ink on alumacore, 78 inches × 44 inches

Untitled (sun scraper), 2018
Website, sun-scraper.com

Untitled (perception wrap), 2018
UV ink on alumacore, 32 inches × 20 inches

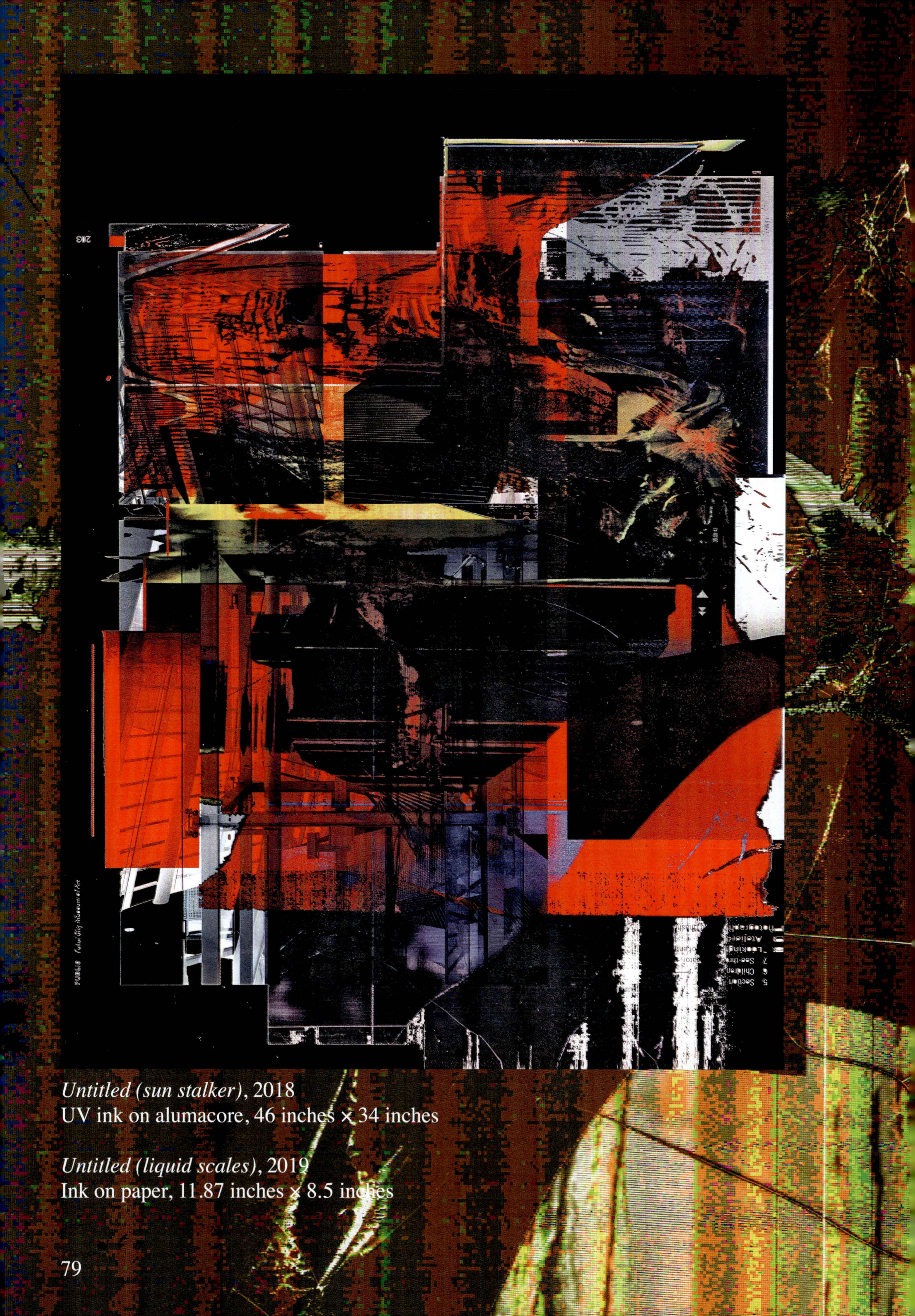

Untitled (sun stalker), 2018
UV ink on alumacore, 46 inches × 34 inches

Untitled (liquid scales), 2019
Ink on paper, 11.87 inches × 8.5 inches

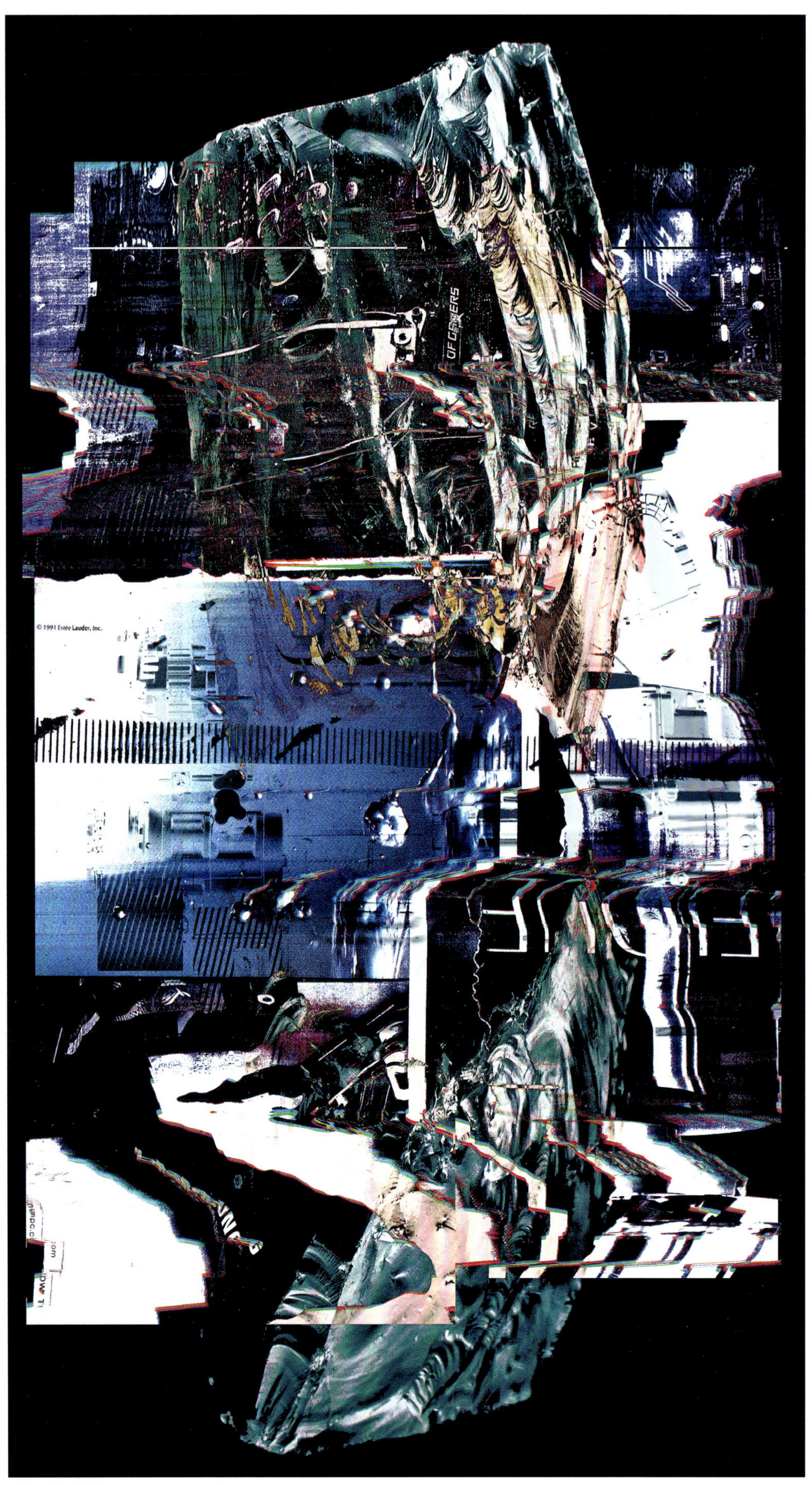

Untitled (liquid foundation), 2019
UV ink on alumacore, 78 inches × 44 inches

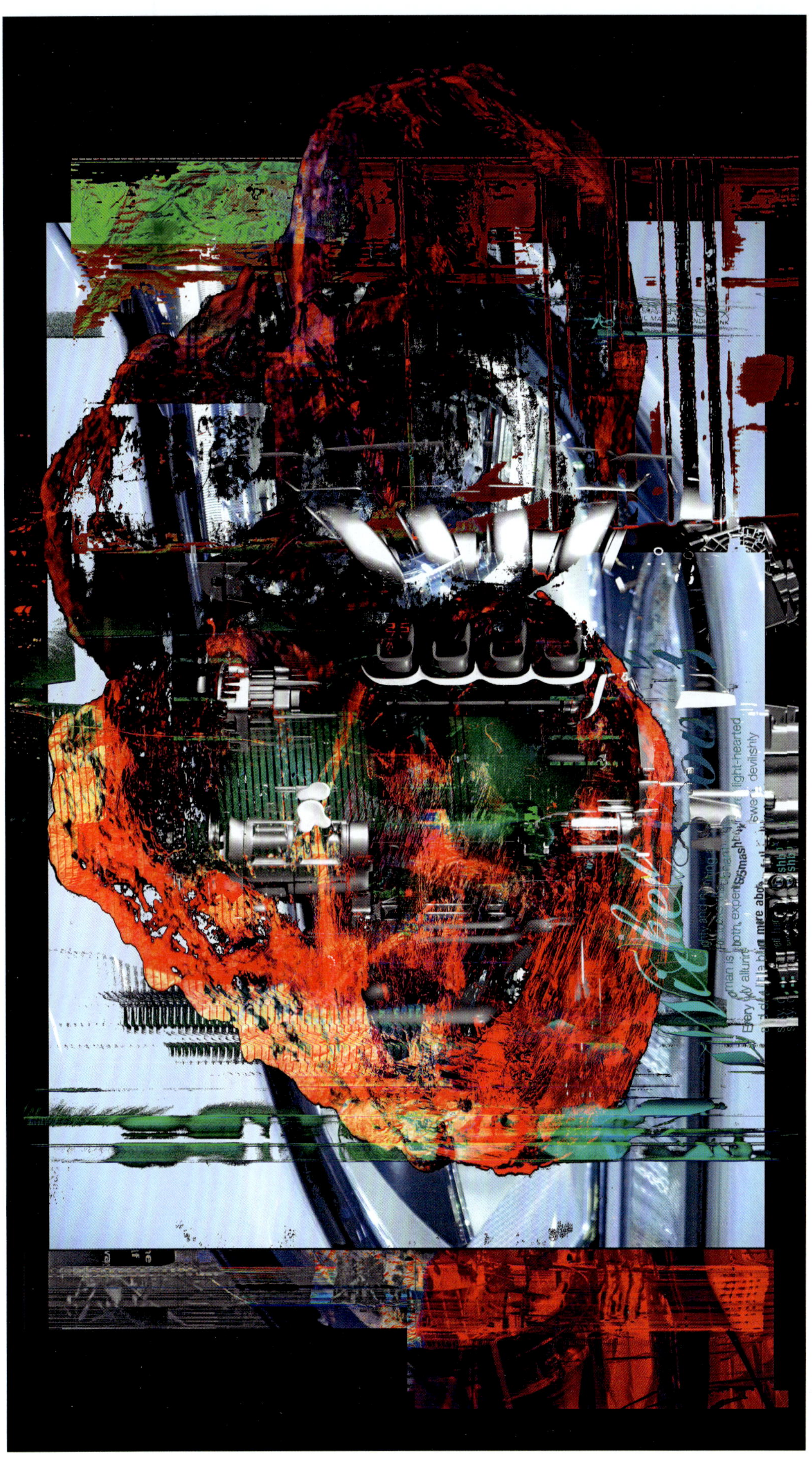

Untitled (hippy crippler), 2019
UV ink on alumacore, 78 inches × 44 inches

Untitled (active user), 2019
Ink on paper, 11.87 inches × 8.5 inches

Untitled (glass partition), 2019
Ink on paper, 11.87 inches × 8.5 inches

Untitled (theranos), 2019
Single-channel video, 00:00:19

Untitled (indirect point blocker), 2019
Single-channel video, 00:00:25

Untitled (casual death), 2019
Single-channel video, 00:00:50

Untitled (active twitch), 2019
UV ink on alumacore, 78 inches × 44 inches

Untitled (infinity scroll), 2019
UV ink on alumacore, 78 inches × 44 inches

Untitled (soft skin), 2019
UV ink on poly chloride vinyl with metal hardware, 96 inches × 48 inches

Untitled (cobalt open), 2019
UV ink on alumacore, 78 inches × 44 inches

Untitled (reality craft), 2019
UV ink on alumacore, 78 inches × 44 inches

Untitled (shallow optics), 2019
UV ink on alumacore, 78 inches × 44 inches

Untitled (synthetic skin), 2019
Single-channel video, 00:00:17

Untitled (drone vision), 2019
Two-channel video, 00:00:33

Untitled (body harvest), 2019
UV ink on poly chloride vinyl with metal hardware, 88 inches × 44 inches

Untitled (spectral land), 2019
UV ink on alumacore, 26 inches × 14 inches

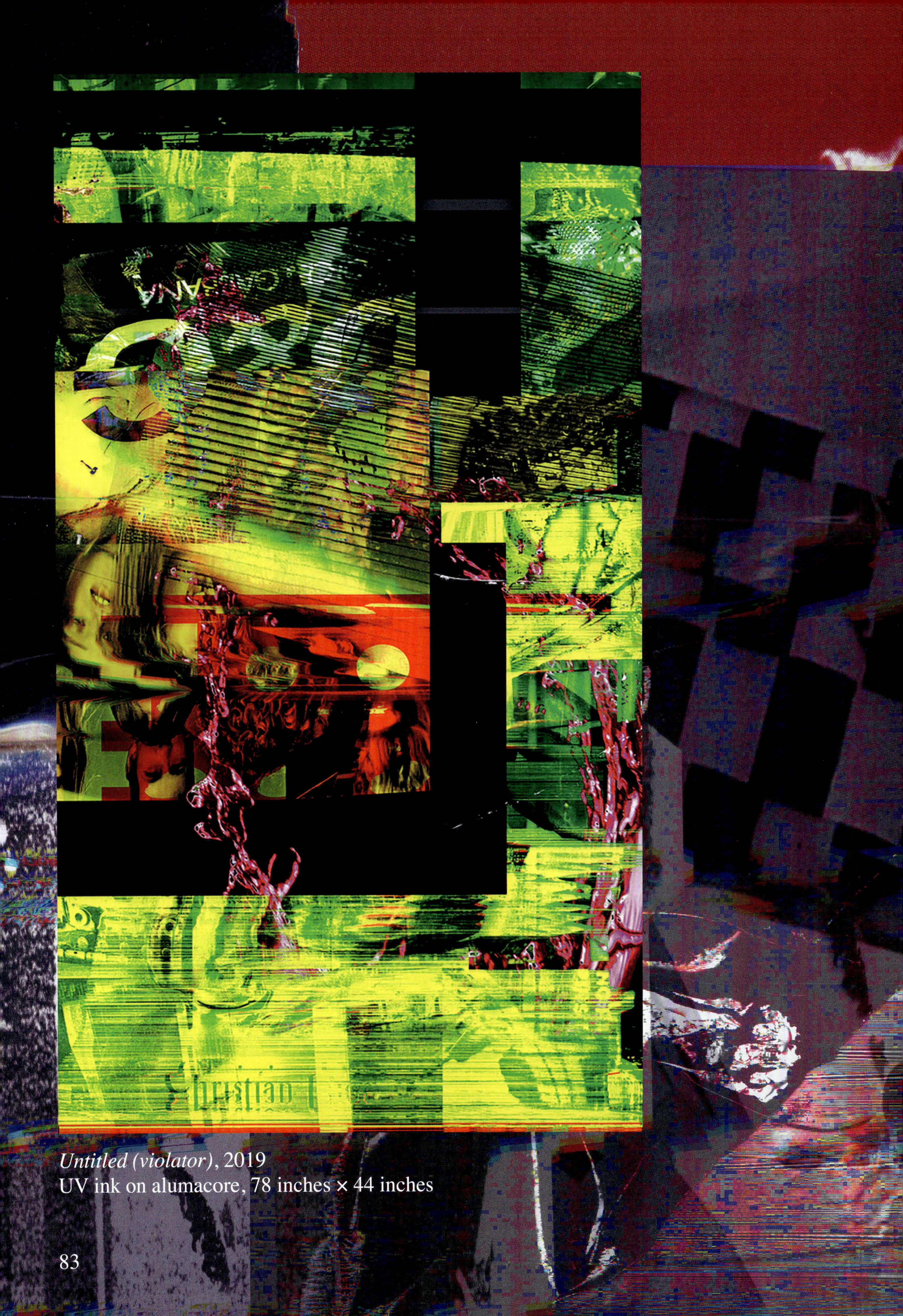

Untitled (violator), 2019
UV ink on alumacore, 78 inches × 44 inches

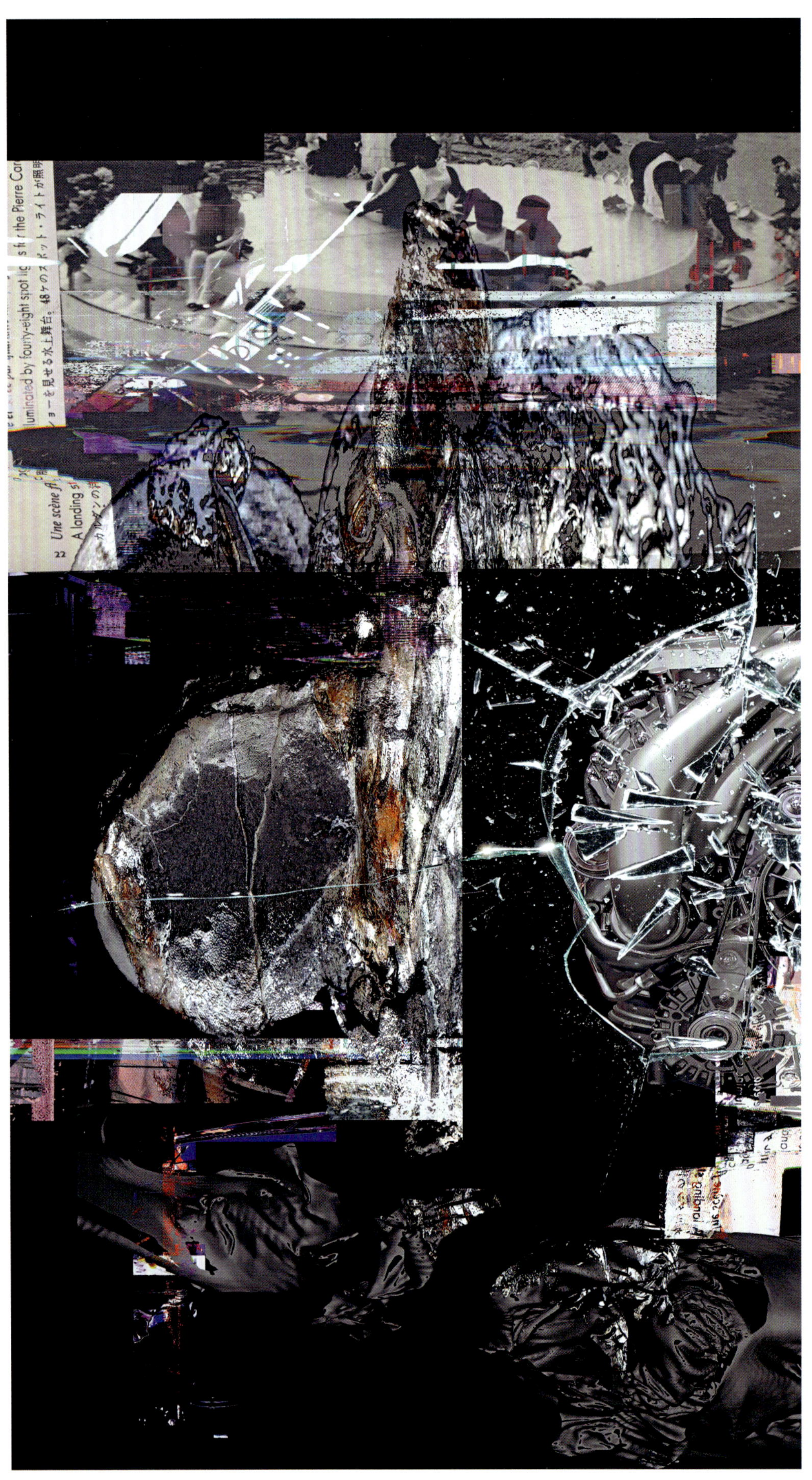

Untitled (new metal), 2019
UV ink on alumacore, 78 inches × 44 inches

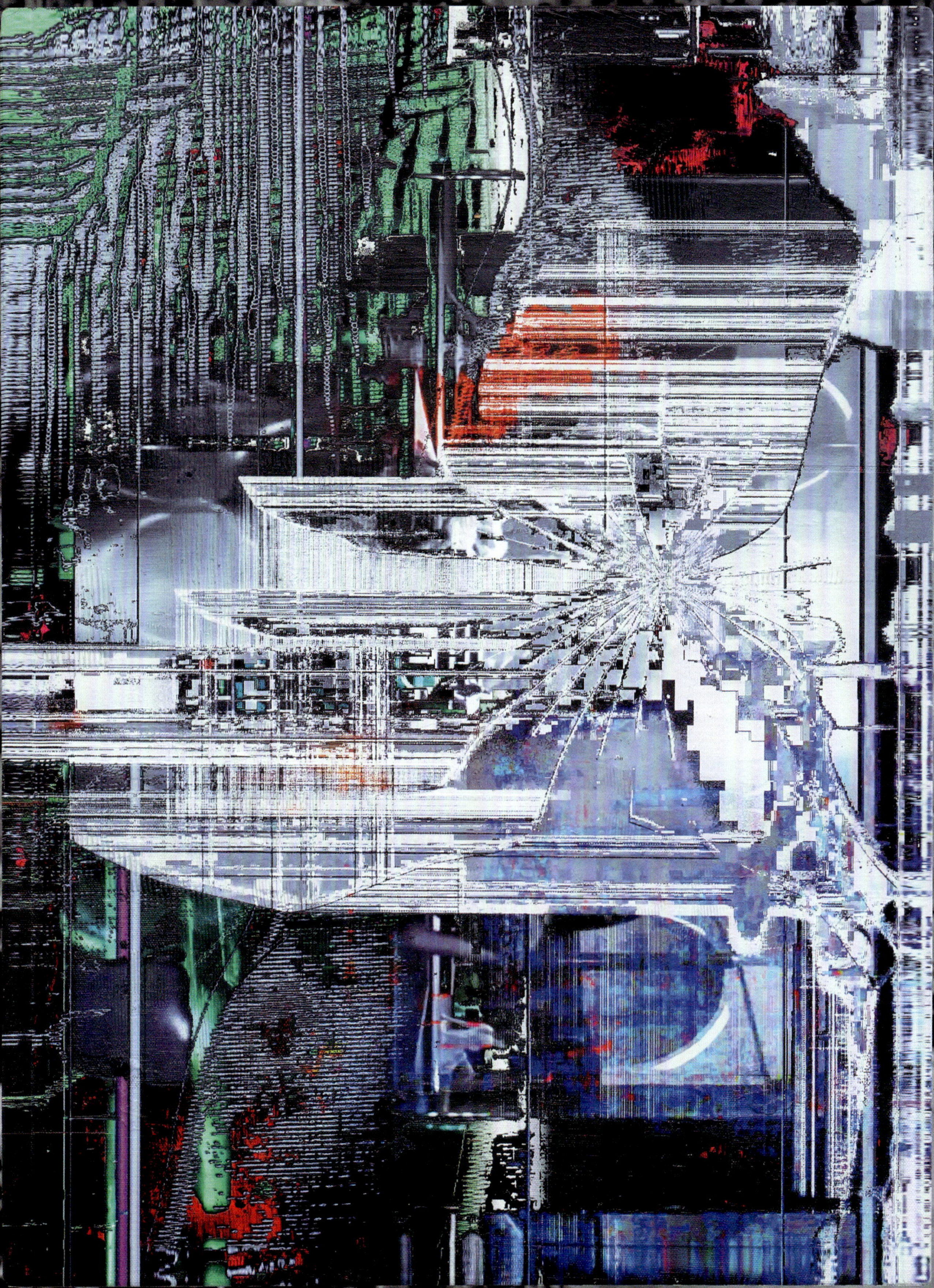

Untitled (zero day exploits), 2019
Acrylic, gesso, UV gel on linen with aluminum stretcher bars, 24 inches × 18 inches

Untitled (cloud flare), 2019
Acrylic, gesso, UV gel on linen with aluminum stretcher bars, 24 inches × 18 inches

Untitled (oil life reset), 2020
Acrylic, polymer, gesso on linen with aluminum stretcher bars, 40 inches × 30 inches

Untitled (instinct mode), 2020
Acrylic polymer, pigment, gesso, UV coating on linen with aluminum stretcher bars
68 inches × 46 inches

Untitled (phantom limb), 2020
Acrylic, gesso, UV gel on linen with aluminum stretcher bars, 36 inches × 24 inches

Untitled (global entry), 2020
Acrylic polymer, pigment, gesso, UV coating on linen with aluminum stretcher bars
68 inches × 46 inches

Untitled (despawn), 2020
Acrylic polymer, pigment, gesso, UV coating on linen with aluminum stretcher bars
68 inches × 46 inches

Untitled (global entry), 2020
Single-channel video, 00:00:06

Untitled (decameron), 2020
Single-channel video, 00:02:03

Untitled (active running), 2020
Acrylic, polymer, gesso on linen with aluminum stretcher bars, 36 inches × 24 inches

Untitled (motherboard), 2020
Acrylic, polymer, gesso on canvas with stretcher bars, 20 inches × 16 inches

Untitled (disk rasp), 2020
Acrylic, polymer, gesso on canvas with stretcher bars, 20 inches × 16 inches

Untitled (breach), 2020
Acrylic, polymer, pigment, gesso, UV coating on linen with aluminum stretcher bars
68 inches × 46 inches

Untitled (titan fall), 2020
UV ink on alumacore, 68 inches × 36 inches

Untitled (flatliners), 2020
UV ink on alumacore, 68 inches × 36 inches

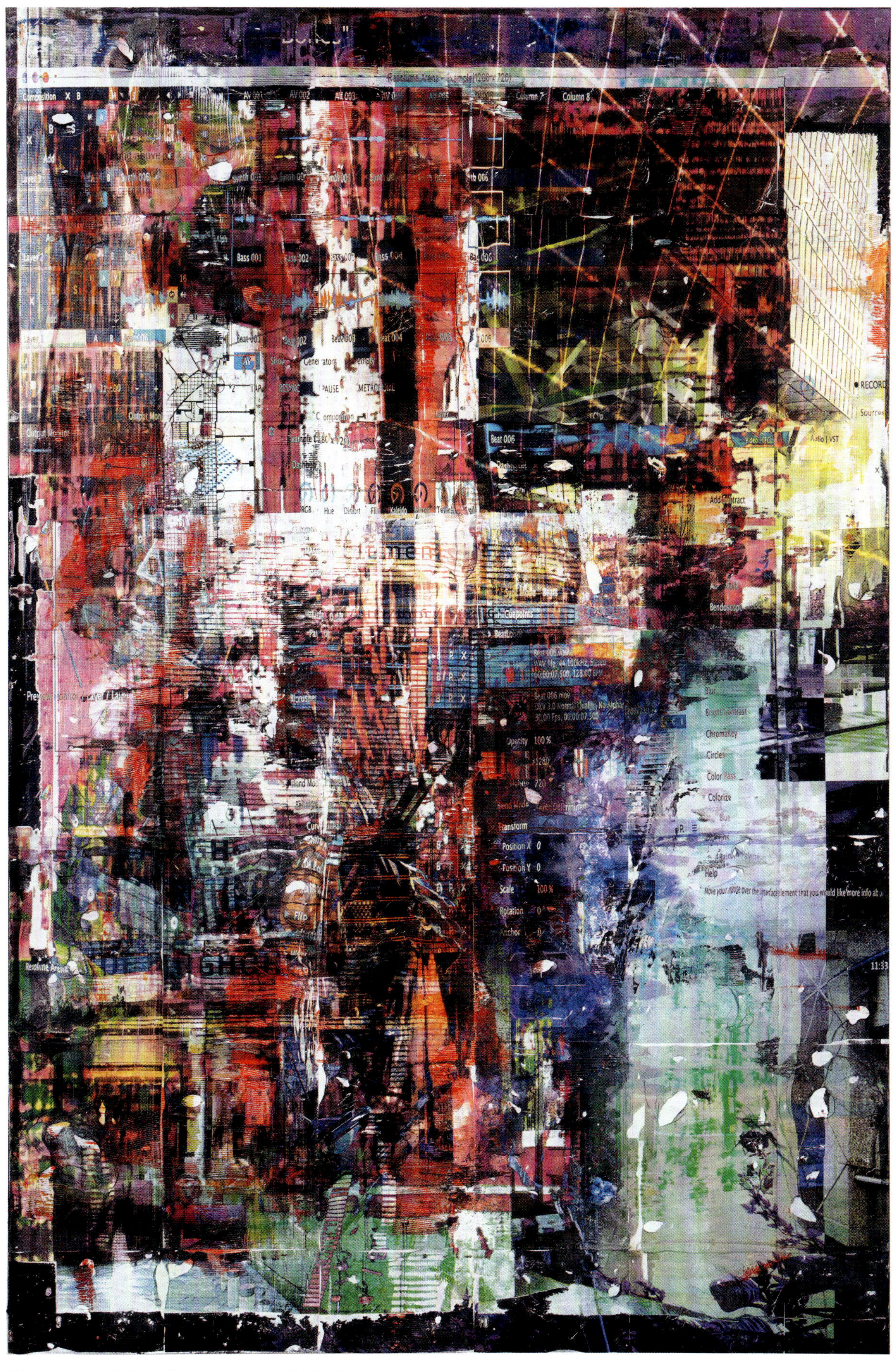

Untitled (bleeding edge), 2020
Acrylic polymer, pigment, gesso, UV coating on linen with aluminum stretcher bars
68 inches × 46 inches

Untitled (bitcrusher), 2020
Ink, acrylic polymer, pigment, gesso, UV coating on linen with aluminum stretcher bars
68 inches × 46 inches

Untitled (glitch hive), 2020
Ink, acrylic, polymer, gesso on canvas with stretcher bars, 20 inches × 16 inches

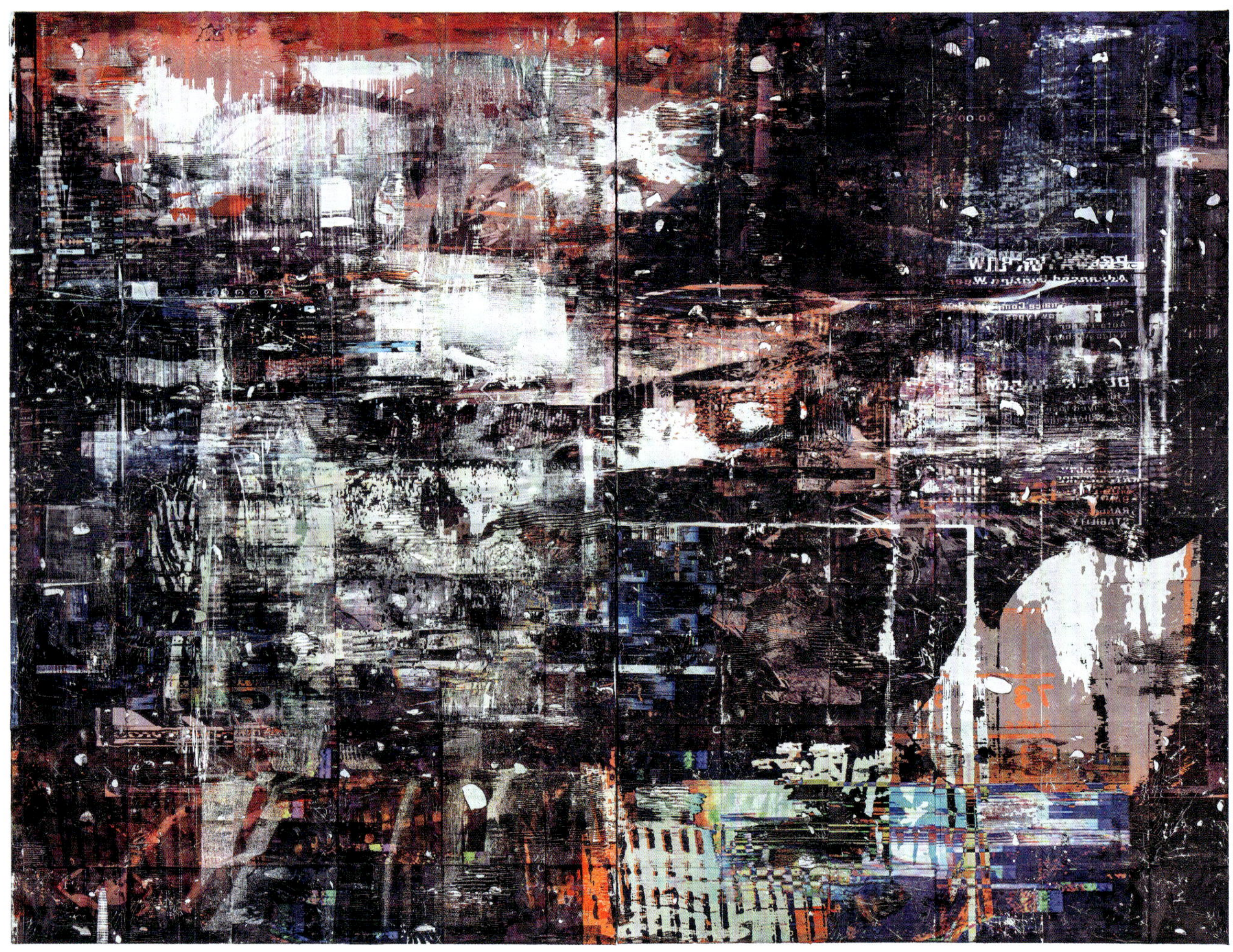

Untitled (leviathan II), 2020
Acrylic polymer, pigment, gesso, UV coating on linen with aluminum stretcher bars
68 inches × 92 inches

Untitled (active user), 2020
Single-channel video, 00:00:37

Untitled (FLR-13), 2020
Single-channel video, 00:01:29

Untitled (simulacron-3), 2020
Single-channel video, 00:01:01

Untitled (drain cartridge), 2020
Acrylic, gesso, UV gel on linen with aluminum stretcher bars, 36 inches × 24 inches

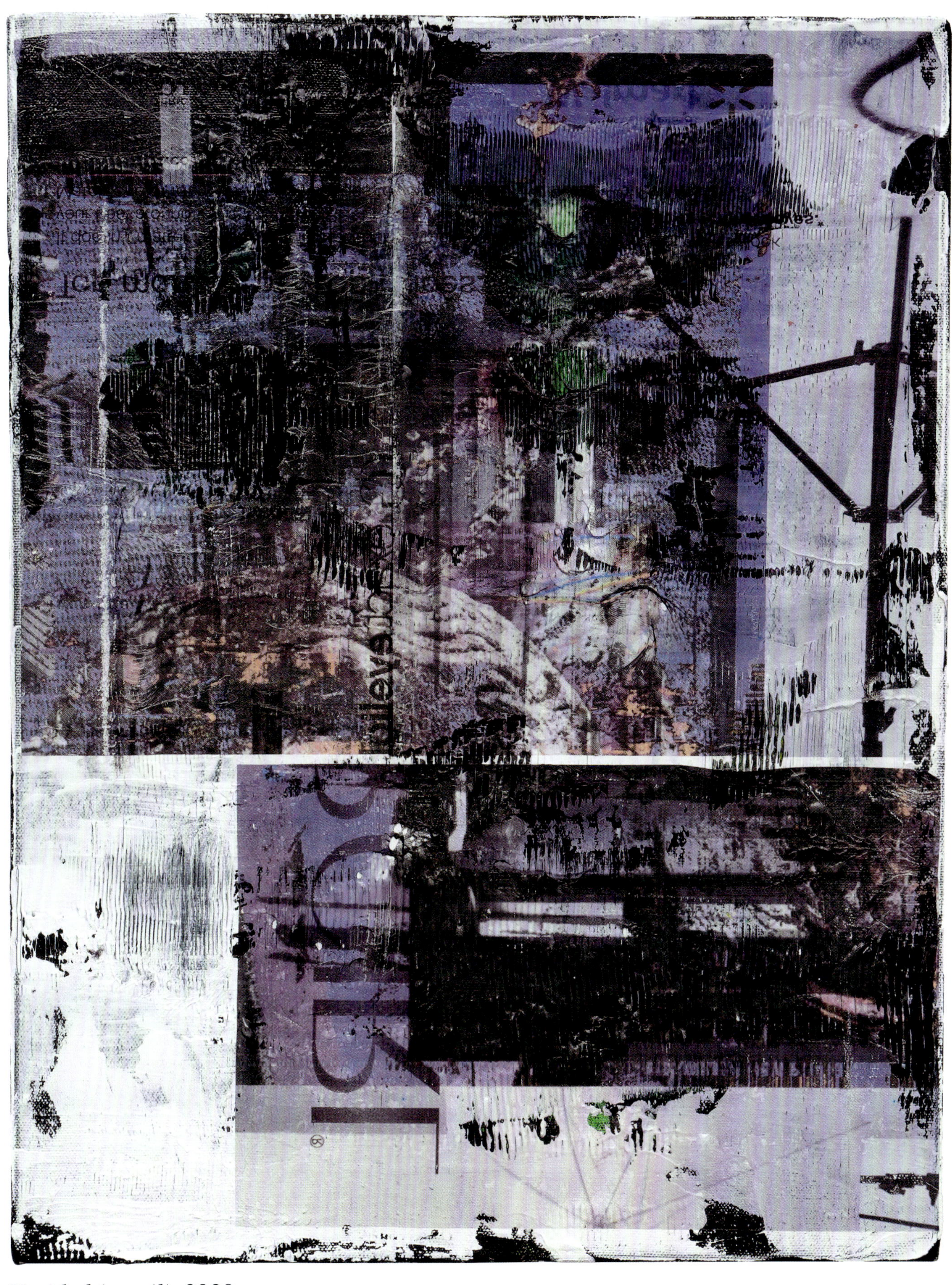

Untitled (recoil), 2020
Acrylic, polymer, gesso on canvas with stretcher bars, 20 inches × 16 inches

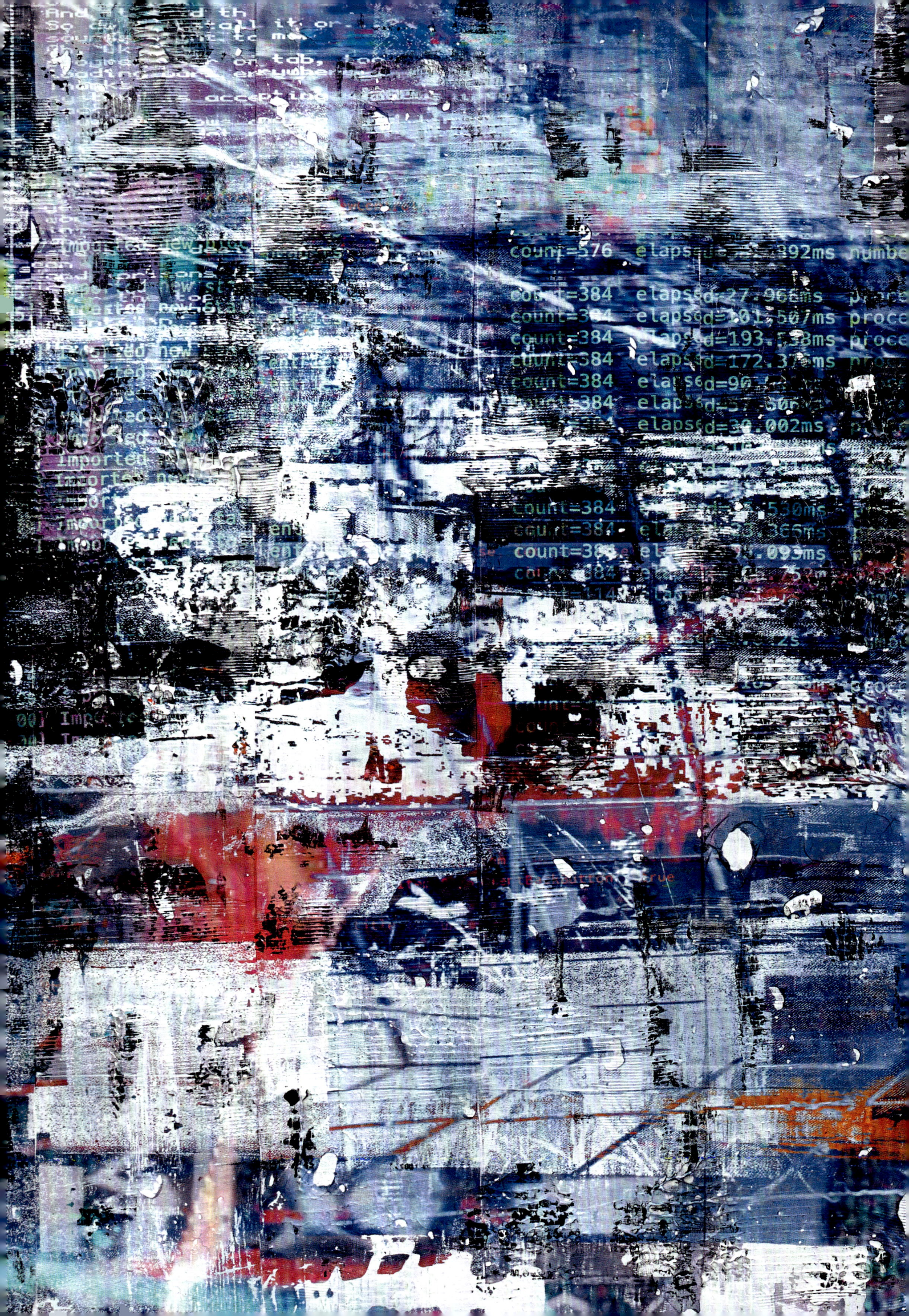

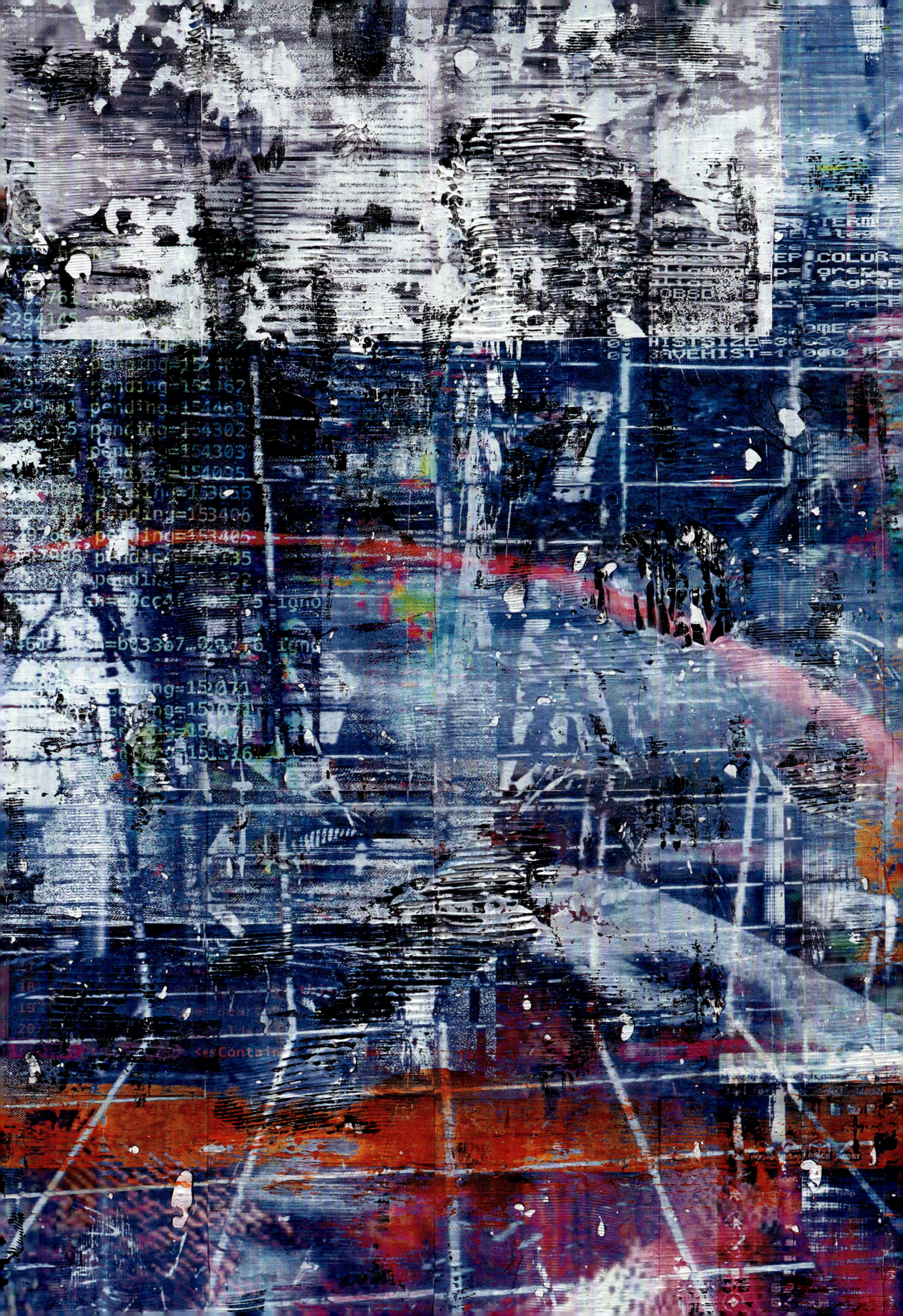

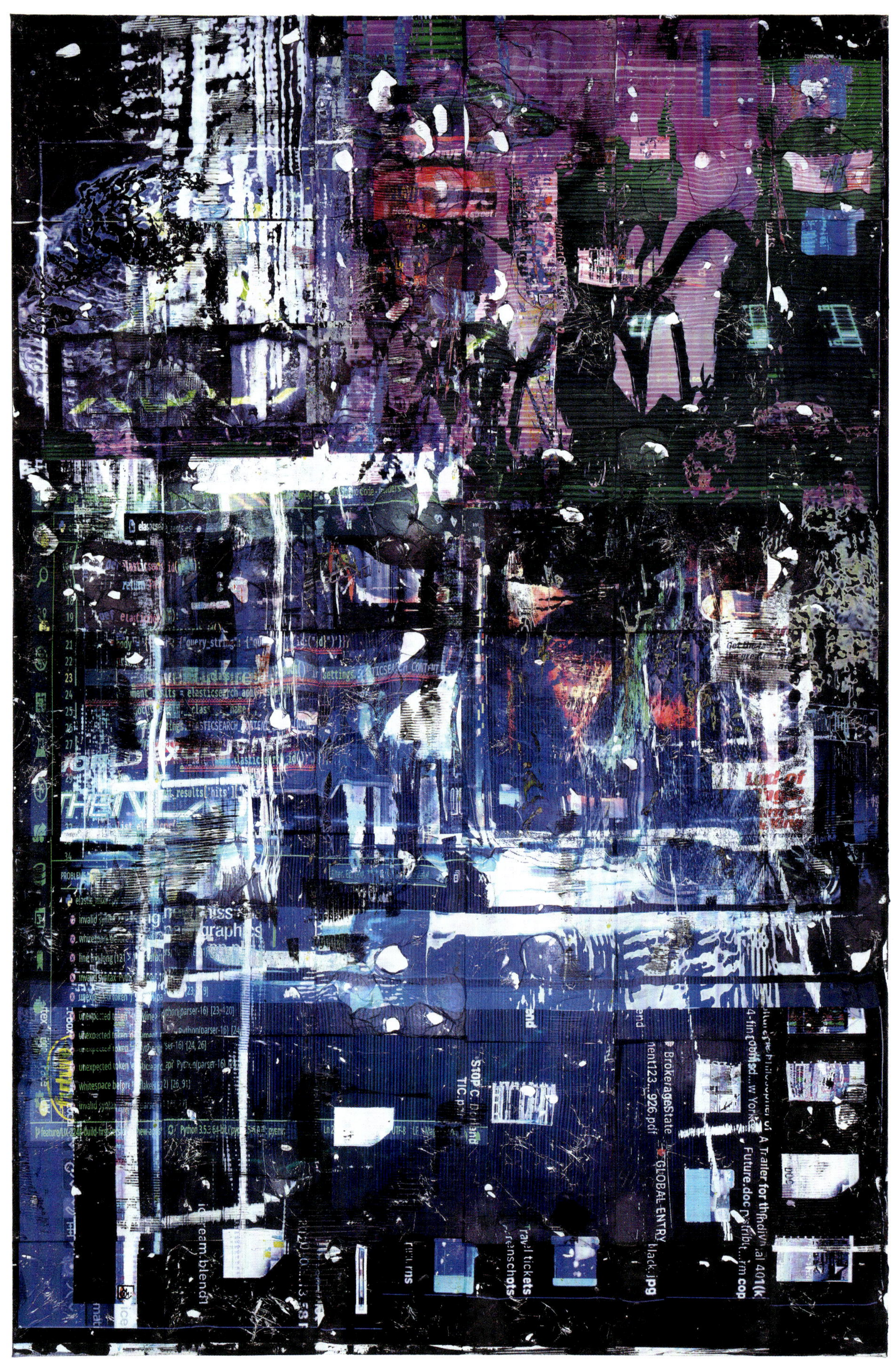

Untitled (brokerage state), 2020
Acrylic polymer, pigment, gesso, UV coating linen with aluminum stretcher bars
68 inches × 46 inches

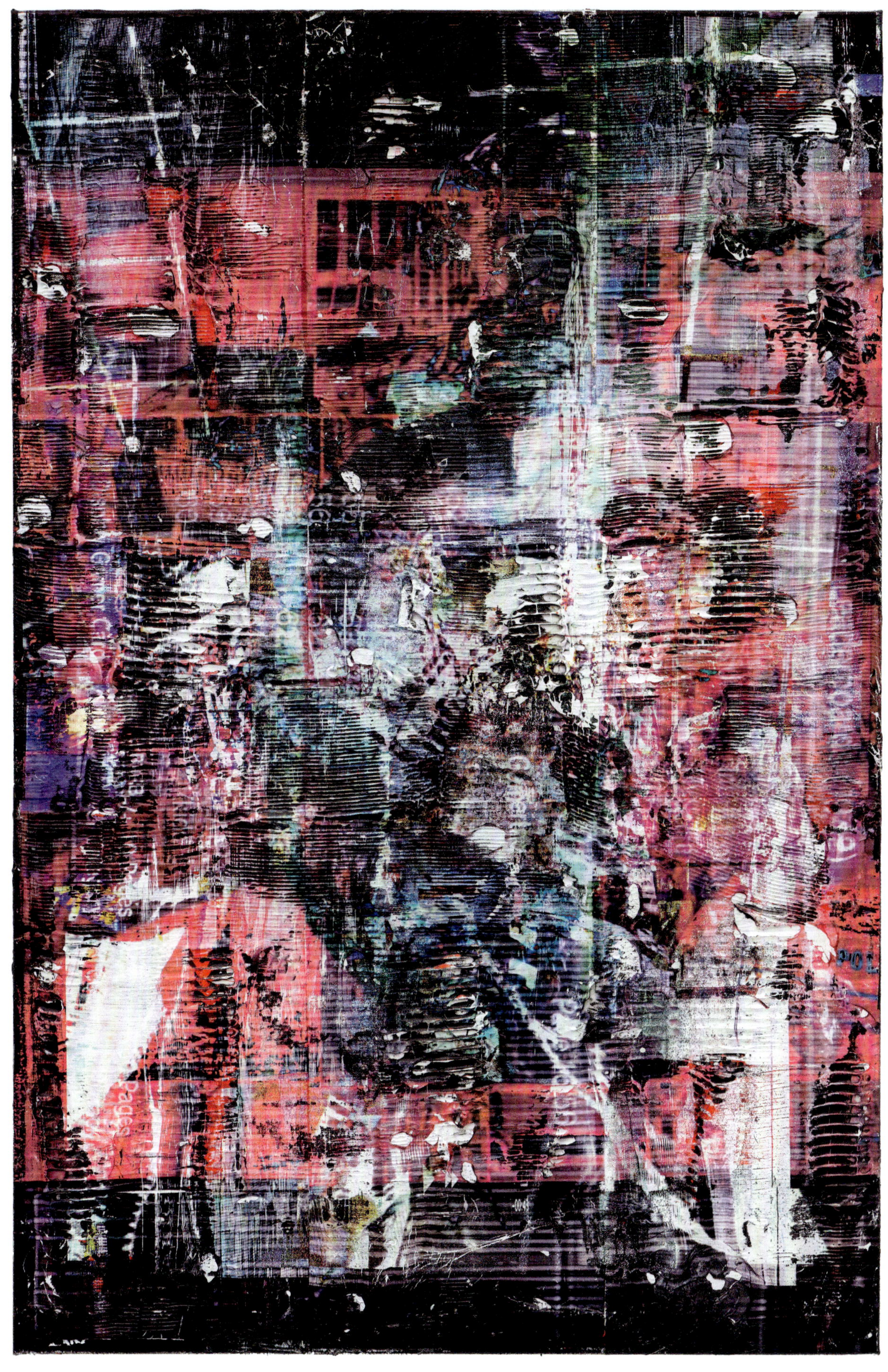

Untitled (subroutine), 2021
Acrylic polymer, pigment, gesso, UV coating linen with aluminum stretcher bars
36 inches × 24 inches

93

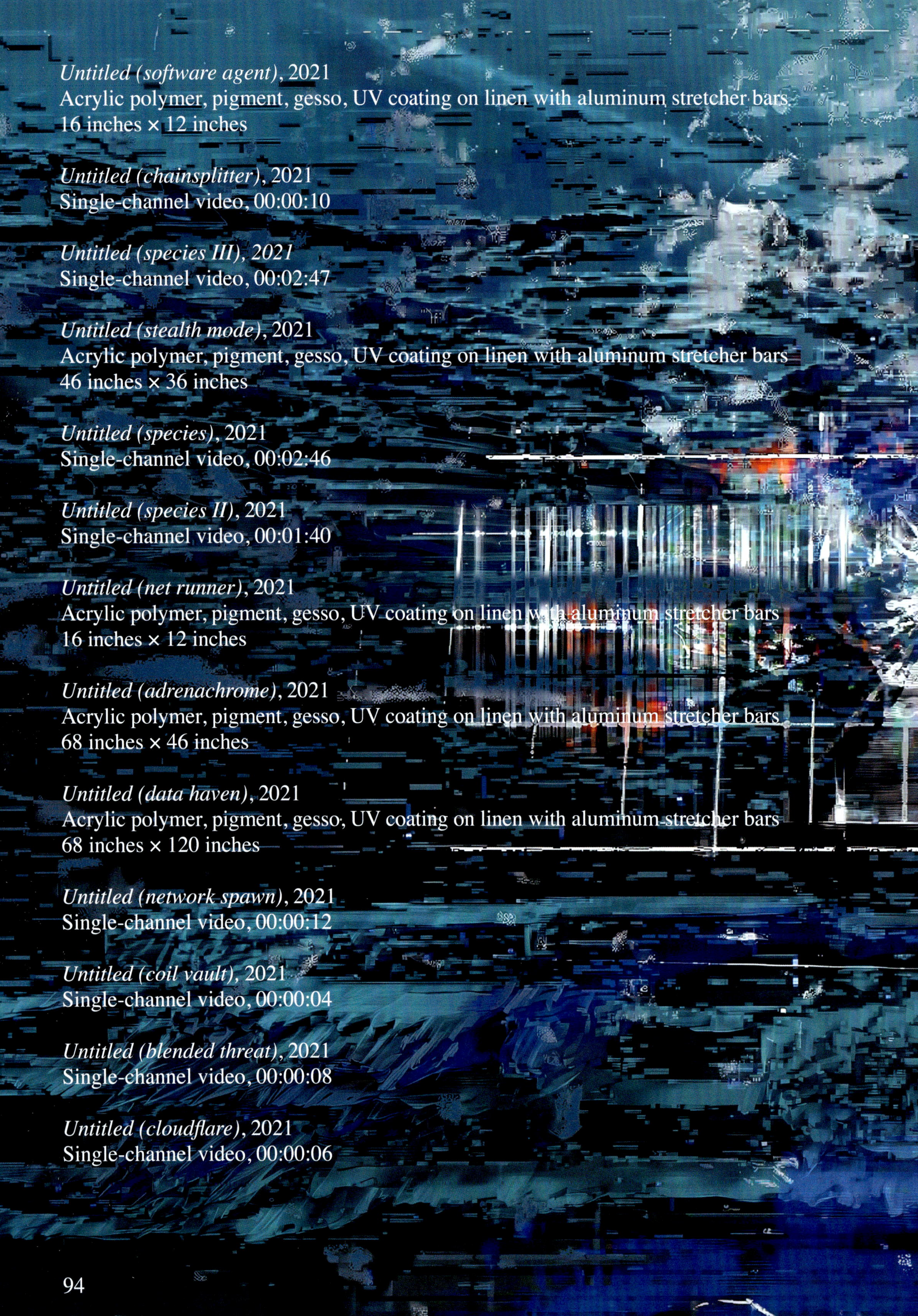

Untitled (software agent), 2021
Acrylic polymer, pigment, gesso, UV coating on linen with aluminum stretcher bars
16 inches × 12 inches

Untitled (chainsplitter), 2021
Single-channel video, 00:00:10

Untitled (species III), 2021
Single-channel video, 00:02:47

Untitled (stealth mode), 2021
Acrylic polymer, pigment, gesso, UV coating on linen with aluminum stretcher bars
46 inches × 36 inches

Untitled (species), 2021
Single-channel video, 00:02:46

Untitled (species II), 2021
Single-channel video, 00:01:40

Untitled (net runner), 2021
Acrylic polymer, pigment, gesso, UV coating on linen with aluminum stretcher bars
16 inches × 12 inches

Untitled (adrenachrome), 2021
Acrylic polymer, pigment, gesso, UV coating on linen with aluminum stretcher bars
68 inches × 46 inches

Untitled (data haven), 2021
Acrylic polymer, pigment, gesso, UV coating on linen with aluminum stretcher bars
68 inches × 120 inches

Untitled (network spawn), 2021
Single-channel video, 00:00:12

Untitled (coil vault), 2021
Single-channel video, 00:00:04

Untitled (blended threat), 2021
Single-channel video, 00:00:08

Untitled (cloudflare), 2021
Single-channel video, 00:00:06

Untitled (blaxxun), 2021
Acrylic polymer, pigment, gesso, UV coating on linen with aluminum stretcher bars
36 inches × 24 inches

Untitled (metadaemon), 2021
Single-channel video, 00:00:06

Untitled (graveyard daemon), 2021
Single-channel video, 00:00:06

Untitled (daemon), 2021
Single-channel video, 00:00:06

Untitled (black sun), 2021
Single-channel video, 00:00:16

Untitled (loopring), 2021
Single-channel video, 00:00:16

Untitled (subroutine), 2021
Acrylic polymer, pigment, gesso, UV coating on linen with aluminum stretcher bars
16 inches × 12 inches

Untited (protocol), 2021
Acrylic polymer, pigment, gesso, UV coating on linen with aluminum stretcher bars
68 inches × 46 inches

Untitled (node run), 2021
Acrylic polymer, pigment, gesso, UV coating on linen with aluminum stretcher bars
16 inches × 12 inches

Untitled (statecraft), 2022
Acrylic polymer, pigment, gesso, UV coating on linen with aluminum stretcher bars
72 inches × 60 inches

Untitled (shardstack), 2022
Acrylic polymer, pigment, gesso, UV coating on linen with aluminum stretcher bars
36 inches × 24 inches

Untitled (memory\shard), 2022
Single-channel video, 00:00:15

Untitled (ÐTX2CP), 2022
Single-channel video, 00:00:11

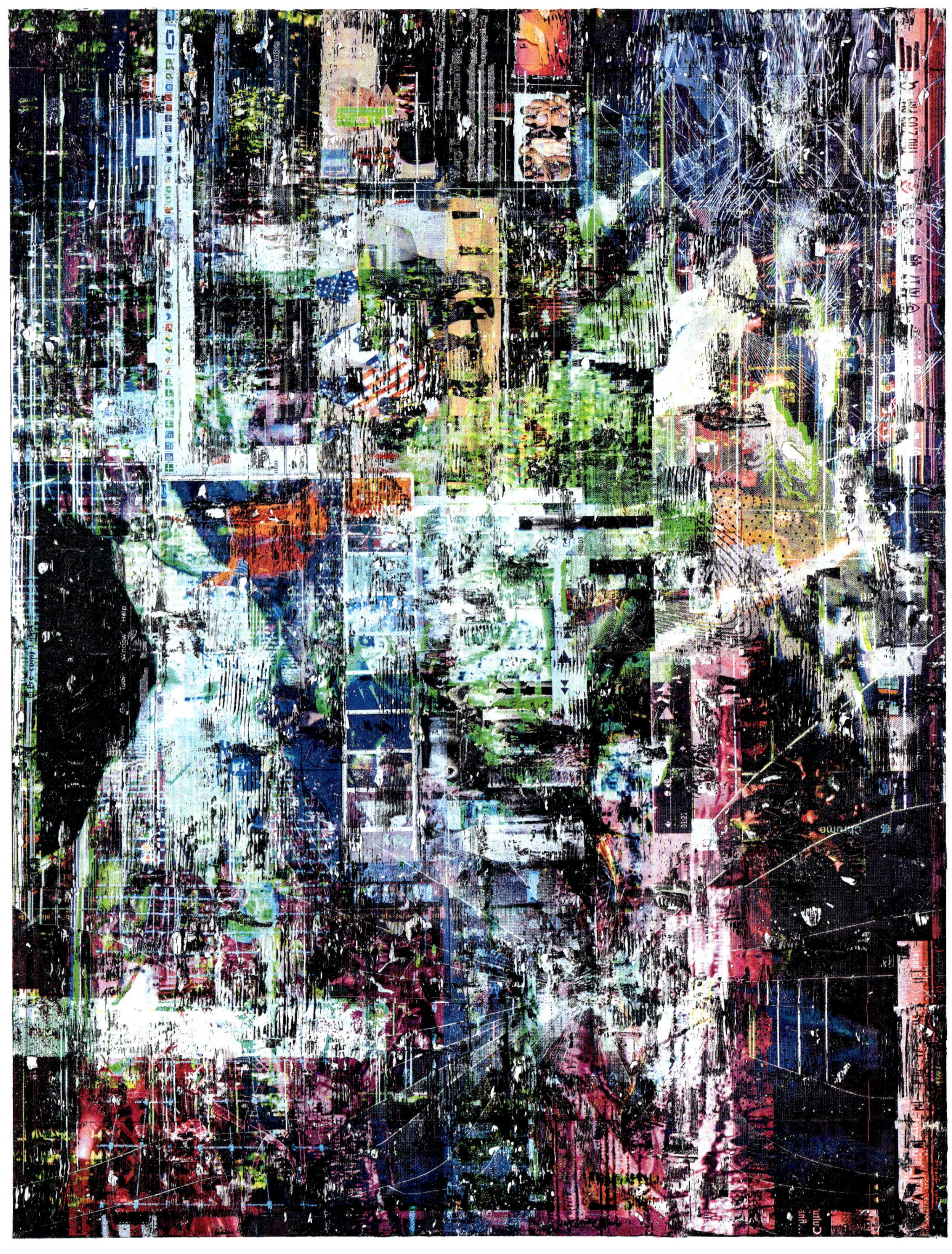

Untitled (chrome accelerator), 2022
Acrylic polymer, pigment, gesso, UV coating on linen with aluminum stretcher bars
84 inches × 66 inches

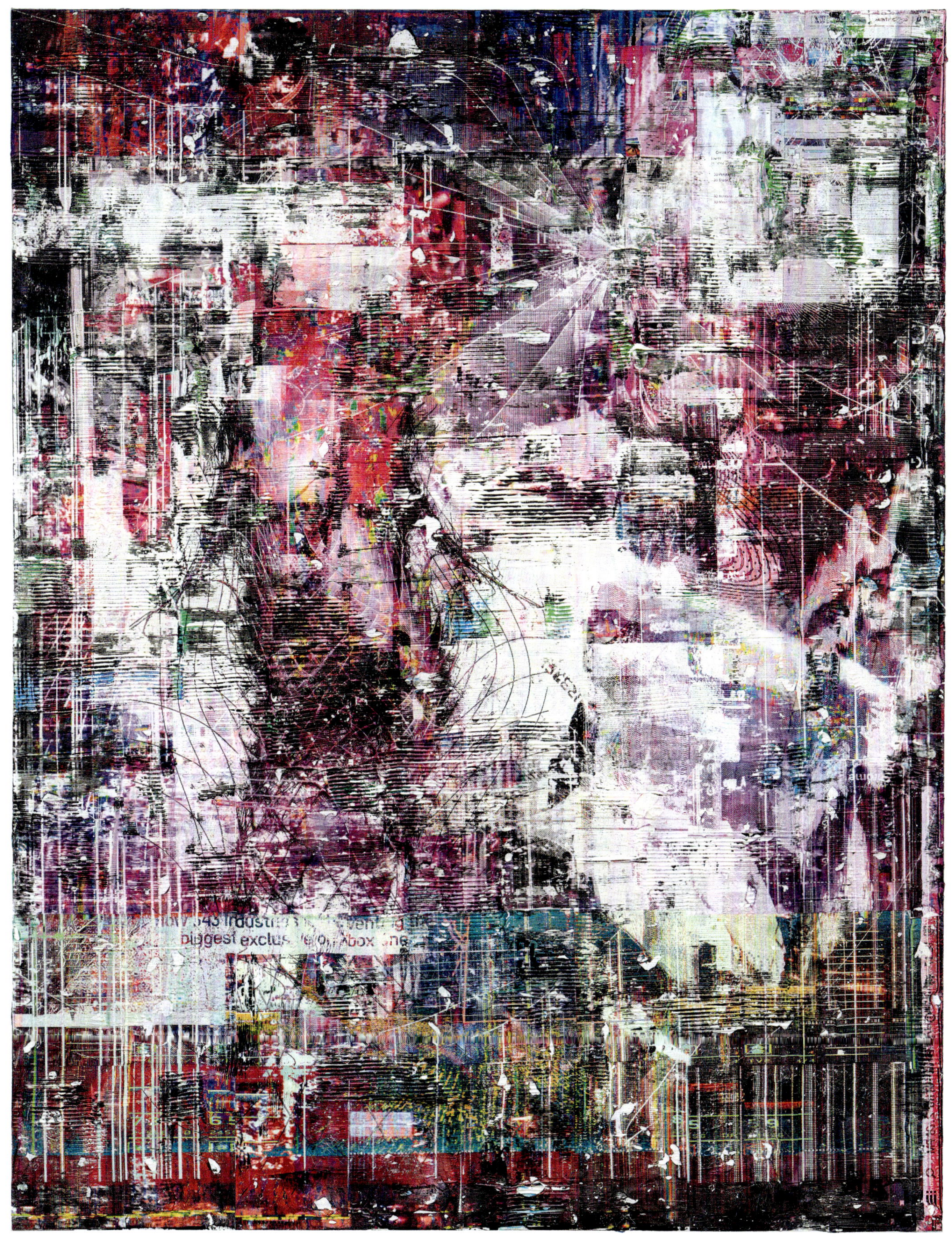

Untitled (shellcode), 2022
Acrylic polymer, pigment, gesso, UV coating on linen with aluminum stretcher bars
84 inches × 66 inches

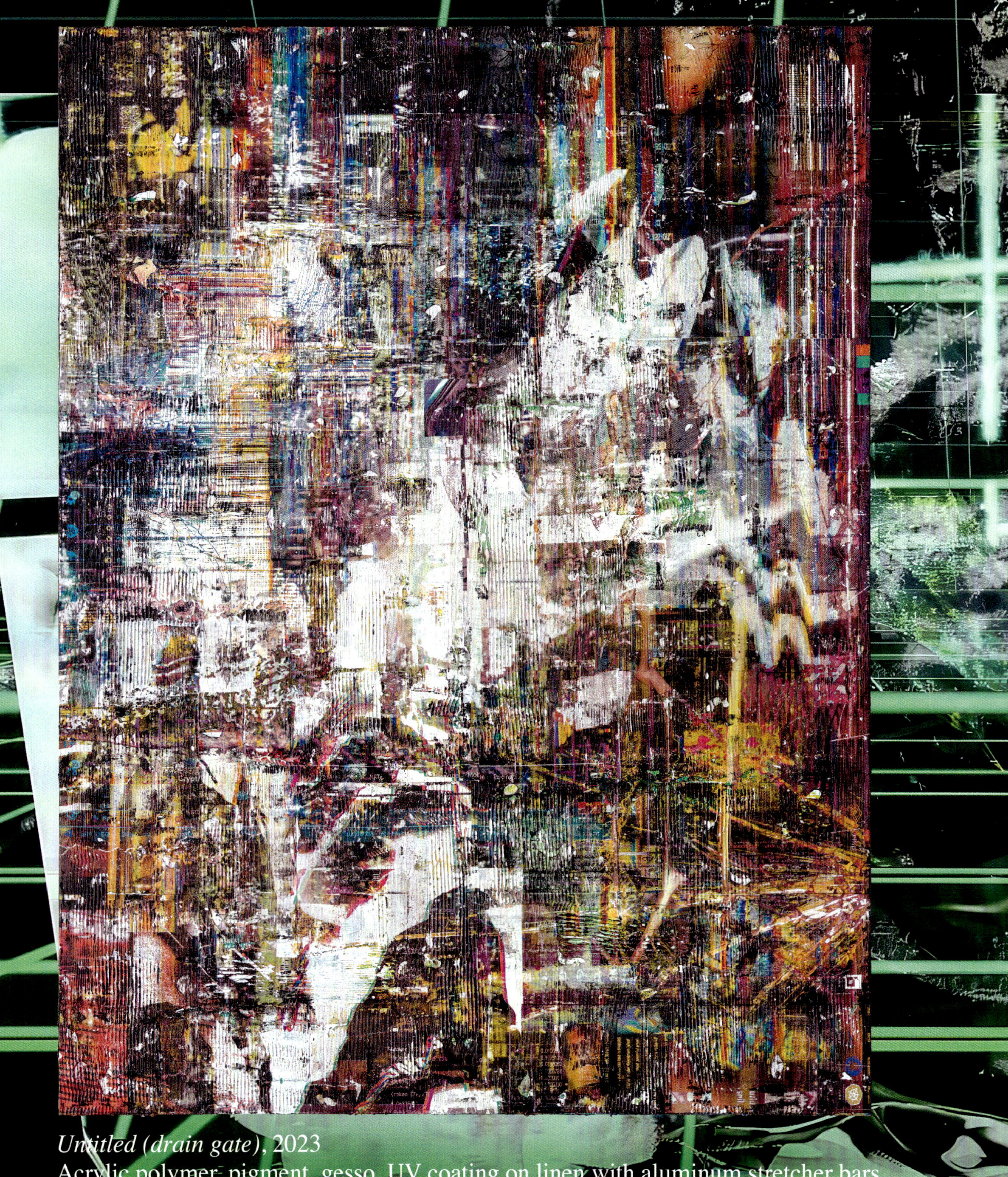

Untitled (drain gate), 2023
Acrylic polymer, pigment, gesso, UV coating on linen with aluminum stretcher bars
60 inches × 78 inches

Untitled (fractured synapse), 2023
Acrylic polymer, pigment, gesso, UV coating on linen with aluminum stretcher bars
68 inches × 46 inches

Untitled (stable diffusion), 2023
Acrylic polymer, pigment, gesso, UV coating on linen with aluminum stretcher bars
68 inches × 46 inches

Untitled (legacy software), 2023
Acrylic polymer, pigment, gesso, UV coating on linen with aluminum stretcher bars
72 inches × 60 inches

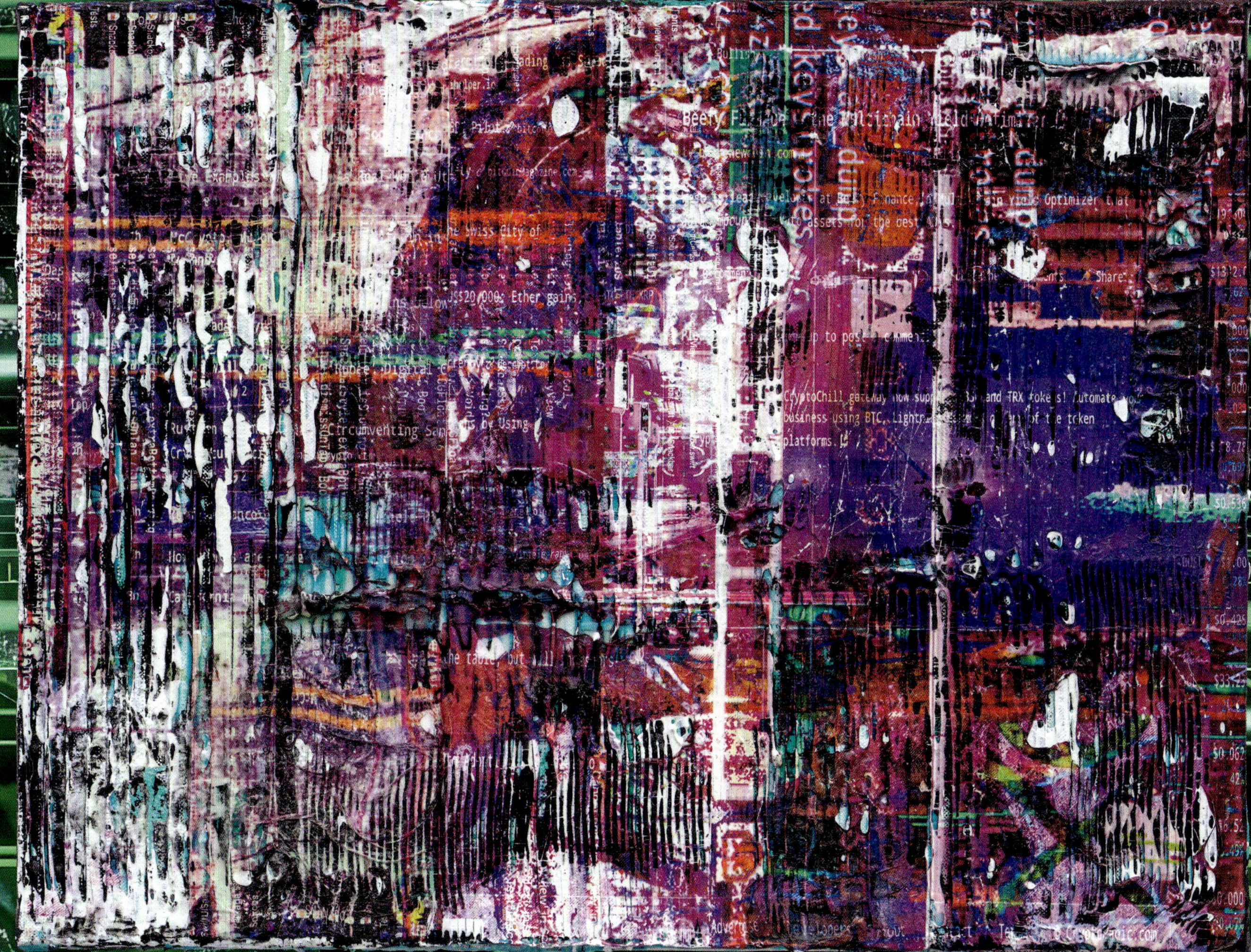

Untitled (keylogger), 2023
Acrylic polymer, pigment, gesso, UV coating on linen with aluminum stretcher bars
12 inches × 16 inches

Untitled (console), 2023
Acrylic polymer, pigment, gesso, UV coating on linen with aluminum stretcher bars
36 inches × 46 inches

Untitled (skinwalker), 2023
Acrylic polymer, pigment, gesso, UV coating on linen with aluminum stretcher bars
68 × 60 inches

Untitled (parallel port), 2023
Single-channel video, 00:00:12

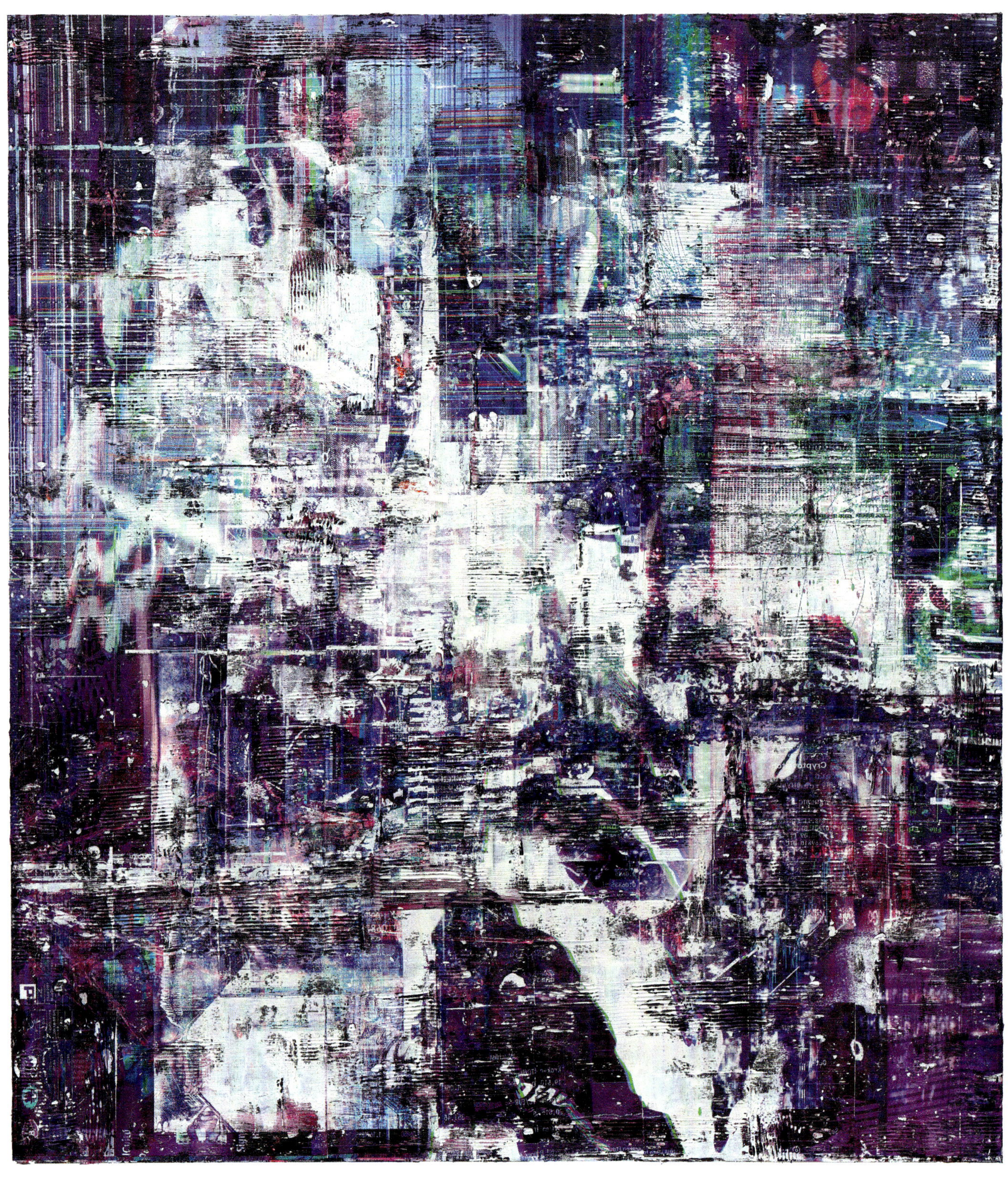

Untitled (screenscrape), 2023
Acrylic polymer, pigment, gesso, UV coating on linen with aluminum stretcher bars
84 inches × 75 inches

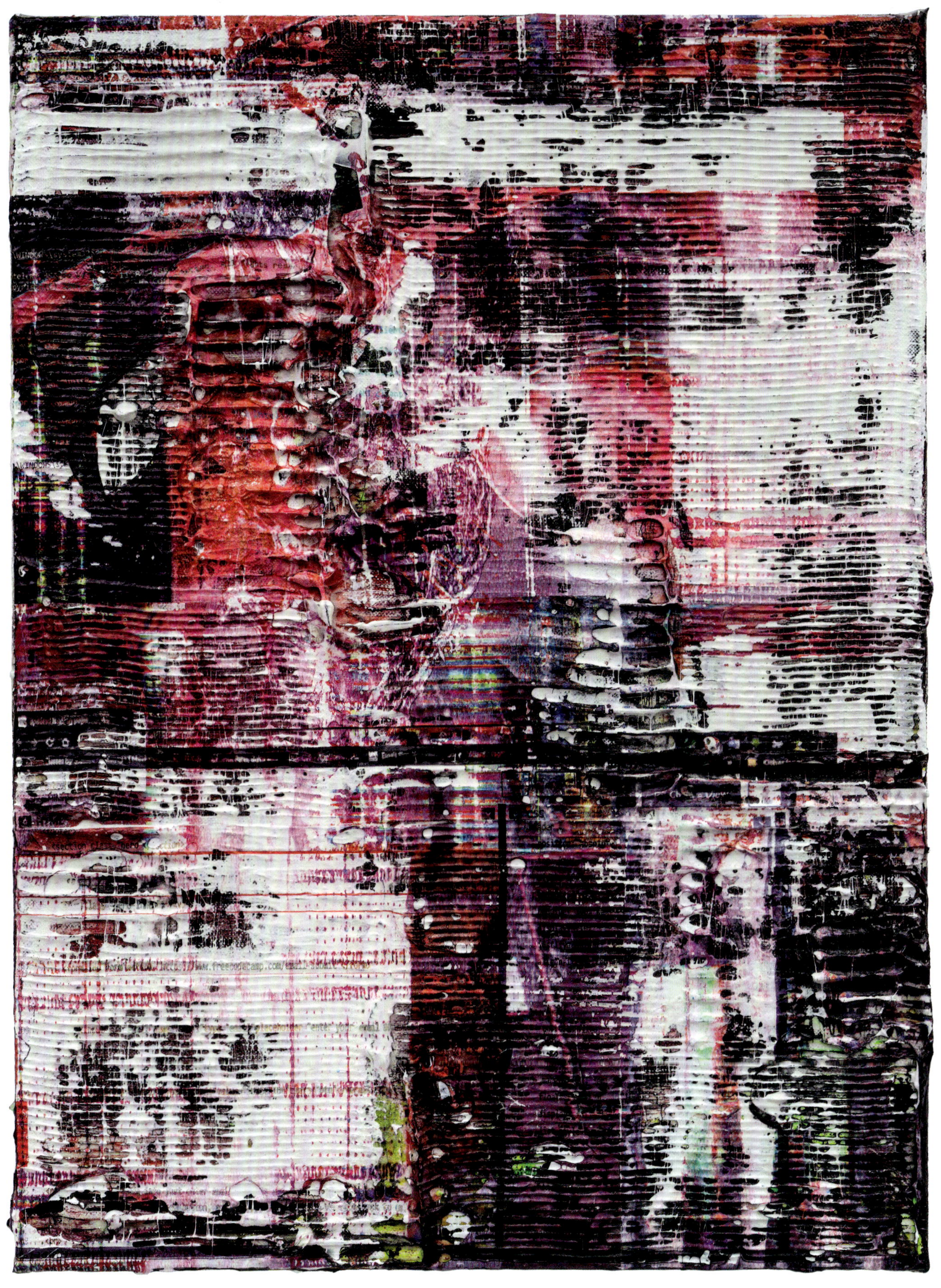

Untitled (relic_ //////), 2023
Acrylic polymer, pigment, gesso, UV coating on linen with aluminum stretcher bars
16 inches × 12 inches

101

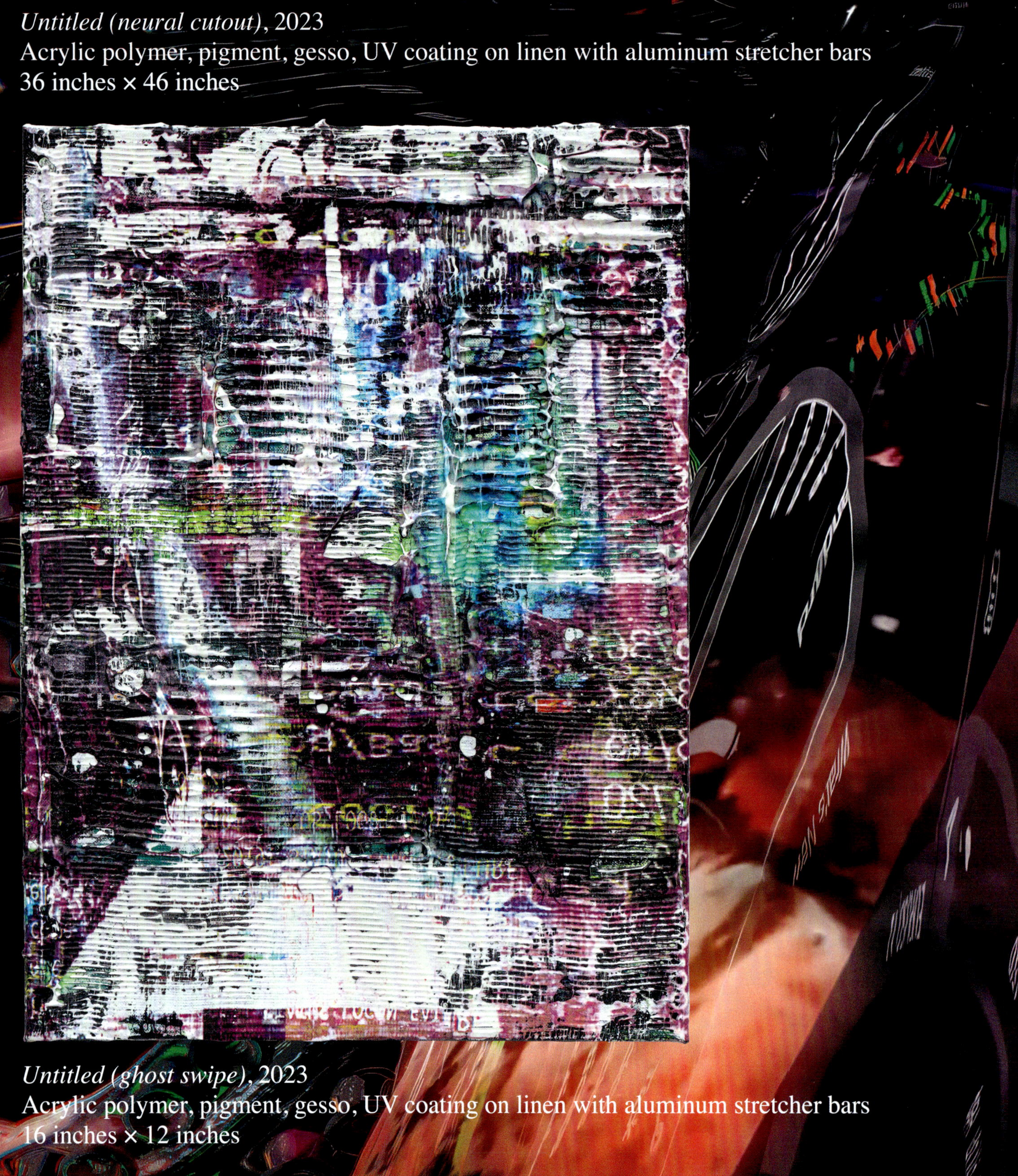

Untitled (neural cutout), 2023
Acrylic polymer, pigment, gesso, UV coating on linen with aluminum stretcher bars
36 inches × 46 inches

Untitled (ghost swipe), 2023
Acrylic polymer, pigment, gesso, UV coating on linen with aluminum stretcher bars
16 inches × 12 inches

Untitled (cipher), 2023
Acrylic polymer, pigment, gesso, UV coating on linen with aluminum stretcher bars
84 inches × 66 inches

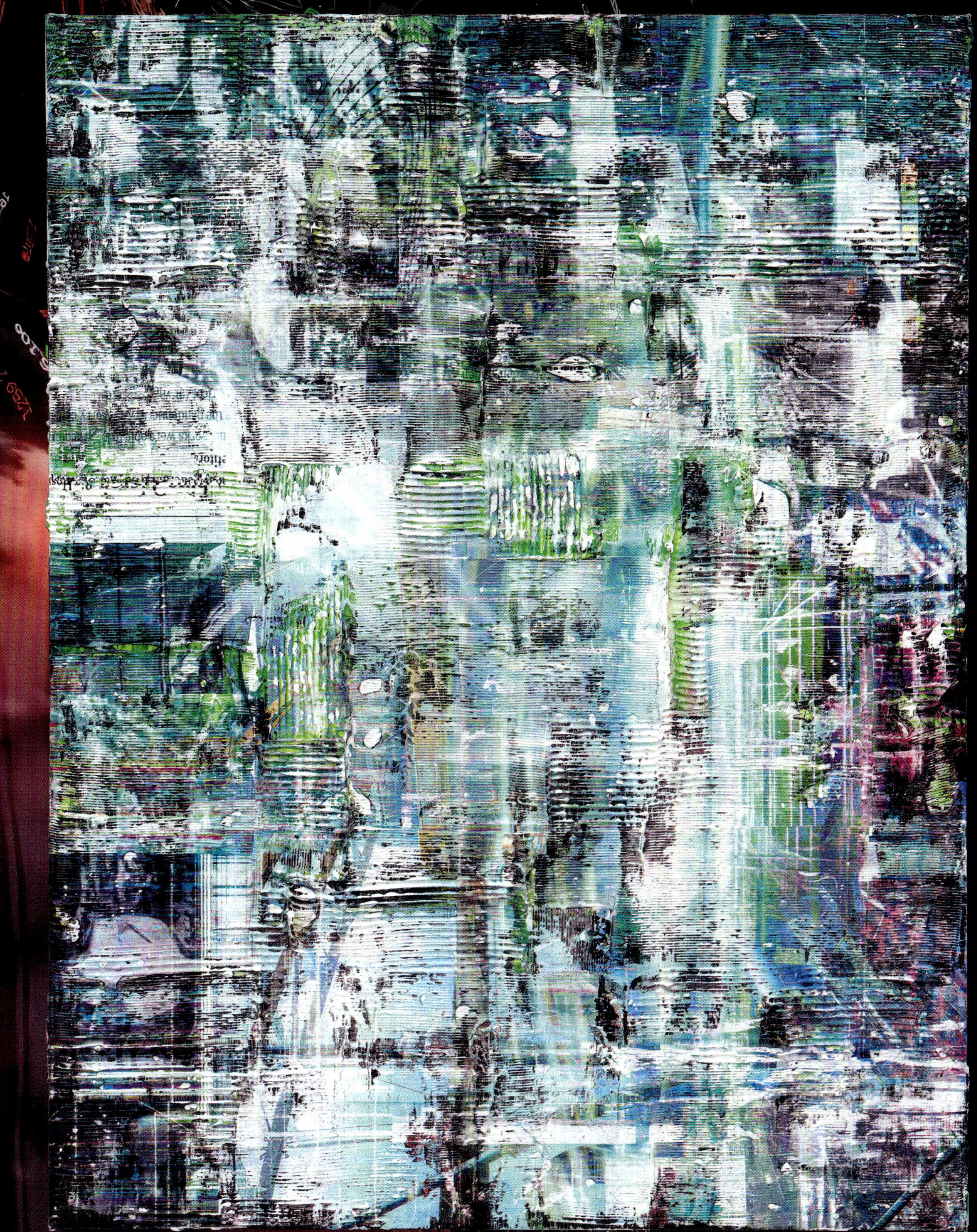

Untitled (aggregator), 2023
Acrylic polymer, pigment, gesso, UV coating on linen with aluminum stretcher bars
46 inches × 36 inches

Untitled (life loader), 2024
Acrylic polymer, pigment, gesso, UV coating on paper, 30 inches × 22 inches

Untitled (passive empire), 2024
Acrylic polymer, pigment, gesso, UV coating on linen with aluminum stretcher bars
72 inches × 60 inches

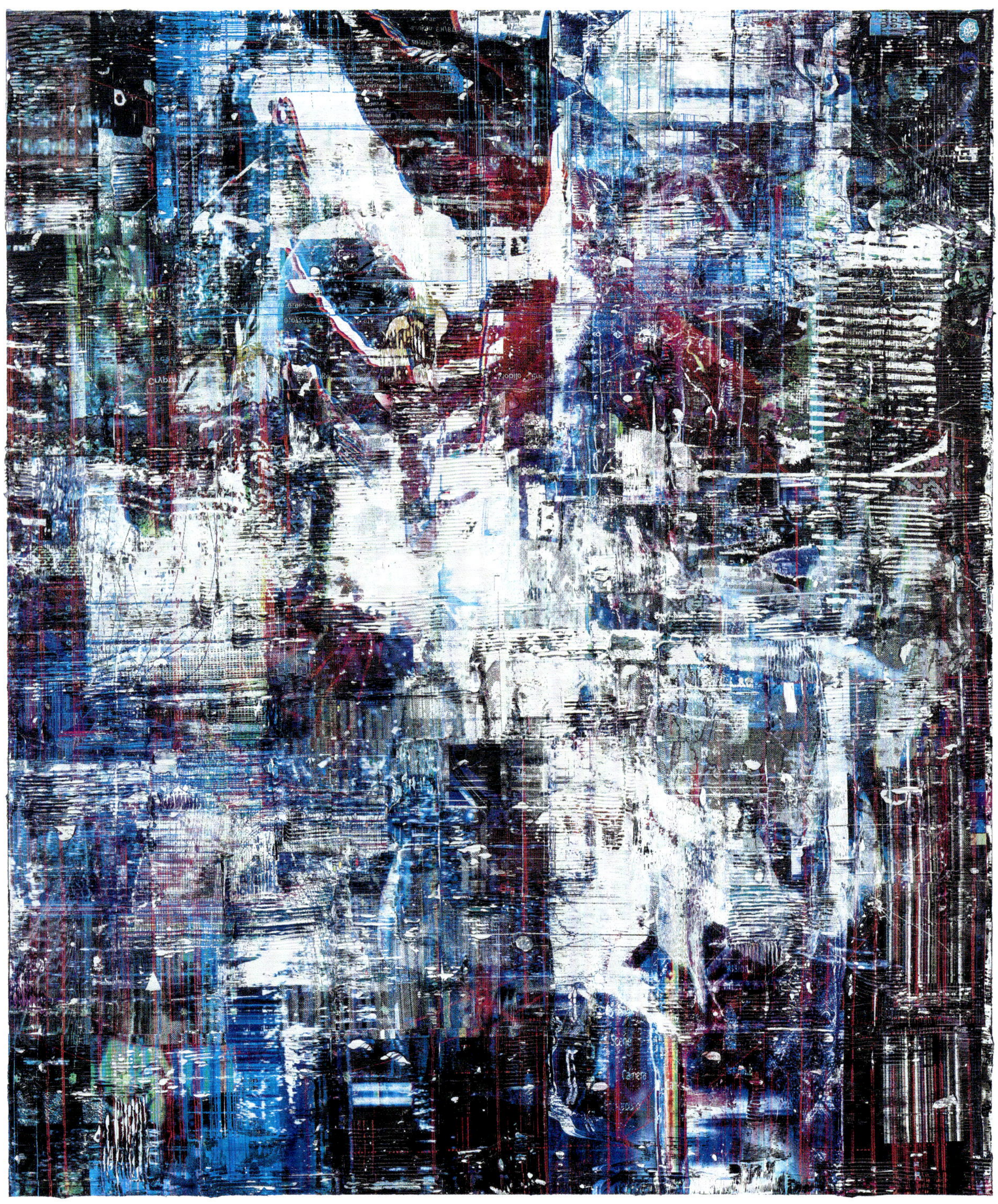

Untitled (necro techno), 2024
Acrylic polymer, pigment, gesso, UV coating on linen with aluminum stretcher bars
84 inches × 72 inches

Untitled (point cloud), 2024
Acrylic polymer, pigment, gesso, UV coating on linen with aluminum stretcher bars
16 inches × 12 inches

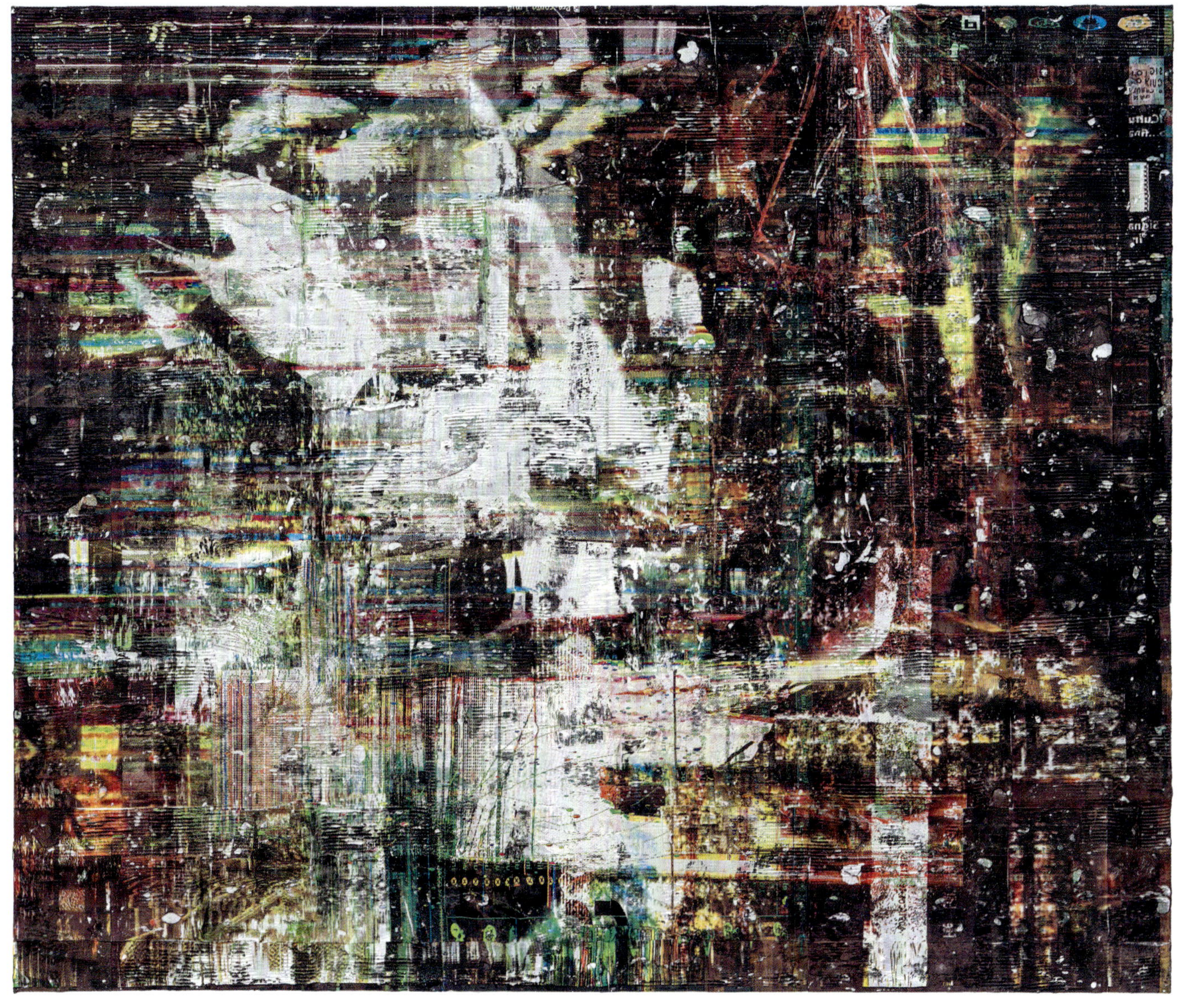

Untitled (night sprawl), 2024
Acrylic polymer, pigment, gesso, UV coating on linen with aluminum stretcher bars
76 inches × 92 inches

Untitled (haptic feedback), 2024
Acrylic polymer, pigment, gesso, UV coating on linen with aluminum stretcher bars
16 inches × 12 inches

Untitled (perception stack), 2024
Acrylic polymer, pigment, gesso, UV coating on linen with aluminum stretcher bars
16 inches × 12 inches

Untitled (background host), 2024
Acrylic polymer, pigment, gesso, UV coating on linen with aluminum stretcher bars
84 inches × 72 inches

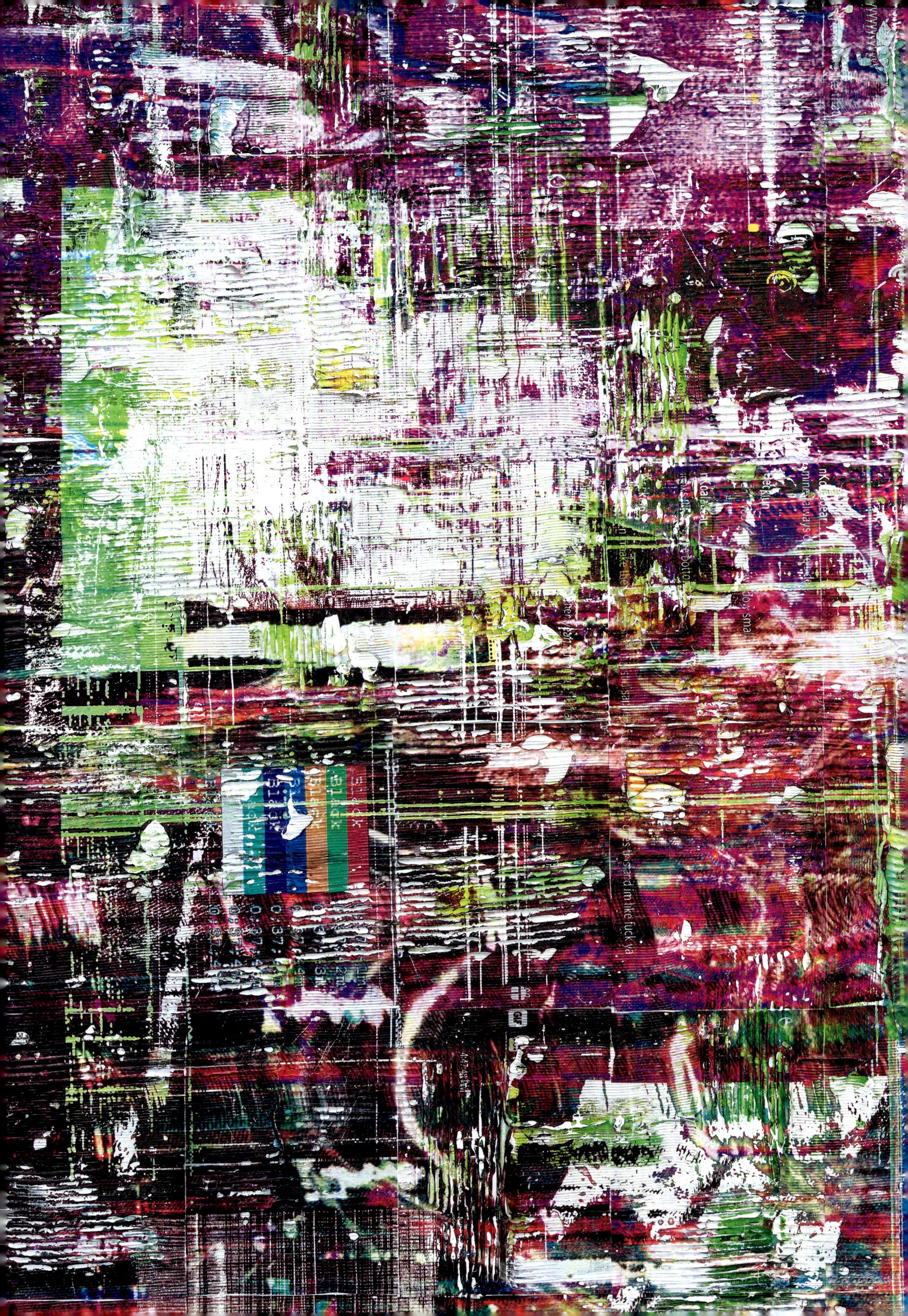

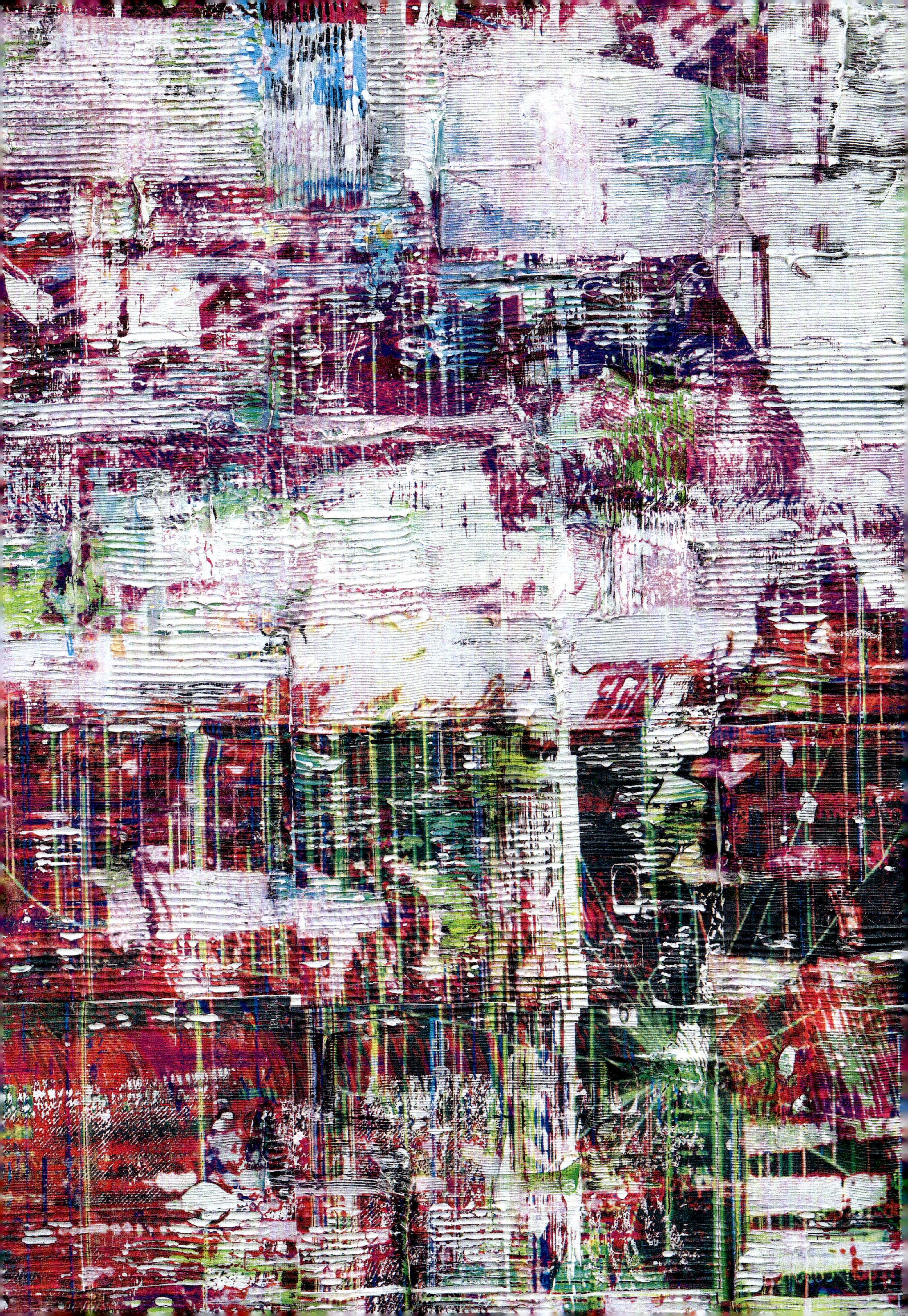

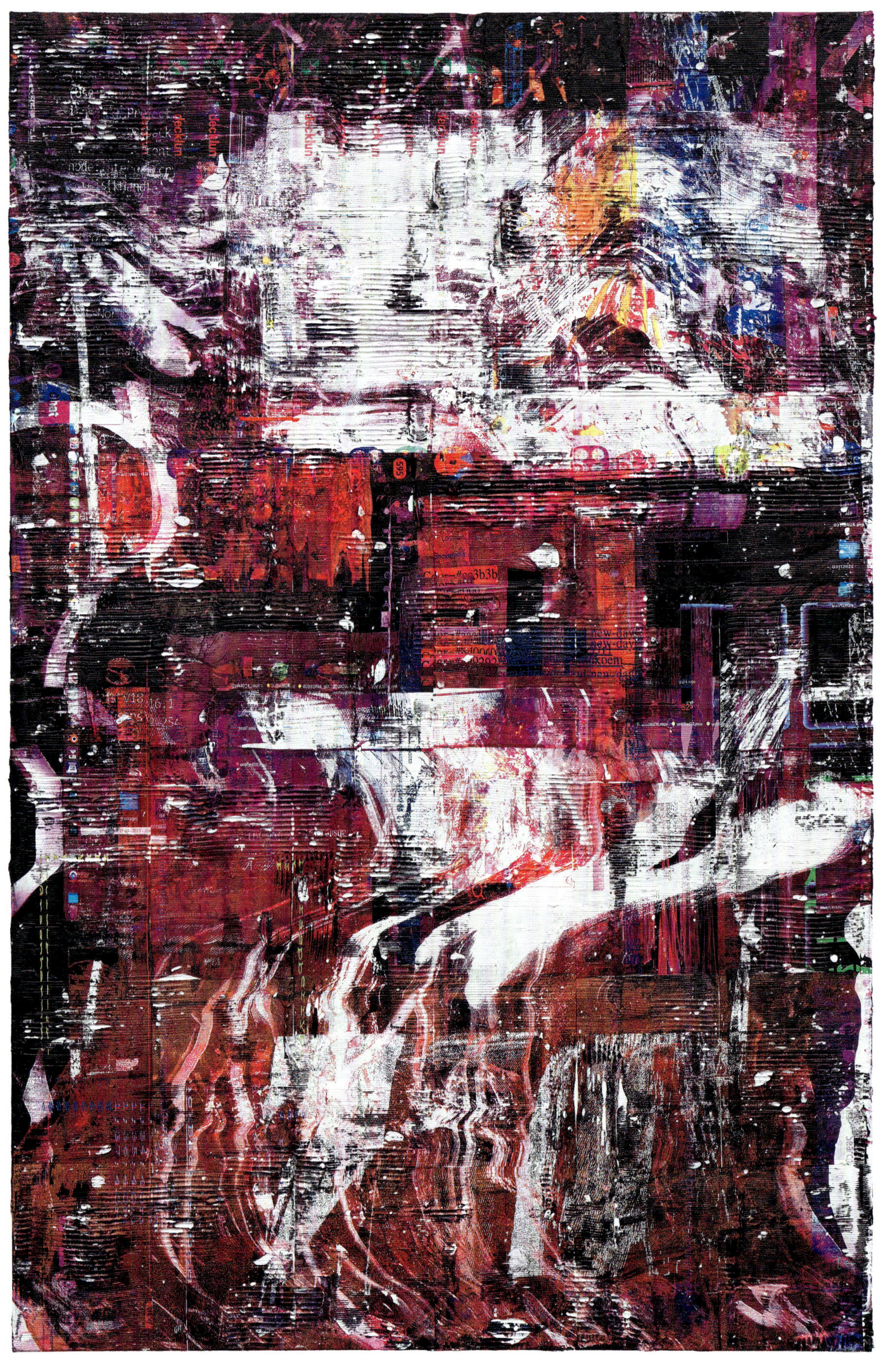

Untitled (harvester), 2024
Acrylic polymer, pigment, gesso, UV coating on linen with aluminum stretcher bars
72 inches × 48 inches

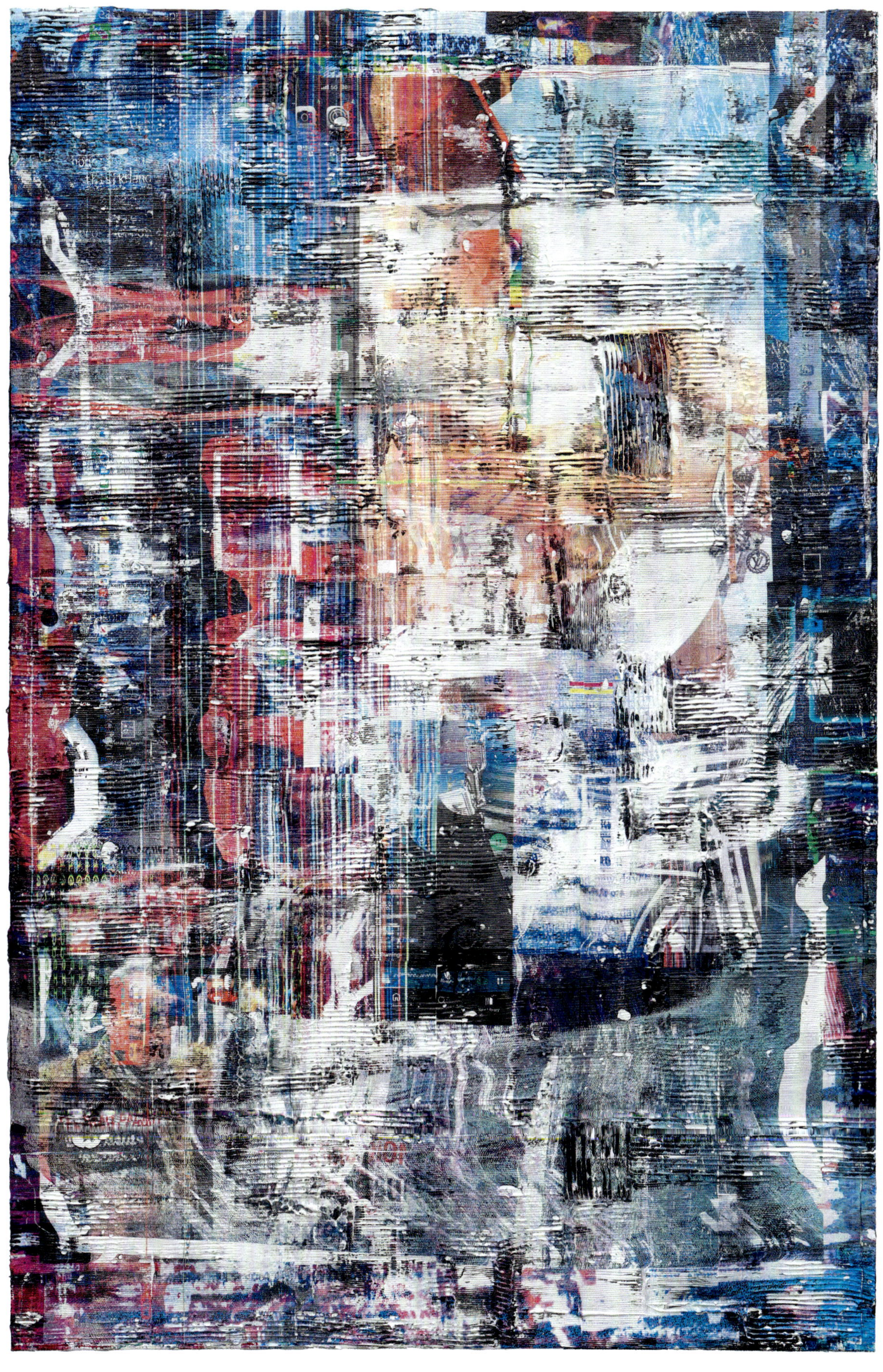

Untitled (service layer), 2024
Acrylic polymer, pigment, gesso, UV coating on linen with aluminum stretcher bars
72 inches × 48 inches

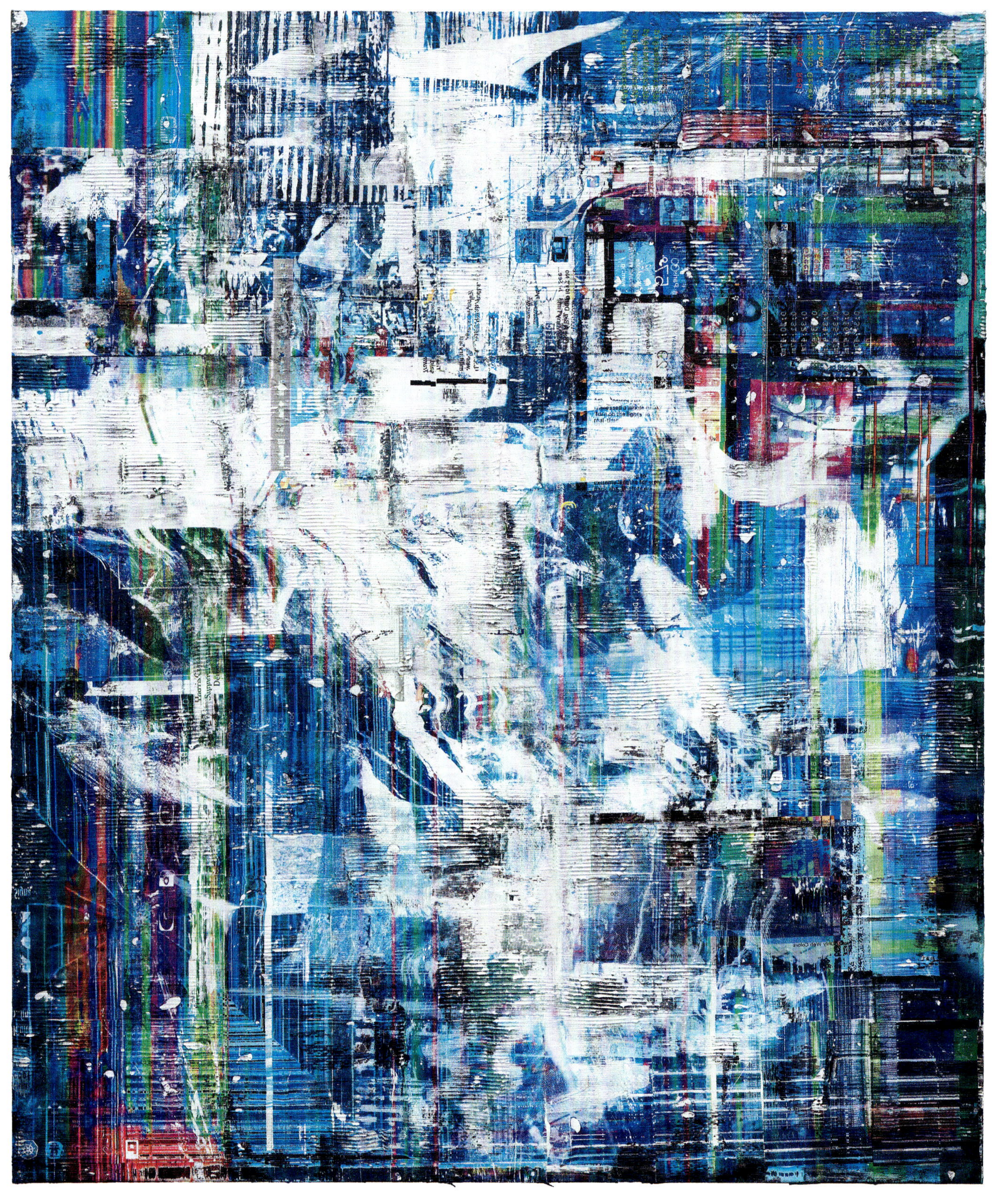

Untitled (hyperscaler), 2025
Acrylic polymer, pigment, gesso, UV coating on linen with aluminum stretcher bars
84 inches × 72 inches

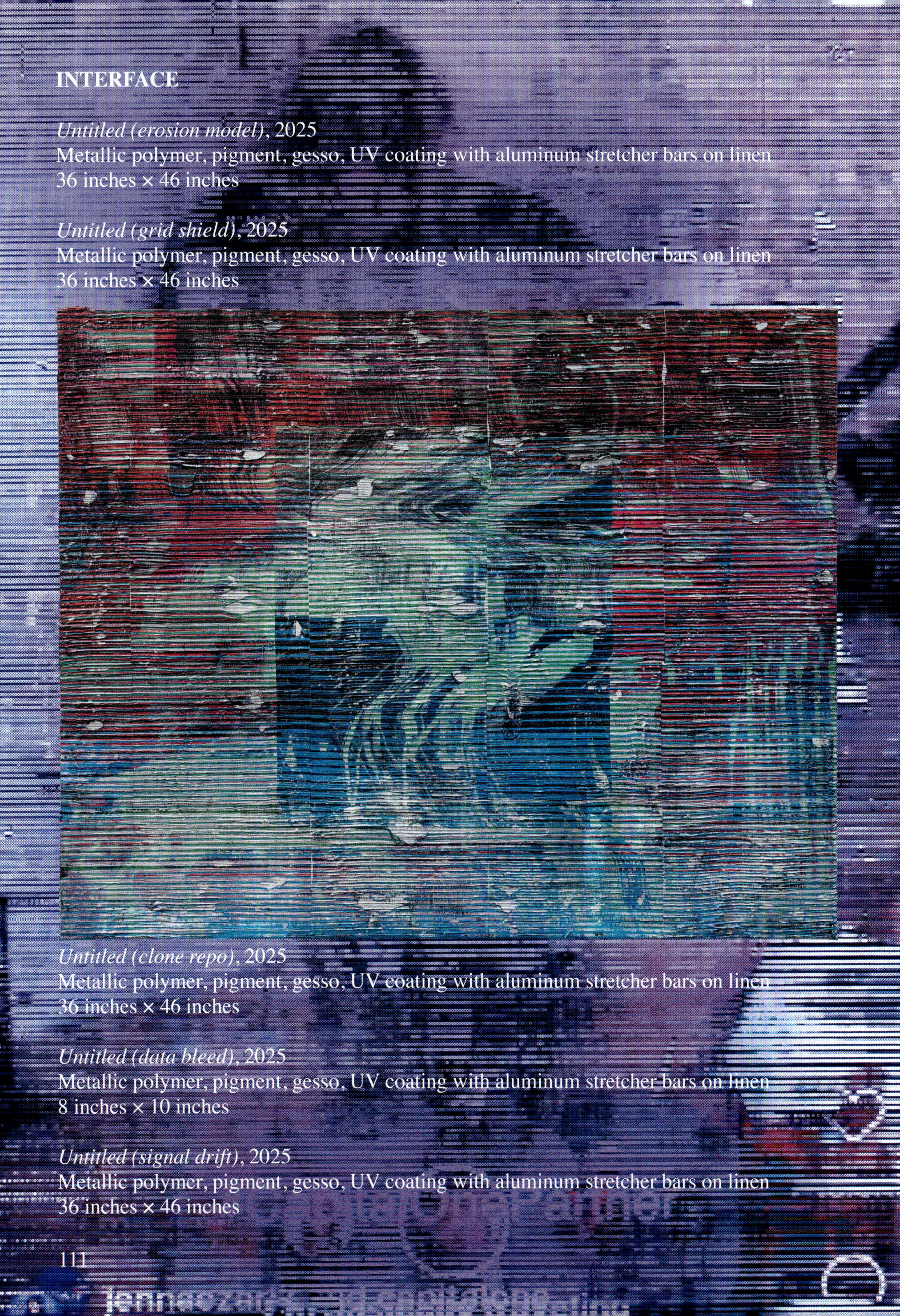

INTERFACE

Untitled (erosion model), 2025
Metallic polymer, pigment, gesso, UV coating with aluminum stretcher bars on linen
36 inches × 46 inches

Untitled (grid shield), 2025
Metallic polymer, pigment, gesso, UV coating with aluminum stretcher bars on linen
36 inches × 46 inches

Untitled (clone repo), 2025
Metallic polymer, pigment, gesso, UV coating with aluminum stretcher bars on linen
36 inches × 46 inches

Untitled (data bleed), 2025
Metallic polymer, pigment, gesso, UV coating with aluminum stretcher bars on linen
8 inches × 10 inches

Untitled (signal drift), 2025
Metallic polymer, pigment, gesso, UV coating with aluminum stretcher bars on linen
36 inches × 46 inches

Untitled (overwrite), 2025
Metallic polymer, pigment, gesso, UV coating with aluminum stretcher bars on linen
36 inches × 46 inches

Untitled (recovery mode), 2025
Metallic polymer, pigment, gesso, UV coating with aluminum stretcher bars on linen
36 inches × 46 inches

Untitled (cipher relay), 2025
Metallic polymer, pigment, gesso, UV coating with aluminum stretcher bars on linen
36 inches × 46 inches

Untitled (residual fill), 2025
Metallic polymer, pigment, gesso, UV coating with aluminum stretcher bars on linen
36 inches × 46 inches

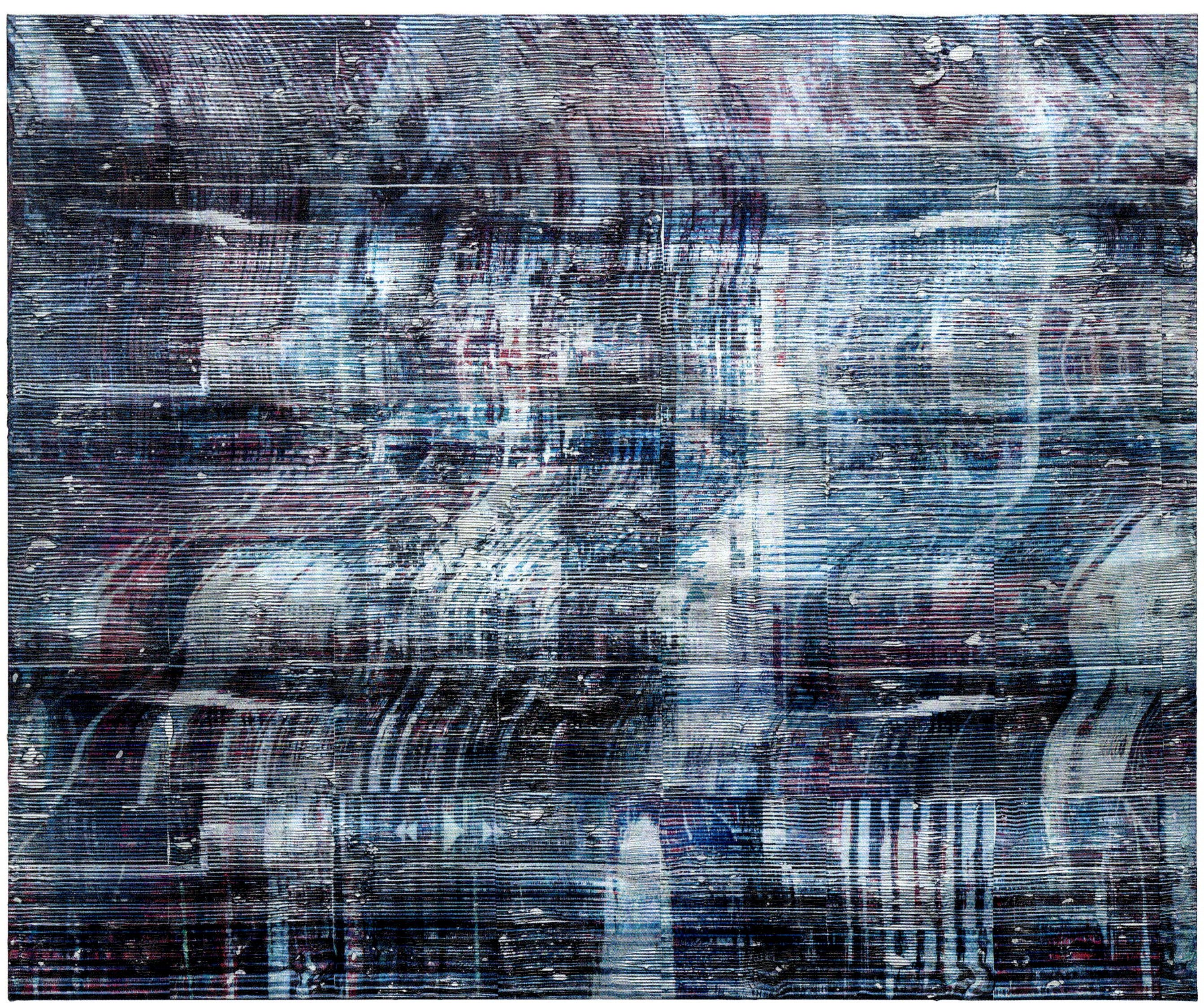

Untitled (gravity core), 2025
Metallic polymer, pigment, gesso, UV coating on linen with aluminum stretcher bars
60 inches × 75 inches

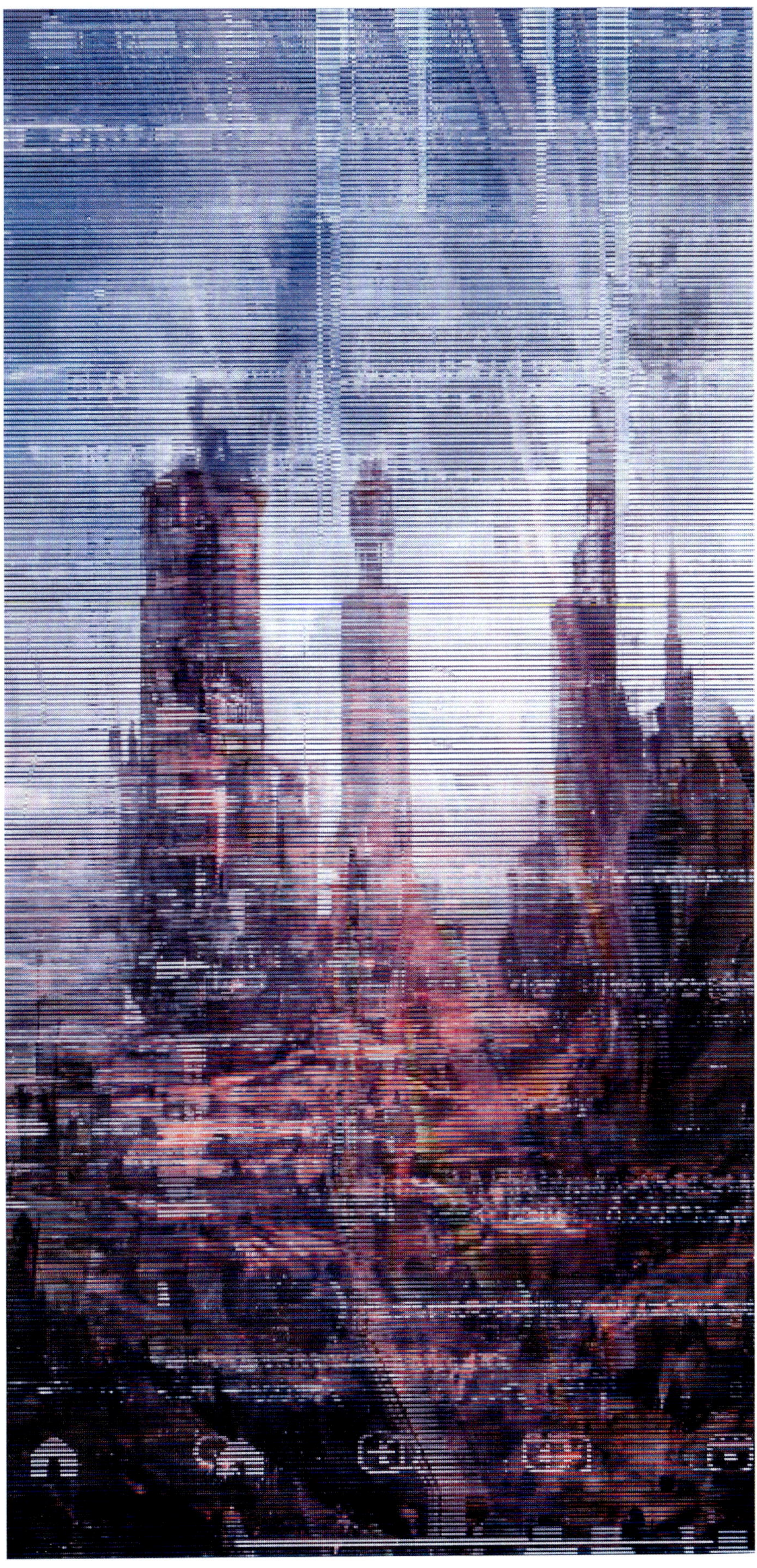

Untitled (server ruin), 2025
Single-channel video, 00:01:20

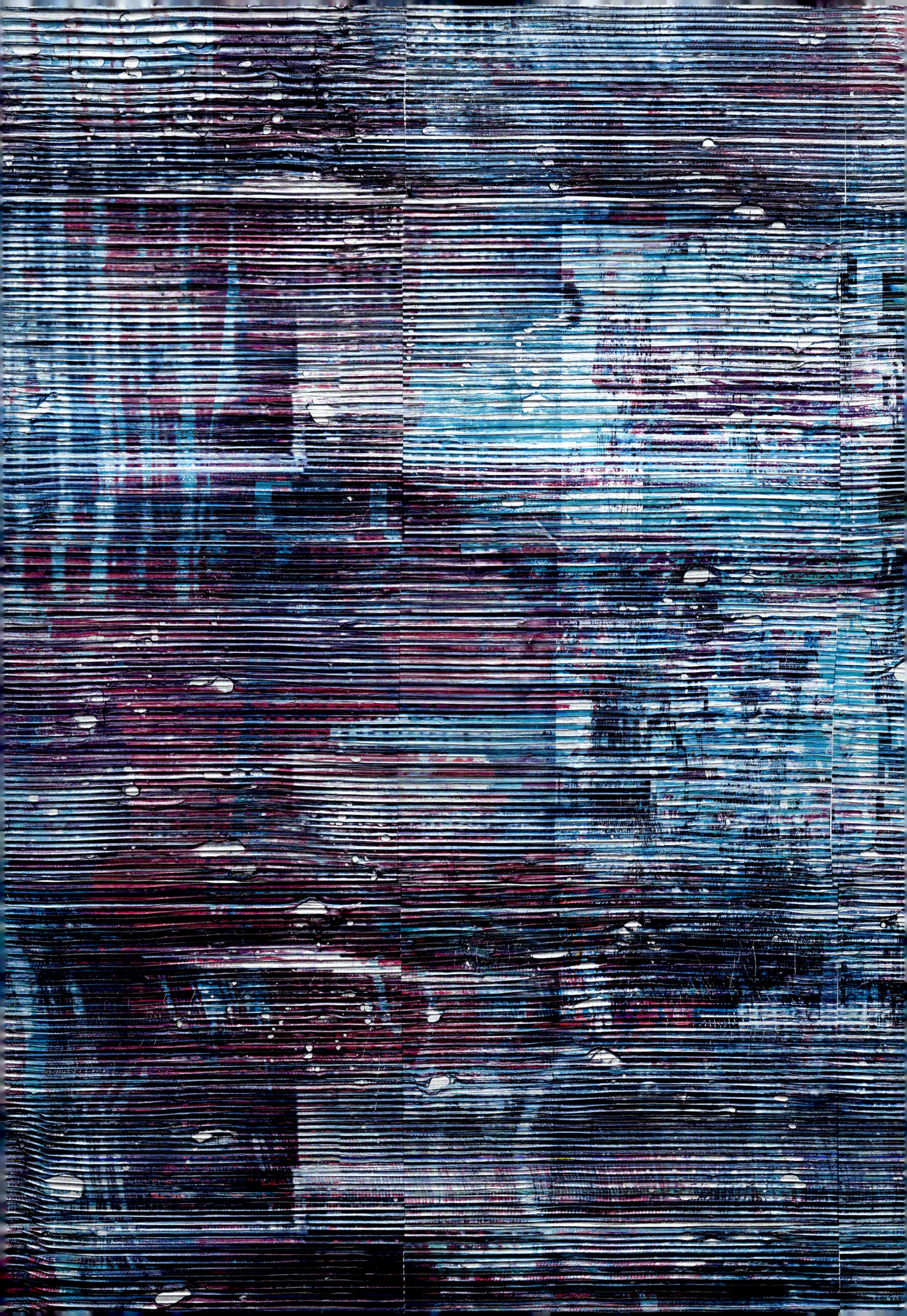

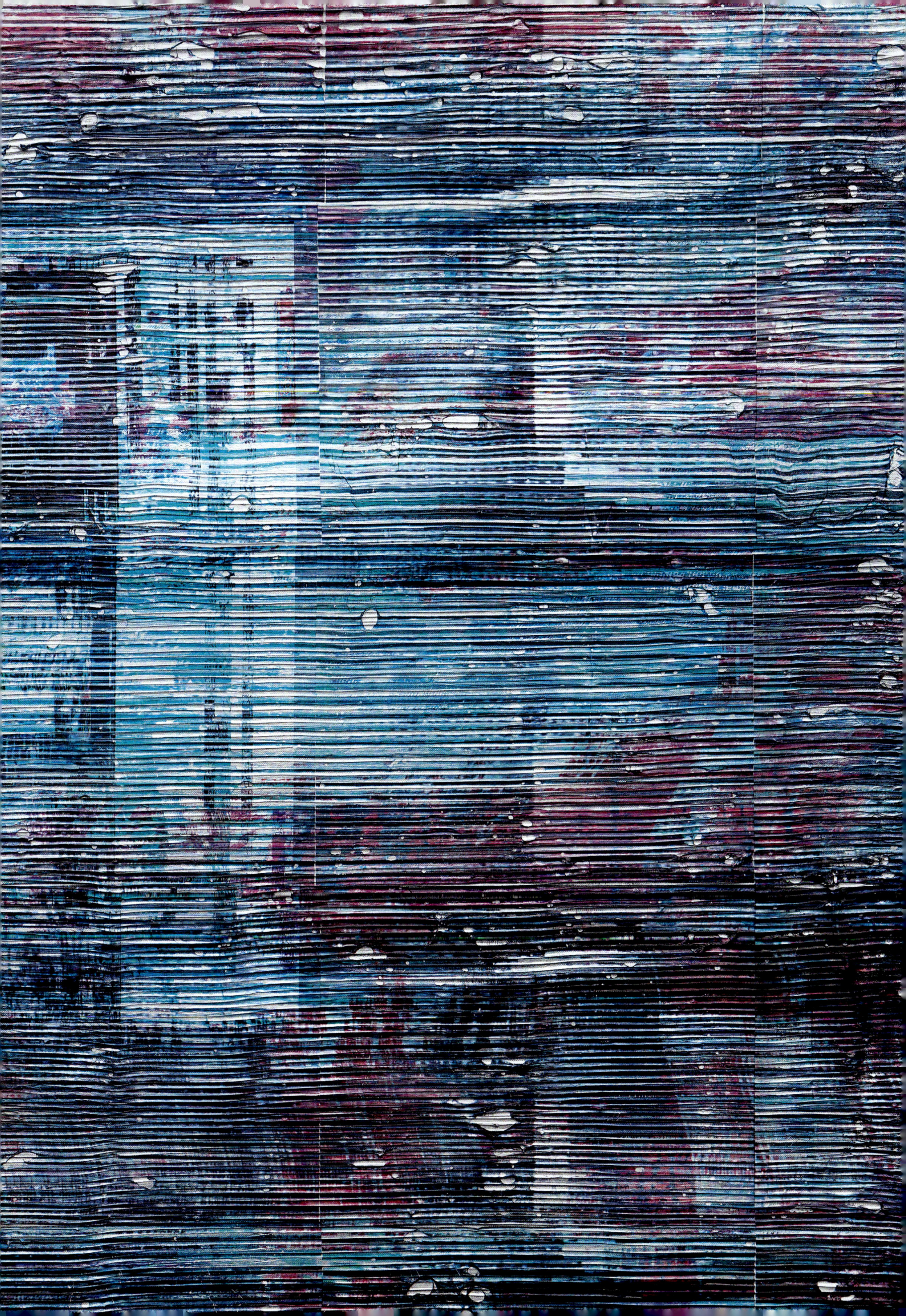

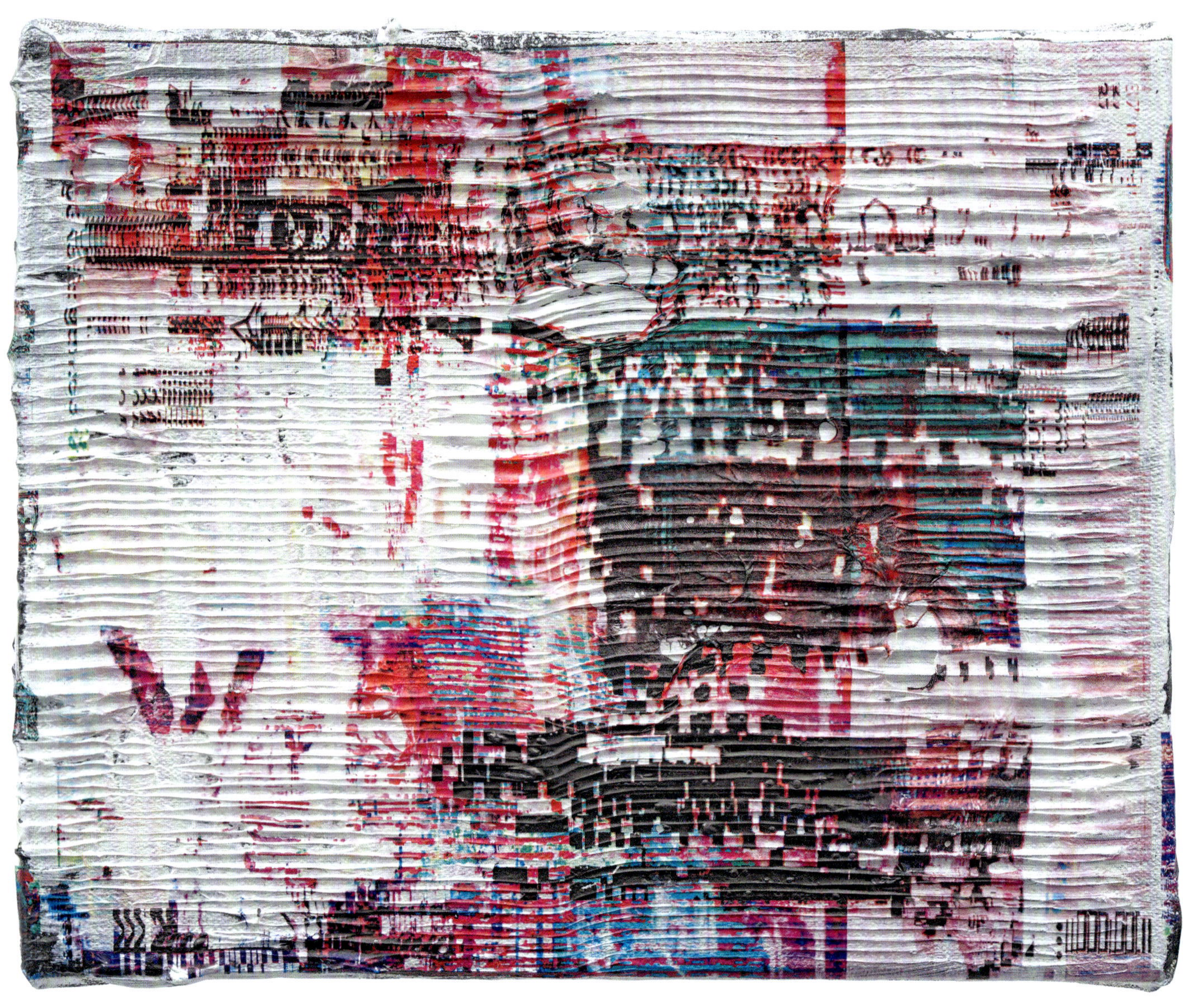

Untitled (fragment), 2025
Metallic polymer, pigment, gesso, UV coating with stretcher bars on linen
8 inches × 10 inches

Page 73:
Untitled (violent ends), 2016 (detail)
UV ink on alumacore, 94 inches × 46 inches

Pages 78–79:
Untitled (overclock), 2017 (detail)
UV ink on alumacore, 78 inches × 44 inches

Pages 82–83:
Untitled (host receptacle, gender recall), 2017 (detail)
UV ink on alumacore, 94 inches × 46 inches

Pages 85–86:
Untitled (snowcrash), 2021 (detail)
Single-channel video, 00:00:06

Pages 90–91:
Untitled (data haven), 2021 (detail)
Acrylic polymer, pigment, gesso, UV coating on linen with aluminum stretcher bars
68 inches × 120 inches

Pages 94–95:
Untitled (chainsplitter), 2021 (detail)
Single-channel video, 00:00:10

Pages 98–99:
Untitled (metadaemon), 2021 (detail)
Single-channel video, 00:00:06

Page 102–103:
Untitled (species III), 2021 (detail)
Single-channel video, 00:02:47

Pages 106–107:
Untitled (background host), 2024 (detail)
Acrylic polymer, pigment, gesso, UV coating on linen with aluminum stretcher bars
84 inches × 72 inches

Pages 111, 117:
Untitled (server ruin), 2025 (detail)
Single-channel video, 00:01:47

Pages 114–115:
Untitled (grid shield), 2025 (detail)
Metallic polymer, pigment, gesso, UV coating on linen with aluminum stretcher bars
36 inches × 46 inches

ACKNOWLEDGMENTS

My deepest thanks to Chris Dorland for his trust, insight, and collaboration throughout this project.

Special thanks to Alison Haage, Stephanie Cash, Sean Yendrys, Elisabeth Rochau-Shalem, Rainer Arnold, the Hirmer staff, and Jean Crutchfield for their support and insight.

And to all whose efforts, in various forms, contributed to the success of this project: A. Alexander Antonopoulos, Damîen Bertelle-Rogier, Geena Brown, Jennifer Chaput, Jack and Jeanette Cohen, David Deutsch, Beth Rudin DeWoody, Tania Fer, Louis and Patrice Friedman, Jordan Goodman, Rhona Hoffman, Camille Houzé, Erin Knutson, Shesna Lyra, Leon Louder, Laura Mitterrand, Jordi Montblanch, Oswaldo Nicoletti, Patrick Reynolds, Grace Robinson-Leo, Colin Ross, Marc Selwyn, Olivia Smith, Simon Watson. Their belief, insight and encouragement have nurtured and sustained this work.

Grateful acknowledgment is extended to the Pollock-Krasner Foundation and the Canada Council for the Arts for their generous support.

With appreciation to Super Dakota, Lyles & King, and Nicoletti, whose collaboration contributed to the realization of this project.

In memoriam: Michael Dorland, Priscilla L. Walton, and Walter Robinson.

"The zero panorama seemed to contain ruins in reverse, that is—all the new construction that would eventually be built. This is the opposite of the 'romantic ruin' because the buildings don't fall into ruin after they are built but rather rise into ruin before they are built. This anti-romantic mise-en-scène suggests the discredited idea of time and many other 'out of date' things."

—Robert Smithson, "The Monuments of Passaic,"
Artforum 7, no. 4 (December 1967): 48–51.

COLOPHON

Chris Dorland: Future Ruins
Author: Robert Hobbs
Graphic design and image selection: Sean Yendrys
Copy editing: Alison Haage, Stephanie Cash
Artwork photography: New Document, Object Studies, Charles Benton, Cary Whittier,
Adam Reich, Lewis Ronald

Hirmer Verlag
Baystrasse 57 – 59, 80335 Munich, Germany
www.hirmerverlag.de / www.hirmerpublishers.com
Managing Director: Kerstin Ludolph
Senior Editor: Elisabeth Rochau-Shalem
Project management: Rainer Arnold

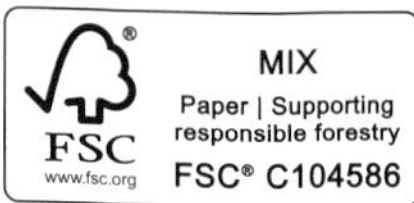

Printed in Germany by Druckhaus Sportflieger GmbH
Prepress: Reproline mediateam GmbH&Co. KG, Unterföhring
Paper: Fines Polar 115gsm, Magno Gloss 170gsm
Typefaces: Times Regular and Bold

ISBN 978-3-7774-4664-6

Bibliographic information published by the Deutsche Nationalbibliothek
The Deutsche Nationalbibliothek lists this publication in the Deutsche Nationalbibliografie;
detailed bibliographic data is available on the Internet at https://www.dnb.de.